THE ORGAN MUSIC
OF JOHANNES BRAHMS

THE ORGAN MUSIC
OF JOHANNES BRAHMS

Barbara Owen

OXFORD
UNIVERSITY PRESS

2007

OXFORD
UNIVERSITY PRESS

Oxford University Press, Inc., publishes works that further
Oxford University's objective of excellence
in research, scholarship, and education.

Oxford New York
Auckland Cape Town Dar es Salaam Hong Kong Karachi
Kuala Lumpur Madrid Melbourne Mexico City Nairobi
New Delhi Shanghai Taipei Toronto

With offices in
Argentina Austria Brazil Chile Czech Republic France Greece
Guatemala Hungary Italy Japan Poland Portugal Singapore
South Korea Switzerland Thailand Turkey Ukraine Vietnam

Copyright © 2007 by Oxford University Press, Inc.

Published by Oxford University Press, Inc.
198 Madison Avenue, New York, New York 10016

www.oup.com

Oxford is a registered trademark of Oxford University Press

All rights reserved. No part of this publication may be reproduced,
stored in a retrieval system, or transmitted, in any form or by any means,
electronic, mechanical, photocopying, recording, or otherwise,
without the prior permission of Oxford University Press.

Library of Congress Cataloging-in-Publication Data
Owen, Barbara.
The organ music of Johannes Brahms / by Barbara Owen.
p. cm.
Includes bibliographical references,
discography, and index.
ISBN 978-0-19-531107-5
1. Brahms, Johannes, 1833–1897. Organ music.
2. Organ music—History and criticism.
I. Title.
ML410.B8O95 2007
786.5092—dc22   2006031572

2 4 6 8 9 7 5 3

Printed in the United States of America
on acid-free paper

IN MEMORIAM

JOHN KEN OGASAPIAN
musician, scholar, friend

Preface

Organ music constitutes but a slight portion of Brahms's splendid and varied compositional output, and it usually receives only scant mention in most studies of his life and work. Like some shorter works of other noteworthy composers, Brahms's small corpus of organ works often tends to be overlooked as a kind of oddity, hard to pigeonhole and regarded as worthy of serious consideration by only a scattered few. In the majority of general discussions of Brahms and his music, the early organ works are often acknowledged (if at all) by little more than a footnote, and the posthumously published set of Eleven Chorale Preludes often rates only a somewhat wearisome "swan song" reference. Yet these beautifully crafted and expressive works are a cherished component of the repertoire of church and concert organists the world over, and most of us dearly wish that Brahms had written more of them.

Nonetheless, no composer's shorter works, regardless of medium, stand apart from the rest of their output nor can they be considered separately from the whole intricate fabric of the composer's life, influences, and artistic development. Brahms's early preludes and fugues for the organ are seminal elements in his lifelong veneration of Bach and study of canon and counterpoint, revealed again and again in the later choral music, chamber works, and larger symphonic compositions. The chorale preludes display not only a mastery of counterpoint but also a wealth of signature "Brahmsian" characteristics in miniature: carefully sculpted melodic lines, chained thirds, inversions, polyrhythms, hidden symbolism, sensitivity to text, and even occasional hints of atonality. As with so many other musical contexts, Brahms has taken this time-honored form and made it uniquely his own.

I do not presume to have added greatly to original research on the subject, but rather I have tried to piece together from a wide variety of sources as complete a picture of this music and its background as possible, and to integrate it into the larger picture of Brahms's life and work. For this reason, I have divided the text into two parts. The first part gives the reader some context that may help to deepen understanding of the music, and the second part discusses the music itself. In the process, there have been conflicting accounts to reconcile, questions to attempt (sometimes unsuccessfully) to answer, and occasional misconceptions to call into question.

At the center of it all is a still slightly unfocused picture of two gifted and very complex human beings—Johannes Brahms himself and Clara Wieck Schumann. As she does to some extent in many other facets of the composer's creative life, Clara—as I must call her in the text, to distinguish her from the ever-hovering ghost of the tragic Robert—seems never far away when it comes to the organ works. Others have noticed this, too, and some have even attempted to explain it in various conjectural ways. I am content to simply accept it as a given, the origins of which may have disappeared forever with the correspondence that Johannes and Clara destroyed by mutual agreement near the beginning of their shared story. But perhaps Brahms said it all when, near the end of his life, he enigmatically linked with a bracket in his notebook the Four Serious Songs, Clara Schumann's death, and the Eleven Chorale Preludes.

All quotations in the text are in English, and, except where a secondary source is cited in the endnote, translations from the German are my own. No musical examples are cited within the text. When dealing with so small a body of work, such illustrations can be of less value than simple references to the pertinent measures in the musical score, where the excerpt can more readily be seen in context. This is particularly appropriate when the entire sum of Brahms's known organ works fits comfortably within a single volume, and an accessible modern urtext edition exists, edited by George S. Bozarth and published in 1988 by G. Henle Verlag. Although the text references (save those related to the early versions of two of the compositions, found only in this edition) can be applied to any available edition, the Henle edition was my point of reference while researching and writing this study.

Acknowledgments

For much of the background, I am indebted to the considerable amount of recent research and insight into Brahms's life, thought, and compositions by Brahms scholars in both America and Europe, which is happily accessible in biographies, anthologies, symposium papers, and periodicals. I am particularly grateful for the seminal studies of Brahms's connections with the organ, organists, and the organ music of earlier composers by Wm. A. Little, Otto

Biba, George Bozarth, and the late Vernon Gotwals, which first piqued my interest and challenged me to continue building on this foundation.

In addition, Wm. A. Little deserves profuse thanks for having taken the time to read a draft of this book and for making corrections and suggestions that clarified certain aspects. Thanks are also due to Max Miller for his perceptive comments on the early contrapuntal works. Yuko Hayashi and Marilyn Mason encouraged me during the early stages of preparation by engaging me to give lectures and master classes on Brahms's music to their organ students, and the students in turn provided useful input. Thanks to a grant from the Ruth and Clarence Mader Memorial Scholarship Fund, I was able to spend a little research time in Brahms's world in Vienna. A note of appreciation is due to Paul Peeters of Göteborg University, Stephen Pinel of the American Organ Archive, and Dr. Uwe Pape of the University of Berlin for locating pertinent information concerning some of the organs mentioned in the text, and also to Astrid Schramek and Otto Biba, Archivist of the Gesellschaft der Musikfreunde, for permission to use a photo by the late Peter Schramek on the cover. For many hard-to-find sources of information, I am particularly indebted to the excellent resources of the Music Division of the Mugar Library at Boston University, the Sibley Music Library of the Eastman School of Music, the Talbot Library of Westminster Choir College, and the A.G.O. Organ Library at Boston University. I wish also to express appreciation to Oxford's anonymous reviewers for their suggestions and thought-provoking commentary, as well as for their encouraging words.

Contents

PART I: BACKGROUND

ONE *The Organ in the Life of Brahms* 3

TWO *Bach, Counterpoint, and Chorales* 33

THREE *Brahms as Revisor* 41

PART II: THE MUSIC

FOUR *The Early Works* 53

FIVE *The Eleven Chorale Preludes* 77

SIX *Interpretation* 121

APPENDIX A *Editions* 139

APPENDIX B *The Organs in Brahms's World* 142

APPENDIX C *Organ Transcriptions of Works by Brahms* 151

Notes 155

Bibliography 167

Discography 177

Index 179

PART I

BACKGROUND

ONE

The Organ in the Life of Brahms

Until fairly recent times, Brahms's organ works have been regarded by many as something of an anomaly. In his biography of the composer (first published in Germany in 1920), Walter Niemann states that, with the exception of the Eleven Chorale Preludes, the organ works "are a side issue, of subordinate interest among the composer's works. Brahms never sounded the real depths of organ composition."[1] In a certain sense, the "side issue" part is true. As a performer, Brahms was known as a pianist, and, as a composer, a writer of symphonic music and songs. Thus his organ works were not initially regarded as being very idiomatic, particularly in the early twentieth century, when radical changes were occurring in organ tonal design, as well as in organ composition and performance. If by "real depths" Niemann meant the massive and symphonically inspired Germanic tours de force of Liszt, Reger, Reubke, Stehle, Rheinberger, or Karg-Elert, then his criticism might be said to be valid. Brahms, as everyone knows, was a superb symphonist when writing for orchestra. But when he composed for the organ, he wrote in classic German organ forms and looked more to Bach and other Baroque masters for his stylistic inspiration. And there are real depths to be plumbed there.

For some time, the notion persisted that Brahms didn't know much about writing for the organ. The noted early-twentieth-century recitalist Lynnwood Farnam is said to have "freely re-arranged the Chorale-Preludes of Brahms, who was not an organist, making them more suitable for the instrument."[2] In 1949 another recitalist, E. Power Biggs, brought out a new edition of the Eleven Chorale Preludes that included alternate versions of 5, 6 (two), 7, and 8 because "the contrapuntal lines must be disentangled for ease of performance and clarity of expression."[3] Even today, players do not always resist the temptation to "lift out" melodies in some of the chorale preludes, although by and large they refrain from doing likewise to similarly constructed works by Bach, Pachelbel, Krebs, and other Baroque masters. By 1912, only a decade after their posthumous publication, no fewer than three editors—among them Brahms's friend Eusebius Mandyczewski—had presumed to arrange the Eleven Chorale Preludes for piano.[4] It is impossible to say at this remove whether they did this because they actually believed them to be more suited to the piano or simply because they wished to make them more accessible beyond the organ loft.

Although in 1934 Gotthold Frotscher, in his book on organ playing and composition, observed that Brahms had an "intuitive sympathy" for idiomatic organ style,[5] as late as 1950 T. Scott Buhrman, editor of *The American Organist*, would still state flatly that "Brahms knew the minimum about organs; a look at his scores shows that."[6] Actually, Brahms's scores look just like those of many of his contemporaries who wrote organ music in the smaller forms, and thirty years later Marilou Kratzenstein could rightly state that Brahms's organ works, though few, "indicate that he understood the instrument very well."[7] Recent research has indeed proven that Brahms had considerably more than a passing knowledge of the organ and was conversant with classical principles of writing for it. Although it is true that he never had formal organ lessons and never held a church position (and passed up the only one known to have been offered—that of *Thomaskantor* in Leipzig), he nonetheless took considerable pains to learn to play the instrument while in his early twenties, even briefly aspiring to give organ recitals. Although he never did reach that level of performance achievement, his personal library contained organ music by several composers, and he is known to have played the organ publicly on a few occasions, although apparently only as an accompanist. This knowledge puts his organ music in a somewhat different light. We must now accept that Brahms was indeed familiar with the prevalent conventions of organ composition and was writing for an instrument that he knew firsthand, and this must be taken into account with regard to understanding and interpreting this small but significant segment of his masterworks.

The Hamburg Period

Seemingly unrelated circumstances often influence events and turning points in a life or a career. Brahms had begun giving piano recitals in his home city of Hamburg while he was still in his teens. Although he also was studying theory and composition with Eduard Marxsen (1806–1887) (who, incidentally, was an organist) and had already written some music, by the time he turned twenty, Brahms appeared to be headed as much toward a career as a concert pianist as that of a composer. If his biographers are to be trusted, Brahms was a somewhat solitary young man, with no close friends to whom he could relate intellectually. This all changed in the spring of 1853, when, following a stint as accompanist to the Hungarian violinist Eduard Remenyi, he made the acquaintance of another Hungarian violinist, Joseph Joachim (1831–1907), the prize student of master teacher Joseph Böhm. Although already an acclaimed virtuoso on his Stradivarius, Joachim was only two years Brahms's senior, and he was to become a lifelong friend and collaborator who inspired some of Brahms's finest violin and string ensemble music. And it was Joachim who, in September of that year, introduced Brahms to Robert and Clara Schumann.

Robert took an immediate liking to the quiet and somewhat reticent "young eagle" and was moved by the depth and quality of his youthful compositions. Only a month later, he penned an enthusiastic article titled "*Neue Bahnen*" ("New Paths") for the *Neue Zeitschrift für Musik*, which lavished praise on the work of this relatively unknown young composer from Hamburg and confidently predicted a distinguished career for him.[8] Then he sent Brahms off to Leipzig with introductions to influential music lovers and a recommendation to the publishers Breitkopf & Härtel. Before long, Brahms had the pleasure of receiving his first publishers' fees, as well as seeing the first of his compositions to appear in print.

Brahms's association with Robert Schumann was tragically short. In February 1854, Schumann's symptoms of mental illness, which had afflicted him sporadically for more than a decade, worsened to the point where he attempted suicide by throwing himself into the Rhine from a bridge, and he was committed to a mental hospital in Endenich. Brahms, Joachim, and Albert Dietrich, one of Robert's students, hastened to Düsseldorf to help Clara Schumann and her children, and after the initial crisis had passed, Brahms stayed on in the Schumann household to help take care of Robert's affairs. Among other things, he undertook to organize (as well as study) the Schumanns' library, which contained a wealth of scholarly books and early music. He remained until shortly after Robert's death in the summer of 1856, by which time his relationship with Clara was maturing into a deeply interdependent friendship that would last until the end of both their lives.

Without the influence of Joseph Joachim and the Schumanns, it is possible that Brahms might never have written anything for the organ. Both Joachim and Robert Schumann had been friends of Felix Mendelssohn and, like him, were admirers of Bach. In 1843, Mendelssohn had founded the Leipzig Conservatory, where Schumann was given a position teaching piano and composition. Organ was also taught there, and pedal pianos were provided for the organ students' practice. Following a stressful concert tour of Russia with Clara in 1844, Robert suffered a nervous breakdown. He gave up his Leipzig position, and in December of that year the Schumann family moved to Dresden. In January, Robert and Clara began a concentrated study of Bach and counterpoint together, initiated by Clara. Although this may have been prompted by the acquisition of a treatise on the subject by Luigi Cherubini, and possibly also by the publication of some of Bach's chorale preludes in 1845, its main purpose was therapeutic. In this, it appears to have been successful, occupying Robert intellectually and creatively while diverting him from some larger projects that threatened to bring on another of his mental breakdowns.[9]

It was not the first time that the Schumanns had turned their attention to counterpoint. In the first year of their marriage, they had embarked on a brief study of Bach's fugues, and Clara noted in her diary that "studying these fugues is really quite interesting and gives me more pleasure each day."[10] What should not be overlooked, though, is that an interest in the organ formed an unobtrusive undercurrent to the Schumanns' shared interest in Bach and counterpoint. Robert's laudatory 1836 account in the *Neue Zeitschrift* of hearing Mendelssohn play Bach's *Schmücke dich* chorale prelude is well known. He was also in attendance at the Thomaskirche in Leipzig on August 6, 1840, when Mendelssohn gave an all-Bach organ recital as a fund-raiser for a memorial monument to Bach erected in 1843, and was effusive in his review of it—"precious jewels, in a glorious arrangement of change and gradation." It is of interest that Mendelssohn closed the program with his own improvisation on the "Passion Chorale," into which he introduced the "B-A-C-H" theme and a fugue. Schumann considered it "such a clear and masterly whole, that if printed, it would have appeared a finished work of art."[11] Whether Clara Wieck was also present on this occasion is unknown, but a little more than a month later, on September 12, a day before her twenty-first birthday, she became Mrs. Robert Schumann.

From the beginning of their marriage, the Schumanns kept a joint diary, fortunately preserved, in which attendance at organ recitals is occasionally mentioned. In July 1841, the newlyweds visited Freiberg, and Clara even played the Silbermann organ there. In March 1842, they paid a visit to friends in Hamburg, prior to a piano concert by Clara, and by chance happened on an organ recital in the Brahms family's parish church, St. Michael's, "with its wonderful organ." Robert reported that "the organist behaved well, but didn't know very much and played unworthy compositions."[12] It is doubtful that a music-loving eight-year-old parishioner named Johannes would have also attended—but an interesting coincidence if he had. In 1843, the Schumanns were living in Leipzig, and Clara briefly noted that on April 18 a "boring" organist named Kloss "gave an organ concert that simply wasn't very edifying." The dedication of the Bach monument next to the Thomaskirche, a few days later on April 23, was undoubtedly more edifying, as it featured an all-

Bach concert at the Gewandhaus, directed by Mendelssohn, who also performed Bach's D Minor Concerto "with customary and yet always surprising mastery."[13]

Perhaps remembering the usefulness of the Leipzig Conservatory's pedal pianos in the study of organ music, the Schumanns decided to acquire one after moving to Dresden in 1845. Soon Clara recorded in her diary: "On April 24 we received a pedal for our piano, on hire, which gave us great pleasure. The chief object was to enable us to practice for the organ. Robert, however, soon found a greater interest in the instrument, and composed several sketches and studies for pedal-piano, which will certainly make a great sensation, being something entirely new."[14] What this makes clear is that this was not a complete pedal piano, but rather a pedal attachment for an existing piano, and that it was rented, not purchased.

Between the beginning of the Schumanns' *Fugenpassion* in January 1845 and its gradual winding down in the summer of 1846, Robert recorded his progress on the B-A-C-H fugues and pedal piano studies in his daybook. But among his daily comments he also recorded their attendance at two organ recitals by their friend Johann Gottlob Schneider, organist of the Lutheran Hofkirche in Dresden, where there was a fine organ by Gottfried Silbermann. Robert found one of Schneider's Bach recitals given in the Sophienkirche in October 1845 especially pleasing.[15] In May, he reported that Clara was playing some of his new pieces on the pedal piano. In March 1846, he was engaged in the final revision of his B-A-C-H fugues. And then, on three days in June, he and Clara spent the morning trying them on an organ, Robert playing—and Clara doing duty as bellows pumper [*Bälgetreter*].[16] Unfortunately, he does not mention which organ this was, but it might even have been Schneider's Silbermann instrument.

The counterpoint study plus the pedal piano produced some very tangible results, the most important of which—from an organist's standpoint—were Robert's *Sechs Studien für den Pedalflügel*, op. 56 (dedicated to his first music teacher, Johann Kuntzch, organist of the Marienkirche in Zwickau); *Vier Skizzen für den Pedalflügel*, op. 58; and *Sechs Fugen über den Namen Bach, für Orgel oder Pedalklavier*, op. 60. Not to be overlooked, though, are Clara's *Drei Präludien und Fugen* for piano, op. 16 (as well as three unpublished fugues, only recently discovered), and Robert's *Vier Fugen für das Pianoforte*, op. 72, which, although not for pedal piano, are obviously the result of the joint counterpoint studies. Only one of these works, Robert's opus 60, is specifically for the organ (even though pedal piano is also cited in the published version). However the pedal piano pieces (opp. 56 and 58) have for some time been usually performed on the organ, to which, despite their more pianistic orientation, they adapt quite well—particularly the canonic *Studien* of op. 56.

Of Clara's three opus 16 pieces, Barbara Harbach has observed that the third, with its chordal Prelude and the long pedal points in the classically constructed fugue, "is so aptly suited for organ that perhaps she intended it for organ."[17] As edited by Harbach, with an independent pedal part, this does make a satisfyingly idiomatic organ work. The pedal attachment (which, according to Robert's daybook, was rented by the month) was used by both Clara and Robert not only in trying out their own compositions but also in studying the organ works of Bach. As Robert recorded, Clara had practiced on the pedal piano, and he himself had tried out his compositions on an organ on at least one occasion. Thus both must have gained some pedal facility as well as firsthand contact with the organ. This episode also seems to have been a musical watershed for both Schumanns, bringing more depth to Robert's compositions and prompting Clara to abandon the "frivolous virtuosity" and "acrobatic feats" of Thalberg and Liszt in her concert programs in favor of Bach, Beethoven, Mendelssohn, and, of course, her beloved Robert.[18]

Although the organ and pedal piano retreated into the background after the Schumanns left Dresden, they still occasionally attended organ recitals. The last such reference in their diary occurs shortly after their first meeting with Brahms, when they were on a concert tour in Holland. On December 13, 1853, they attended a recital by an organist named Van Eyken in either Rotterdam or Amsterdam. Robert enthused over the "lovely organ and masterful playing" and recorded that four of his own works—two of the B-A-C-H fugues and two of the *Skizzen*—had been performed, along with works of Bach, Mendelssohn, and Gade.[19] This may have been one of the very few times (if not the only time) that Robert heard his own organ music played in a recital.

For Clara, thoughts of organ playing reentered the picture in the summer of 1854, following Robert's suicide attempt and commitment to the sanatorium in Endenich in February, and again involved his organ compositions. In her diary, she wrote that one day, when she was walking with Brahms, she suddenly decided "to learn to play the organ sufficiently to be able to play some of Robert's things to him when he is well. . . . The idea pleased me so much that I lay awake half the night thinking of what I was going to play, and how I would entice Robert into the church where he would find me playing the organ."[20] Could she perhaps, while on that walk, have told Brahms about having heard some of Robert's organ pieces performed in Holland only a few months earlier? We can only wonder what church she may have had in mind for her own performance of them.

Brahms had returned to Hamburg in the fall, but he, too, had been working on his organ playing. In November 1854, he wrote to Clara, "I've found something pleasing here. You can play the organ, for in Böhme's music store there stands a *schottische* [one] with two manuals and (unfortunately) a pull-down [*angehängten*] pedal. I play it often with great pleasure."²¹ The term *angehängt* refers to a pedalboard that has no independent pipes and is simply permanently coupled to (or hung from) the lower keys of one of the manuals, which are pulled down when a pedal note is played. Brahms may have regarded it as "unfortunate" because it provided no 16' tone or because it could not be used to play an independent pedal solo line. This limitation is probably the reason that the pedal parts in his A minor and G minor preludes and fugues were written in such a low register, so as to avoid crossing the bass line with the tenor line (because both lines would have sounded at 8' pitch on this organ). It is noteworthy that when Brahms later revised the A-flat Minor Fugue and *O Traurigkeit* chorale prelude for publication, he raised the pedal line in several places. He would have been aware that the published versions of these pieces would be played on organs with 16' pedal stops, and the pedal line thus would sound an octave lower than it did on the music store organ (where he must have still been practicing when he wrote the early versions), eliminating any problem with part crossing.

But why did he refer to this organ as *schottische* (Scottish or Scotch)? It stretches credulity to think that a music store in Germany, where organ builders were plentiful, should import an organ from Scotland, where native builders were at the time quite scarce, and too small to have done any exporting. However, it turns out that the term has nothing to do with the organ's origins. Just as English speakers sometimes use the word "Scotch" pejoratively to denote someone or something stingy or cheap, so, too, did the Germans. According to a definition unearthed by Wm. A. Little in Johann Christoph Adelung's late-eighteenth-century dictionary, *schottisch* was a colloquial term used to describe careless or shoddy workmanship. Thus Brahms—who could speak the Low German dialect of Hamburg when he chose, and whence this colloquialism may have come—is simply telling Clara that he's found this convenient, if nondescript, little practice organ. As Little suggests, Brahms is really "speaking *ironically* when he says he is delighted to be practicing away on this crumby, jimcrack instrument,"²² as surely it would have seemed in comparison to some of the church organs that he and Clara must have heard.

As Clara was planning a visit to Hamburg, Brahms promised her some practice time on the instrument in Böhme's music store while she was there. Clara must have eventually decided to tell Robert about her organ study after all, for when she sent him a copy of Brahms's *Ballade*, op. 10, in January 1855, he responded, "Doesn't this please you more, my Clara, than the organ?"²³ The *Ballade* was a piano work, but Brahms would soon be working on his first organ fugues. In May, Brahms was in Düsseldorf, but Clara was away from home, on an extensive concert tour of England that would last until July. Brahms had sent her an organ fugue, presumably the one in A minor, and wrote, "I am practicing it just now, things are going considerably better with the organ! By the time you return, not a bit sooner, I will have progressed enough to play it for you. Is organ-playing so hard for you, too? Probably not. I have not played for Grimm."[24] Brahms's question suggests that Clara had also recently been practicing on an organ, but where it was located is unknown. And organ playing may indeed have come easier to Clara, thanks to her previous experience with the pedal piano. As any organ teacher knows, pedal playing is usually the most daunting hurdle for a pianist aspiring to be an organist.

On May 24, in response to her just-received "lovely long letter" from England, Brahms wrote Clara a rather rambling reply. He is concerned about Clara's health, encourages her to cut short her tour and come home (which she didn't), and agonizes over whether it would be proper for him to join her there (which he didn't). He gloomily talks about writing wills and asks Clara to keep all his letters together (as he does with hers). Then he rather candidly reveals at least part of his motivation for working so diligently on his organ playing: "I have already thought about the possibility that I could become a passable organ virtuoso by next year, then we could tour together, and I should hang up piano-playing on a nail, and always travel together with you."[25] Young Brahms was, at least in this period, clearly infatuated with this gifted and intelligent older woman. After mentioning some eyeglasses she had promised to send him—Brahms was nearsighted—he refers again to their organ playing: "organs in concert-halls are very possible for us, perhaps next year." Later in his letter, he mentions a "cherished volume of music" that he plans to send, and he states that he is enclosing a revised copy of his fugue.[26] This was presumably the early draft of the A-flat Minor Fugue, which has survived among Clara's papers.

The comment about concert hall organs is a bit curious, considering the date. Although organs had been built for British concert halls since the 1830s, they were somewhat slower in appearing on the continent. There was no organ in the Düsseldorf Tonhalle before the Schulze instrument of 1866. However, what is said to have been the first concert hall organ in Germany was built by Peter Tappe of Verden for the Hamburg Tonhalle in 1845.[27] Brahms must surely have known about this organ, and this was perhaps what he had in mind. It is probable, too, that Brahms was aware that there were concert hall organs in England; during the 1840s, Mendelssohn had given organ recitals at London's Exeter Hall and Birmingham's Town Hall, as well as in some churches. Although in later life Brahms had strong objections to crossing the English Channel, the thought about joining Clara in England expressed in his 1855 letter suggests that he had no compunction about doing so at that early date.

For Brahms at this time, there was yet another motivation for learning the organ besides fantasizing concert tours with his beloved Clara, and this involved his friend Joseph Joachim. Early in 1856, Brahms, Joachim, and Clara engaged in a study of Bach and counterpoint reminiscent of that essayed by Robert and Clara a decade earlier, and it may even have been instigated by Clara. Brahms and Joachim committed themselves to a weekly exchange of studies in strict counterpoint, canon, and fugue, and many of these were submitted to Clara for criticism as well. Brahms was still practicing on the organ, and as his skill as a contrapuntist developed, he began to assay organ fugues. On June 5, he sent Joachim copies of his fugues in A minor and A-flat minor, saying, "I have been practicing the organ lately, from which these come."[28]

The A-flat Minor Fugue particularly satisfied him, and he sent a copy of it to Clara on Robert's birthday, June 8, 1856 (having already sent her the A Minor Fugue on his own birthday a month previous). Perhaps these gifts were partly in response to Clara for having dedicated her Three Romances (op. 21) to him a year earlier, although he was also eager for her comments on them. Joachim, who had teasingly addressed Brahms as "Herr Hopeful Cathedral-Organist" in one of his letters, proved a painstakingly honest sounding board throughout these contrapuntal exchanges, praising what was good but not hesitating to make suggestions concerning details that he found questionable. Despite some minor criticisms, he seems to have been particularly impressed with the Prelude and Fugue in A Minor.

On June 17, 1856, in London's Hanover Square rooms, Clara had the pleasure of giving the first English performance of Brahms's piano compositions—a Sarabande and Gavotte "in the style of Bach," written in 1855.[29] This was indeed the first performance of any of Brahms's compositions in the British Isles, later to become a hotbed of Brahms appreciation. Shortly after Clara's return in July, Brahms played both the A Minor Prelude and Fugue and the A-flat Minor Fugue for her, but whether on the piano or on the organ is unknown. Some writers have speculated that the Schumanns might still have had a pedal piano,[30] but the pedal attachment they had in Dresden was rented, and there is no concrete evidence that they either owned or rented a similar one after their move to Düsseldorf in the fall of 1850. Yet in October 1853, very shortly after Brahms's arrival, Clara had recorded in her diary that she had played some of Robert's B-A-C-H fugues for Brahms.[31] These may, of course, have been her own pedal-less transcriptions of the works. In 1896, her transcriptions of three of Schumann's *Skizzen für den Pedal-Flügel* (op. 58) were published in London, but it is not improbable that these transcriptions had been made much earlier, and that she had transcribed the "B-A-C-H" fugues as well. Brahms is known to have played one of the *Skizzen* in a piano recital early in 1857, but whether he or Clara transcribed it is unknown.

Nonetheless, the presence of a pedal piano in the Schumanns' Düsseldorf residence, although nowhere specifically mentioned, cannot be ruled out and could account for at least some of the instances in which Brahms played his organ pieces for Clara. In early July, Brahms had written to Adolf Schubring, to whom he had lent some manuscripts of recent compositions for appraisal, asking for their speedy return, "as I have no copy of the fugues and must practice them."[32] Considering the date, he must have been referring to the two works he planned to play for Clara, both of which have substantial pedal parts but could have been practiced on either an organ or a pedal piano. Of course, one cannot rule out simple transcription to an ordinary piano, as Brahms did with Bach's organ works. Both he and Clara also played Robert's pedal piano pieces in their concerts, and most likely both were quite capable of transcribing from the originals at sight. Yet the fact remains that whenever either Brahms or Clara refers to actually practicing organ music, the only instrument ever specifically mentioned is the organ.

Clara's previous reference to hoping to "entice Robert into the church" to hear her playing his organ compositions suggests she may have had access to one of the church organs in Düsseldorf, but if so, there is no clue as to which one. The Schumanns and Brahms would have heard on at least one occasion the fine 1755 König organ in St. Maximilian's Church, located not far from the house the Schumanns had rented in the Poststrasse. In October 1853, shortly after Brahms arrived at the Schumanns', Robert conducted a performance of a mass by Moritz Hauptmann in this church; the organ was probably involved in the accompaniment, and Brahms was presumably in attendance.[33] Another Düsseldorf organ they might have encountered was the 1766 Teschemacher organ in the Lutheran Church in the Bergerstrasse. Tonally, both of these instruments were in the eighteenth-century Rhenish tradition, which, like that of Thuringia and Saxony, incorporated—along with the classical principal chorus—an ample complement of 8' and 4' stops, including strings (Gamba, Salicional, Unda Maris) and flutes, some of which were harmonic (overblowing). The St. Maximilian organ was the larger of the two, with three manuals and thirty-nine registers, and its third manual was enclosed—an "Echo Oberwerk."[34] The Teschemacher organ was a two-manual instrument of twenty-one registers, with only a coupled pedal and no enclosed division, but again with a good selection of 8' and 4' colors.[35]

The explorations of counterpoint, Bach, and organ composition served the three friends in more than one way. For Brahms, they deepened his understanding of counterpoint and sharpened his skills in that discipline; doubtless they likewise did so for Joachim, even though composition soon became subordinate to performance and conducting in his career. And for both Brahms and Clara, they surely also provided a needed diversion from their growing concerns about Robert Schumann, as his physical condition and mental state continued to worsen. It all came to an end in July 1856. On the twenty-third, Robert's physician summoned Clara to the sanitarium and told her that her husband was in his last days. Going with her, Brahms found Robert in such a horrifying state that he persuaded Clara not to see him. Four days later, they went to Endenich again; this time, Clara did see for the last time her beloved husband, who, although incoherent and feeble, smiled at her and tried to embrace her. Two days later, Robert Schumann, one of the nineteenth century's finest composers, was gone. He was buried on July 31 in Bonn, with Brahms, Joachim, and his student Albert Dietrich among his mourners.

Brahms stayed with Clara for a short while afterward, escorting her and two of her children (with his sister Elise as chaperone) to Switzerland for her health, but the close little circle of friends in Düsseldorf shortly broke up. Joachim went to Hanover, Dietrich to Bonn, and Clara and her children to Berlin, from which she launched—from financial necessity, as well as a desire to promote the music of Robert Schumann and Brahms—her demanding career as a concert artist. Brahms, thanks to a recommendation from Clara, had secured a pleasant and undemanding part-time court appointment in Detmold, where he directed a choir, played the piano in concerts, gave piano lessons, and had ample free time for both composition and visits to Hamburg.

Brahms was in Hamburg in late October 1856, and his thoughts seem to have briefly returned to his contrapuntal work. In December, he wrote to Clara, saying, "Everybody is greatly pleased with my A Minor Fugue. On Sunday I shall try it again on the organ."[36] Unfortunately, he doesn't amplify on who "everybody" was, or what organ he tried the piece on. Otto Biba suggests that he may have played it in a church service,[37] but in view of Brahms's reference to "trying" the piece, this seems highly unlikely. Possibly he could have gone to some church after a service—perhaps St. Michael's, where he knew the pastor and where he might have bribed the organ blower to stay a little longer. However, he may simply have gone to Böhme's music store, where he had practiced on previous stays and may have had access when the store was closed for business. This appears to be Brahms's last mention of playing the organ in any of his known correspondence, although he completed the Prelude and Fugue in G Minor for organ a few months later and possibly also tried it out on an organ.

Brahms had gone to Detmold in October 1856 but continued to occasionally spend some time in Hamburg, first with his family and, after 1858, in a friend's pleasant villa in the suburb of Hamm. The last three years with the Schumanns had been an intense and maturing time for the young composer. During this short period he had met the woman he worshiped but could not have, and he had witnessed the tormented death of the gifted composer who had so unselfishly promoted his cause. He had also deepened his understanding of Bach and the Lutheran chorale and matched wits with Joachim as together they plumbed the intricacies of counterpoint. And on top of all this, he had labored—possibly not entirely successfully—to master a new instrument. The organ may well have been forever linked in his subconscious with the emotional intensity of this period.

Perhaps this is why, in the relatively secure and stress-free period that followed, the organ began to recede into the background as Brahms reorganized his life and plunged with new confidence into revising earlier works and composing new ones. To Clara, he wrote, "How laboriously I had to climb and toil over many things that I now feel that I can take in my stride."[38] Now he began thinking more seriously about orchestral and chamber music composition. The result was the two Serenades (opp. 11 and 16), the First String Sextet (op. 18), and the completion of the First Piano Concerto (op. 15), begun during his time with the Schumanns.

There is no further mention of the organ from Brahms or anyone connected with him until two years after his move to Detmold. But by the summer of 1858, or probably earlier, Brahms had completed another organ piece. This was not a fugue but rather a short chorale prelude on the Good Friday chorale *O Traurigkeit, O Herzeleid*. A copy dated July 1858 was left as a gift to his piano student Friedchen Wagner before Brahms left for a short stay in Göttingen.[39] Although the full text of the chorale has to do with Good Friday, it is hard not to associate its opening words—"O sadness, O heart-sorrow"—with Brahms's lingering feelings over the loss of Robert Schumann. Indeed, it is probable that the piece was begun shortly after Schumann's death, for the pedal part of the earliest surviving holograph suggests that it had been written when Brahms was still practicing on the little music store organ with the *angehängten* pedal in Hamburg.

Julius Otto Grimm (1827–1903), a composer, conductor, and teacher, was Brahms's friend and a member of the Schumann circle. Brahms mentions him in his 1854 letter to Clara in which he described his progress on the organ, noting, "I have not played for Grimm." But possibly on other occasions he did play for his friend. In any case, Grimm was aware of Brahms's organ-playing ability, for in late June 1858, he invited Brahms to Göttingen, where he was then directing a small choral society, the Cäcilienverein. Clara was visiting there, and—as if Brahms needed any further incentive—Grimm added, "You can also play the organ here—and help me perform a couple of Bach cantatas, if you are willing to accompany on the organ."[40] Brahms went to Göttingen in July and possibly did as Grimm asked, although we do not know the location of the Bach performance or what sort of organ was there. However, Brahms's lyrical choral work, *Ave Maria* (op. 12), is said to have been written, or at least begun, while he was in Göttingen and perhaps even sung by Grimm's chorus. Although subsequently scored for strings and woodwinds, the accompaniment was originally written for organ, and the work was later sung by Brahms's Frauenchor in this version.

It is curious, then, that when Grimm again requested Brahms to accompany his chorus on the organ in the fall of 1858, Brahms responded rather gruffly, "Organ-playing isn't possible. Why such experiments? You have a very good organist there, and I can neither find my way around the pedalboard nor the stops."[41] One possible interpretation might be that Brahms had had some unpleasant experience (perhaps with an unfamiliar type of organ?) on his previous encounter. Even if he had reservations about his pedal playing, he could have accompanied choral music just as well on manuals only. Of course, it might also have been simply that Brahms, who was doing quite a bit of composing at this time, couldn't see any reason to interrupt his work to go to Göttingen just to do a bit of accompanying (probably gratis), especially when he knew that Grimm already had a good organist at his disposal.

One further instance of Brahms as organist occurs less than a year later. Brahms grew up in the parish of St. Michael's Church in Hamburg. Pastor von Ahlsen had married his parents and baptized little Johannes, who was later confirmed there at the age of fifteen. During Brahms's lifetime, this large and imposing church had a notable organ built between 1769 and 1771 by J. G. Hildebrandt, Gottfried Silbermann's godson, whose father was Silbermann's successor.[42] It was a three-manual organ of sixty-eight speaking stops, with an impressive façade in which pipes of the pedal 32' principal were displayed. Its physical and tonal design reflected the progressive central German style rather than that of the earlier Schnitger-influenced Hamburg school. Its divisions were not disposed in the older *Werk-Prinzip* arrangement, and along with the classic principal chorus and upperwork, each division was well supplied with foundation tone, including strings and a variety of colorful flute and reed stops.[43] Although he never made any mention of it in his later correspondence, Brahms must certainly have heard this splendid instrument on more than one occasion in his youth, even if he rarely (if ever) attended a church service as an adult. The church may have also had a smaller organ on the north side, although sources concerned with the larger organ give no details of it.

Brahms seems in any case to have been friendly with Pastor von Ahlsen and his family, and in May 1859 he was asked to accompany a small chorus of women for the wedding of the pastor's daughter Jenny. Two separate accounts mention this event. Chorus member Marie Völckers stated plainly in her diary: "Brahms played the organ, and after the ceremony he asked the ladies if they would like to sing some of the songs he had composed."[44] This was the genesis of the Hamburger Frauenchor that Brahms directed for several years, and for which he wrote some of his earliest choral works. What is unknown about this incident is whether Brahms played for the entire service or simply accompanied the chorus, conducted by his friend Karl Grädener, director of the Hamburg Akademie chorus. Wm. A. Little suggests that the church's regular organist probably played for most of the service and that Brahms's role in the wedding music was limited to accompanying the chorus.[45] But depending on the musical content of the rest of the ceremony, which may have comprised only a few chorales, it is not impossible that Brahms was indeed the only organist involved. Even today it is not unusual for a German Lutheran wedding party to simply process and recess to chorales—as this writer once observed in no less notable a venue than St. Thomas's Church in Leipzig. And Brahms was certainly quite capable of playing chorales on the organ.

Thanks to the Hamburger Frauenchor, Brahms continued to have occasional encounters with the organ. Although rehearsals were usually held in Friedchen Wagner's home, the group sometimes sang in St. Peter's Church. This was one of Hamburg's oldest churches, which until the great fire of 1842 housed a much-rebuilt seventeenth-century organ. After the church was rebuilt, a two-manual organ was installed in 1848 by the Hamburg builder Johann Gottlieb Wolfsteller, who added a third manual division in 1852. Wolfsteller is regarded as a conservative builder whose work grew out of the late-eighteenth-century style, but in 1857, perhaps to keep up with changing trends, he enclosed the new third manual in a swell box.[46] This was the organ that Brahms knew, although it was replaced by a larger Walcker instrument in 1884.

In June 1859, one of the Frauenchor's first performances was given in St. Peter's Church, where they sang Brahms's *Ave Maria* and two newly composed four-part motets, *O Bone Jesu* and *Adoremus*. He reported the event to Clara, whose response indicated that organ accompaniment was involved: "How did you like the songs which you tried with the organ on June 9? Aren't they very difficult? Did your girls sing them well?"[47] One other question might well be asked: Did Brahms accompany them on the organ (perhaps at rehearsals), or did someone else play? In August, Brahms wrote to one of his singers in Detmold, "Some very pleasant pupils detain me [in Hamburg] and, strangely enough, a ladies' society that sings under my direction, till now only what I compose for it. The clear, silver tones please me exceedingly and, in the church with the organ, the ladies' voices sound quite charming."[48] We could wish that Brahms had extended his commentary to some description of the organ, but we must be satisfied that it proved a good accompanimental instrument for the "clear, silver tones" of his chorus.

Franziska Meier, one of the Frauenchor singers, noted in her diary that by the end of August, the group was rehearsing two new works that eventually became part of Brahms's *Marienlieder* (op. 22). She had not taken part in the earlier performance at St. Peter's Church, but Brahms promised another, and she quotes him as saying, "I think we will repeat that at the earliest opportunity. Everybody enjoys singing with organ accompaniment so much."[49] The Frauenchor seems to have had free use of the church and its organ, and Meier indicates that some of its members, including Mme. Nordheim, one of the older singers who occasionally joined them, and even Brahms's sister Elise, took turns treading the bellows for the rehearsals.[50] She also quotes Brahms as saying that he preferred the acoustics of St. Peter's Church to those of the larger St. Michael's for his singers. Their numbers were rapidly growing, and they continued to inspire him to compose new music.

By the end of August, the Frauenchor was rehearsing his *Psalm XIII* (op. 27), completed only a week earlier, and Brahms wrote to Clara, "As it has organ accompaniment, we shall again sing in church—this and my *Ave Maria*—I have at least forty girls now."[51] *Psalm XIII* has a quite independent organ part—more so than that of the *Ave Maria*, for it interacts and alternates with the voices and provides a climax at the end. Perhaps having a good organ for his choir's concerts had inspired Brahms to write something with a more ambitious accompaniment at this juncture. Brahms later added some ad libitum string parts to it, while retaining the obbligato organ accompaniment. The Frauenchor sang these and some other pieces in St. Peter's Church on Monday, September 19, and this time we know from Meier's account that Brahms directed and the church's organist, Georg H. F. Armbrust, accompanied on the organ, assisted by Meier's sister Camilla as stop puller and page turner. Apparently the chorus first attempted to sing from the ground floor, but there were communication problems between director and organist, the latter being in the loft above, where it was impossible to see Brahms's conducting. But the girls eventually agreed to regroup in the rather narrow organ loft, and the performance was a success.[52]

Brahms gave up his Detmold post in 1860, moved back to Hamburg, and continued to direct the Frauenchor sporadically (occasionally spelled by Grädener) until his move to Vienna in 1863. He afterward retained many fond memories of "his girls," their performances, and the social times they enjoyed together (suitably chaperoned by Frau Grädener), and he stayed in touch with some of them in later years.

The Vienna Period

Brahms, a North German to the core, had cherished hopes of finding a secure musical position in his native city of Hamburg. But these were dashed when the attractive position of conductor of the Hamburg Philharmonic

Society, for which Joachim and other supporters had recommended him, was awarded instead to his friend the singer Julius Stockhausen. Brahms first visited Vienna in the fall of 1862 to give a piano concert, in which he included a transcription of a Bach organ work. He returned to Vienna in January 1863, and in March he was appointed conductor of the Wiener Singakademie. He held the position only a year, but it was a year marked by performances of Bach's Christmas Oratorio and other Bach works, along with early works by Italian and English composers and pieces by Schumann and himself.

In the first concert that Brahms directed, on November 15, 1863, the Singakademie performed works by Bach, Beethoven, and Schumann, as well as some of Brahms's own four-part folk song arrangements. The location of the concert is unknown, but it must have been a church or another venue with an organ. The Bach work was the cantata *Ich hatte viel Bekümmernis* (BWV 21), and Karl Geiringer observes that Brahms took the trouble to write a special organ part for this, preserved in the Singakademie's archives, which "clearly shows the artist's conception of how the older music should be performed. The organ supports the choir and the orchestra, intensifies the important crescendos, and supplies the necessary fullness of tone and harmony."[53] It was not the only time that Brahms did this. Michael Musgrave notes that "for his performances of Handel at the *Gesellschaft der Musikfreunde*, Brahms added expression marks and organ parts, though these were never published." He also wrote his own organ part for Mozart's *Offertorium de Venerabili Sacramento* for another concert there,[54] and in 1875 he is known to have written out an organ part to another Bach cantata for his friend Philipp Spitta.[55] Such instances confirm that Brahms regarded the organ as an important element in some of the older choral music, as well as occasionally in his own.

After his move to Vienna in 1863, Brahms made no further mention of organs in his surviving correspondence with Clara Schumann, but she did. Indeed, Clara's interest in the organ seems to have noticeably exceeded that of Brahms. Previously, in March 1859, she had written to him about attending a recital played by her old acquaintance Johann Gottlob Schneider on the noted Silbermann organ in the Dresden Hofkirche; she was rather critical of Schneider's performance of Bach, which she regarded as somewhat mannered and "not noble enough." She then admonished Brahms: "Keep on playing the organ!"[56] There is no real evidence that he did, however.

In September 1862, Clara was in Lucerne, where we again catch a glimpse of her continuing interest in the organ as she writes to Brahms: "A magnificent new organ has been built here, which was dedicated today; various organists played, Kirchner and Stockhausen sang, Hegar, a very pleasing violinist, played, all accompanied by the organ." This was a four-manual, seventy-stop organ in the Hofkirche, built by German-trained Friedrich Haas of Lucerne, considered at the time to be the leading Swiss organ builder. According to Clara, it had "a new stop, which imitates the human voice, which charmed everyone, but is unfortunately so weak that occasionally it requires great effort to hear it." Undoubtedly, this was a Vox Humana, a soft reed stop rather popular at the time. Stockhausen sang an aria from *Faust,* after which Kirchner—an organist as well as a singer—improvised on it.[57] The following year, Clara reported hearing their mutual friend Kirchner play the organ in Winterthur and stated that she was "particularly charmed" by his organ playing.[58] Clara was perhaps also a bit charmed by Kirchner himself; some biographers have suggested that she may have had a brief and very discreet affair with him around this time.[59]

Soon Clara encountered something quite different from large German church organs. While in Paris in the 1830s, Clara had met a gifted young singer, Pauline Garcia, and a friendship of long standing was begun. Pauline, sister of the renowned Maria Malibran, also became a successful operatic diva, and in 1840 married Louis Viardot, impresario, art critic, and director of the Théâtre Italien in Paris. The Viardots acquired an opulent Paris residence that included a salon for informal concerts, for which the noted Parisian organ builder Aristide Cavaillé-Coll built an organ of two manuals and sixteen stops in 1851.[60] Despite its relatively small size, it was a *multum in parvo* of French Romantic tone colors. The Viardots moved to a residence in Baden-Baden in 1860 and brought with them the organ from the Paris salon. In 1862, Clara Schumann and two of her daughters came to visit, and Pauline and other friends persuaded her to take up residence near Baden-Baden during the summer. There is no question that the idea appealed to her, for in her diary she wrote that she had been leading "a really dreadful life," on the road concertizing most of the time, but "always in doubt where to go in the summer." Baden-Baden thus held great appeal as "a refuge with leisure and seclusion for my study," as well as a congenial colony of people involved in the arts.[61] As a result, in 1863 Clara purchased a modest country house there that comfortably accommodated her family, three pianos, and occasional visitors.

In the fall of 1864, Clara attended an informal concert in the salon of the Viardots' home, during which Pauline played the organ. Reporting the event to Brahms, she declared that the organ "sounded wonderful" and gave much pleasure—but that "Mad. Viardot can't play the pedals" and only played the D-Major Fugue (BWV 850) from Bach's *Wohltemperierte Klavier.* The organ was also used to accompany harp, violin, and voices. Then she added, "Ah, why couldn't I have such an organ ... and then when you came and played on it, what divine music that would be!"[62] This was wishful thinking, of course; the Schumann home (and finances) hardly compared with that of the Viardots. But it confirms Clara's lingering interest in organs and reveals nostalgia for their joint encounter with organ playing a decade earlier.

Brahms visited Clara in Baden-Baden several times and also knew Pauline Viardot. He even composed a little serenade for her and conducted some of her students' performance of it under her window on her birthday in July 1864. Later, in 1870, she sang the solo part in the premiere performance of Brahms's *Alto Rhapsody* (op. 53).[63] During his summer visits to Baden-Baden, Brahms is said to have attended some of the Viardot soirées, and it is not improbable that he, too, had occasion to hear the Cavaillé-Coll organ before the Viardots (and the organ) returned to Paris in 1872, after the end of the Franco-Prussian War. Of all the organs that Brahms may have heard, hardly any still survive in anything resembling their original state. However, the Viardots' Cavaillé-Coll does still exist, having been moved in 1885 (with some modifications) to the Collegiate Church of Notre-Dame in Melun, where it remains in use.[64]

Brahms spent the next few years traveling, living briefly in Zürich, and then returning to Vienna in 1866. From this point on his interest in the organ, nostalgic or not, seems to have diminished almost (but not quite) to the vanishing point. Before 1864, as we have seen, Brahms wrote four organ works (Prelude and Fugue in A Minor, Prelude and Fugue in G Minor, Fugue in A-flat Minor, and the Chorale Prelude on *O Traurigkeit*) that can be positively dated, as well as two choral works with organ accompaniment (*Ave Maria* and *Psalm XIII*). Two additional compositions are also attributed to this period. Although the *O Traurigkeit* chorale prelude can be documented as having been written in 1858 or before, the fugue that accompanied it when it was finally published in 1882 has not. Although it was probably sketched out earlier, it is not mentioned in any correspondence or other source prior to 1873.

The other composition—and, with *Psalm XIII*, a convincing example of Brahms's fluent grasp of independent organ accompaniment—is the moving *Geistliches Lied* (to Paul Flemming's text *Lass mich nur nichts nicht dauern*), op. 30. It is usually assigned to the year 1864, when its first known performance occurred in July at St. James's Church (Jakobikirche) in Chemnitz, but, like *Psalm XIII*, it had its origin earlier, during Brahms's period of contrapuntal experiments, and the "consolation" theme of the text is suggestive of a Schumann connection. The accompaniment is unquestionably for the organ, even being written on three staves (as is that for *Psalm XIII*), although piano is given as an alternate accompaniment. In 1860, Clara observed that although the organ really helps the whole, the piano "appears too dry" to be suitable.[65] Certainly only the organ, with its sustained sound, allows the accompaniment to flow seamlessly with the voices in this work, and the percussive nature of the piano indeed makes it too "dry" for the task.

In their style, craftsmanship, and musical maturity, these choral works with organ accompaniment have a strong kinship to the *Deutsches Requiem*, the beginnings of which can be traced at least as far back as 1861, and which was virtually completed (with the exception of the fifth movement) by 1866. Although assumed by many sources to have been inspired by the death of Brahms's mother in 1865, Max Kalbeck and others make a better case for the *Requiem* having been initially conceived in honor of Schumann. Yet it is hard not to see the added fifth movement, at least, as a touching tribute to the composer's mother, particularly because it is the only movement written after her death.

The first three movements of the *Requiem* were performed in Vienna in December 1867, with orchestra only, and were not particularly well received. However, on Good Friday of 1868, the work was, excepting the yet-to-be-written fifth movement, performed in the Bremen Cathedral, where Schulze had built a large organ in 1849. By this time, an organ part had been added to the full score, which had also been reworked in other respects. The first published edition of the orchestral parts of the *Requiem* included an organ part "fully worked out by the composer."[66] From the opening bars (where the pedal doubles the contrabass in the repeated notes), the organ plays at least part of the time in all but the fifth movement, which was added shortly after the Bremen performance. Vernon Gotwals finds that the organ is required to play for about a third of the time during the entire *Requiem*, and it is probable that this is why Brahms wished the first real premiere to be performed in a venue with a good organ.

Brahms used a sustained low D, played on the pedals, to undergird the muffled drumbeats of the fugue in the third movement. Writing to his old teacher Marxsen after the organless Vienna performance in 1867, Brahms observed of this passage: "When I can't have the use of an organ, it doesn't sound right."[67] Pedal points occur elsewhere in the score, and in several places Brahms uses the pedals alone to reinforce the low strings; in one instance, to reinforce a double bass line, Brahms wrote "*Orgel!*" in his conducting score, presumably for the Bremen performance.[68] Elsewhere, the organ is employed in a variety of carefully thought-out ways, all confirming Brahms's understanding of the instrument. Full *forte* organ chords are called upon for emphasis of certain words, especially in the second and sixth movements. But elsewhere, soft *piano* chords reinforce choral and string parts, as in the first, fourth, and seventh movements. In some of these softer examples, Brahms specified manuals only, and in a couple of instances he wrote "*oben*" above the notes, apparently in reference to the upper (and expressive) manual. An occasional diminuendo in these places can refer only to the use of the expression pedal. In some fugal passages (e.g., the third movement, where it also holds a long pedal point) the organ doubles all or most of the chorus parts.

Siegfried Ochs (1858–1929), the conductor of the Philharmonisches Chor of Berlin, soon added the *Requiem* to his chorus's repertoire and also underscored the importance of the organ part. He stated that an "instruction that is apt to meet with lack of understanding is the *Orgel ad libitum:* it appears to be rather unimportant whether the organ is used or not. According to a recollection of the publisher, the *ad libitum* was placed there because at the time the work was published one could not expect to find an organ in every concert hall, and [Brahms] was afraid that the piece might never be performed at all." Ochs, who subsequently conducted the *Requiem* many times, observed that in the crescendo of the second movement, where the trumpets do not initially play and the strings drop to a low register, "the only support can come from the organ, which should make use of the crescendo pedal."[69]

The presence of an organ part may well have encouraged some early church performances of the *Requiem,* as in Lübeck's Marienkirche in 1872 and 1873.[70] Although organs were soon to proliferate in German concert halls, at the time the work was written, Brahms's concern about their absence was valid. Performance venues in 1869 included Leipzig, where there was no concert hall organ prior to 1884, and Zurich, where the first organ was not installed in the Tonhalle until 1872. And although the first performance in Vienna, in 1871, occurred in the new hall of the Gesellschaft der Musikfreunde, this was a year prior to the installation of an organ there. However, the *Requiem* was performed there on several subsequent occasions, undoubtedly with organ.

A lesser-known work, the *Triumphlied,* op. 55, written in 1870–1871, is also scored for orchestra and "*Orgel ad libitum.*" Manuscript organ parts for performances directed by Brahms in 1874 in the same Vienna hall (by this time equipped with an organ), and fairly well authenticated as having been written by Brahms, exist for this work. It is obvious that the organ plays an important role in the *Triumphlied,* which begins with three *forte* chords for organ and orchestra, the organ part being marked *Volles Werk* (full organ). The organ continues to be an indispensable part of the scoring throughout, although not in as subtle a manner as in the *Requiem;* here its role consists largely of emphatic forte and fortissimo chords, which must surely have provided added excitement. Interestingly, the organ part in the manuscript includes some registration directions, although it is not known whether these were written in by Brahms or by the organist who performed from it. They seem to have to do largely with dynamic changes: "with Trumpets," "without 16' and 4' with Trumpets" (suggesting that the 16' and 4' pitches had previously been employed), and, in one instance, "without 4', *pp*" (suggesting only quiet 8' stops).[71]

In 1872, Brahms was appointed director of the prestigious Gesellschaft der Musikfreunde. This organization owned what was then the finest concert hall in Vienna, the Grosse Musikvereinsaal, familiarly known as the Goldene Saal for its brilliantly gilded decorations, built in 1870. In the same year, a contract was signed for a three-manual, fifty-two-stop organ from the distinguished Weissenfels builder Friedrich Ladegast, and it was completed just a few months after Brahms assumed the directorship.[72] The stoplist of this organ reveals a fairly conservative but colorful Romantic instrument, which had for its third manual division a substantial enclosed *Echowerk*. This organ remained in use throughout Brahms's subsequent residence in Vienna, although it was extensively rebuilt and enlarged in 1904.

Brahms's connections with the Ladegast organ, ordered before his arrival by a committee that included Anton Bruckner, who was then teaching organ at the conservatory, are somewhat vague. Hermann J. Busch reports what may be an urban legend to the effect that while the organ was being installed, Brahms stopped by to look at it, but Ladegast did not know who he was "and therefore prevented him from inspecting the work."[73] A slightly different version is related by Alexander Koschel of the Ladegast-Kollegium, although without citing a source. According to this version, Brahms came to the hall while the tonal finishing was in progress but was refused admittance by Ladegast. An official of the hall saw this incident and said to Ladegast, "But you can't turn him away!" Ladegast asked why, and the official responded, "Because that's Herr Brahms."[74] The original source for this story is probably Emile Rupp's 1929 history of organ building, in which he relates that although Brahms was already "well known among his votaries and the Bruckner-adversaries," Ladegast did not recognize him. Thus when Brahms made an apparently impromptu appearance in the hall at an "unsuitable hour," he was "unceremoniously dismissed like any other ordinary mortal."[75] Rupp (who does not suggest that Brahms came to "inspect the work") appears to have heard this story from someone associated with Ladegast; if true, it suggests that Brahms showed at least some interest in the new organ. But was Brahms so reticent that he would not have introduced himself to the organ builder as the new director of the Gesellschaft der Musikfreunde? This organization was, after all, the owner of the organ. Possibly, though, he may simply have realized that he was intruding on some very busy people and was content to retreat without further words.

The Ladegast organ was completed on November 5, 1872, and first heard publicly at Brahms's own inaugural concert on November 10. A featured work was Handel's *Dettingen Te Deum*, and a reviewer noted that the organ part, played by court organist Rudolf Bibl, had been prepared and scored by Brahms.[76] Rudolf Quoika claims that Anton Bruckner played it,[77] but it is likely that he confused this concert with the formal debut of the organ in a solo recital on November 15, when Karl August Fischer of Dresden played a program of works by J. S. Bach, Mendelssohn, and Liszt, followed by Bruckner, who demonstrated various stops and combinations and closed with an improvisation on the Austrian national anthem.[78] There can be little doubt that this concert, which received a very lukewarm review in the *Allgemeine Muzikzeitung*, was planned not by Brahms but by Bruckner and his organ committee. Despite his coolness toward Bruckner and dislike of Liszt, Brahms was present—but only to conduct the Singverein in two unaccompanied Renaissance motets by Johannes Eccard and Heinrich Isaac.[79]

Brahms presented a concert of his own on December 6, described in a letter to Joachim. It included the Organ Concerto in D Minor by Handel, a double chorus by Mozart accompanied by violins and organ, a Gluck aria sung by Amalie Joachim, a single work for organ solo, Bach's Prelude and Fugue in E-flat Major (BWV 552), and Brahms's own *Triumphlied*, which included an organ part—and was, incidentally, the only contemporary work on the program.[80] The organist for this occasion was Samuel de Lange Jr. of Rotterdam, an acquaintance and supporter of Brahms who shared his interest in earlier music (as well as his distaste for Liszt). Brahms's friend, Theodor Billroth was there, and was hugely impressed with it, particularly the *Triumphlied*, which "made a wonderful impression here with organ and a colossal choir ... it is monumental music." Indeed, the performance of that work was so stirring that it gave Billroth "goosebumps" [*Gänsehaut*].[81] Those frequently interjected *forte* and *fortissimo* organ chords doubtless heightened the effect of certain passages.

The *Triumphlied*, a pièce d'occasion written to commemorate the victory of the Prussians over the French (1870–1871), is rarely performed today, although it was understandably popular in its day. It includes two chorale-based movements and ends with a hallelujah chorus. Not everyone was quite as enthusiastic as Billroth. In 1887, Hugo Wolf (a Wagner supporter and therefore inclined to be cool toward Brahms) wrote it off in a review as "a Handelian impersonation, unfortunately rather tiresome."[82] There is no denying the Handel influence, and it should be remembered that one of the works played at Brahms's inauguration was a closely related work, Handel's *Dettingen Te Deum*, composed to commemorate England's victory over the French at Dettingen in 1743.

Brahms, who seems to have had an aversion to long-term professional commitments, as well as to the jealousy and intrigues that often go with them, stayed in his position with the Gesellschaft der Musikfreunde only until the spring of 1875. During his time there, though, he directed a number of choral performances that featured Bach, Handel, and other earlier composers, as well as his own compositions: in addition to the *Triumphlied*, there were his *Requiem, Schicksalslied, Alto Rhapsody,* and some folk song arrangements. Save for that first concert in the Musikvereinsaal, however, the new organ was relegated to merely an accompanimental role in subsequent concerts Brahms directed, although the Bach Prelude and Fugue in E-flat was presented again on February 28, 1875—in an orchestral arrangement![83] Nonetheless, Brahms would have had other opportunities to hear the rich sonorities of the Ladegast organ in the splendidly warm acoustics of the Goldene

Saal, both during and after his directorship—certainly in any performances of his *Requiem* and *Triumphlied,* and presumably in Handel and Bach choral works as well. Scores of several of these exist with an organ part written in Brahms's own hand. In his score for Handel's *Saul,* the organ part contains such directions as *Man. III, Pedal, Solo,* and *Coppel* (coupler).[84] Had he ever been inquisitive enough to have tried the Ladegast organ himself, he probably would have told Clara of it—and perhaps he did, but he left no record of it. But although we find little concrete evidence that Brahms ever displayed much curiosity about organs generally, it seems quite clear that he had a good understanding of the instrument and its uses, both solo and accompanimental.

Several writers have attempted to suggest that Brahms's last organ works may have been influenced by some of the newer Viennese church organs, such as the 1858 Buckow instrument in the Piaristenkirche, the large 1878 Walcker in the Votivkirche, or the even larger 1886 Walcker in St. Stephen's Cathedral. Robert Schuneman, Holger Gehring, Hermann Busch, and others cite the first two as examples of "Brahms organs," Busch rather cautiously suggesting that Brahms at least "had the opportunity" of hearing them.[85] However, Bruckner's connection with the Piaristenkirche was probably enough reason for Brahms to avoid it, and if Brahms was present at the organ dedications in St. Stephen's or the Votivkirche (which surely must have been gala musical events), no reference has ever surfaced. Curiously, no one has attempted to link Brahms with the eighteenth-century organ (enlarged in 1847) in the Karlskirche, a building Brahms could see from the window of the workroom in his lodgings at No. 4 Karlsplatz. Brahms admired this impressive edifice for its Baroque architecture and had to walk past it to go to the Gesellschaft der Musikfreunde's buildings a short distance away. But he was no more likely to have heard this organ (save possibly at Bruckner's funeral) than those in any of the other Catholic churches.

Brahms, though not much of a churchgoer, was still at heart a North German Lutheran, part of the small Protestant minority in Vienna. If his compositions are any indication, his orientation with regard to organs and organ music—as well as to some of his choral music—was Lutheran. If he ever attended a church service in Vienna at all, it would have been in the Lutheran Church in the Dorotheergasse, with its modest two-manual Deutschmann organ, variously dated at 1808 or 1820, the attractive casework of which still graces the church's rear gallery. Bruckner played this organ for a friend's wedding in 1890, but there is no evidence that Brahms ever played it. However, the pastor of the church at the time Brahms first came to Vienna was Gustav Porubsky, a friend from Hamburg who was the father of one of his Frauenchor singers, and one of the Grädeners may have been the organist there during Brahms's early Vienna years. Some of his Viennese Lutheran friends were also associated with this church, and even if Brahms never attended the Sunday *Gottesdienst* there, he might still have been present at a friend's wedding or funeral and would thus have heard the organ on such occasions.

Vienna's most notable church organs were housed in the large Catholic churches, and Bruckner was at the time the doyen of Catholic church music in the city. Although it is not impossible that Brahms may at some time have heard some of these organs during his long residence in Vienna, it is too much of a stretch of the imagination to suppose that he ever had the occasion (or desire) to actually play any of them. Wishful thinking is no substitute for factual documentation, and statements such as that made recently in a major organists' periodical referring to the "organ in the Votivkirche, where Brahms is said to have practiced,"[86] besides having no foundation in fact (or even urban legend), are irresponsible and misleading. After the early 1870s, Brahms became so involved with composing and conducting that he virtually gave up performing on the piano in public, and according to several accounts, he was no longer seriously practicing even his primary instrument. Students and those for whom he occasionally played informally noted sloppiness and lack of concern "over such little trifles as hitting the wrong notes."[87] If Brahms let his piano playing slip, it is hard to imagine why he would have either needed or wanted to practice on any organ. And if he ever did, the organs in the Gesellschaft der Musikfreunde's building (which included a ten-stop Ladegast practice organ, as well as the large concert hall organ)[88] would have been closer and more accessible. Indeed, the only organ in Vienna whose sound we know with certitude that Brahms actually heard was the Ladegast instrument in that organization's Grosser Vereinsaal.

Although Brahms is not positively known to have composed any solo organ works (with the possible exception of the *O Traurigkeit* fugue) for nearly forty years after 1858, his use of the organ in solo and concerted accompaniments to choral works during the 1860s and 1870s shows that he could still put his knowledge of the organ to practical use. It should also be remembered that two of his earlier organ compositions were eventually published, although without opus number: the Fugue in A-flat Minor in 1864 and in 1882 the Chorale Prelude and Fugue on *O Traurigkeit, O Herzeleid*, both having been noticeably revised from the earliest known manuscript versions. The other two preludes and fugues, quite as estimable in different ways, did not see publication until the twentieth century, when they were found among the papers of Clara Schumann. Brahms possibly never knew that she had preserved them.

After 1875, when he relinquished his directorship at the Gesellschaft der Musikfreunde and began to be known as a composer of larger-scaled symphonic works and in increasing demand as a conductor, the organ is a virtually blank page in Brahms's life until 1896. The publication of the *O Traurigkeit* pieces in 1882 shows that he hadn't forgotten some of his earlier organ compositions and that he set enough store by these particular ones to deem them worthy of publication. It is interesting, too, that when he played piano recitals before and during his early years in Vienna, these sometimes included his transcriptions of Bach's organ works. Bach's youthful Prelude and Fugue in A Minor (BWV 551) was performed in a concert given in Cologne in 1865; its bravura opening and the fact that most of the pedal parts can be fairly easily played by the left hand make it particularly adaptable for performance on the piano. In 1868 a reviewer of one of Brahms's concerts expressed admiration for these transcriptions, stating that Brahms knew "how to create the closest possible organ effect on the piano" with his "excellent legato" and "mastery of large sonorities."[89] Indeed, by the 1880s, when A. Maczewski contributed a biographical sketch of him to the first edition of *Grove's Dictionary*, it appears that Brahms had made something of a reputation for himself in such performances, for Maczewski states that "in his execution of Bach, especially of the organ works on the piano, he is acknowledged to be quite unrivalled."[90] Analyzing programs of nearly a hundred of Brahms's piano recitals given over a span of forty years, musicologist Raymond Kendall found frequent appearances of transcribed Bach organ works such as the Toccata in F Major (BWV 540) and the "St. Anne" Prelude and Fugue in E-flat Major (BWV 552) as well as the previously mentioned A Minor.[91] Possibly Brahms also at some time performed his friend Carl Tausig's piano arrangement of Bach's *O Lamm Gottes unschuldig* (BWV 656, from the "Great Eighteen" chorale preludes), for it is dedicated to him.[92]

Brahms is known to have played some transcribed Bach organ works in informal gatherings, as well as in recital. The young English composer Ethel Smyth, visiting Brahms's friends the Herzogenbergs in Leipzig, happened upon one of these impromptu performances in the 1870s and later wrote, "I like to think of Brahms at the piano, playing one of his own compositions or Bach's mighty organ fugues."[93] Although Brahms had long since put aside his youthful aspirations as an organ recitalist and returned to the piano, he had clearly not forgotten the Bach organ works he had presumably once studied— or the organ sonorities that he is credited with re-creating on the piano.

In 1880, Brahms began spending some of his summers in the spa village of Bad Ischl. In 1888, Matthias Mauracher built an organ of three manuals and thirty-three stops in the parish church of St. Nicholas there, replacing a smaller two-manual, seventeen-stop organ built in 1825; the Mauracher organ was subsequently rebuilt and enlarged in 1910. In July 1890, the kaiser's daughter was married in the Ischl church, and the organist for the ceremony was Anton Bruckner, who improvised on the Austrian national anthem (*Kaiserhymne*) and Handel's well-known hallelujah chorus.[94] Brahms had gone to Ischl in June and might have been there at the time but was probably quite uninterested in royal weddings—especially when they included another rehash of Bruckner's *Kaiserhymne* improvisation. Considering how many summers Brahms spent in Ischl, however, it is not improbable that he may have at least heard the organ in the parish church on a few occasions. Again, one writer attempts to connect "the Ischl organ . . . with the name of Johannes Brahms," although stopping short of suggesting that Brahms may have actually played it.[95] And there is no reason to think that he ever did.

In June 1896, shortly after Clara Schumann's funeral, Brahms, while visiting some friends in Vienna, played some of his first seven chorale preludes for them on the piano. A week later, he played them for a pupil in his residence in Ischl, likewise on the piano. Indeed, nowhere is there any evidence that Brahms either played or even heard these chorale preludes on an organ—unless, of course, earlier drafts of some of them were actually begun in the 1850s, when he was learning to play the organ, and then put aside, along with so many other things. But then there really was little need for Brahms to try or to hear these pieces on the organ. He had played his own compositions on an organ when he was in his twenties and had apparently played the music of Bach as well. Moreover, he had heard various organs played by others—in St. Michael's and St. Peter's churches in Hamburg, in the Bremen Cathedral, in the concert hall of the Gesellschaft der Musikfreunde in Vienna, perhaps in the Viardots' salon in Baden-Baden and the Lutheran Church in Vienna, and possibly in other places that are unrecorded, such as Winterthur, Lucerne, or Ischl.

Even after his brief early episode of writing solo works for the organ, he had written choral music with idiomatic organ accompaniment and had written and arranged organ parts in concerted works. He had even arranged Bach's organ music for the piano. Brahms knew the organ and its music, even though he had been out of close contact with it for decades. He knew what organs sounded like, what they could and couldn't do, and the proper way to write for them. If, as seems likely, he never physically heard his chorale preludes played on an organ, the remembered sonorities of the instrument surely resonated clearly in his mind as he wrote or revised them in later life.

Coda: Organists in Brahms's Life

From all evidence, Brahms had relatively little contact with organists and organ composers. Wm. A. Little notes that despite Brahms's youthful connections with St. Michael's Church in Hamburg, he never mentioned (and possibly never had any contact with) the church's organist from 1840 to 1886, G. D. W. Osterholdt.[96] He did later know Georg Armbrust (1818–1869), the organist of St. Peter's Church in Hamburg, who accompanied his Frauenchor for some concerts, and he stayed in touch with him occasionally later on. Karl Reinthaler (1822–1896), the organist of the cathedral in Bremen, collaborated with Brahms on a few occasions, including the first full performance of the *Requiem* (minus the as-yet-unwritten fifth movement) at the cathedral and a later performance of both the complete *Requiem* and the *Triumphlied*. If an anecdote related by Schauffler is authentic, Brahms is said to have written Reinthaler jokingly prior to the performance of the latter work, "We'll let the chorus sing whatever it likes. You will accompany them on the organ as loud as Bismarck alone deserves, and I will beat time for the whole business."[97] For some years thereafter, Brahms and Reinthaler corresponded, and when the Chorale Prelude and Fugue on *O Traurigkeit* was published in 1882, Brahms sent Reinthaler a copy.

Contacts with organists were no more frequent after Brahms settled in Vienna, where the prominent organists were mostly Catholic and presumably members of the Bruckner cadre. Although Brahms obviously was acquainted with Bruckner, who taught organ at the conservatory connected with the Gesellschaft der Musikfreunde, the relationship between the two was cool, and they seem to have taken pains to stay out of each other's way. It is interesting to note that although Bruckner was well known as an organ teacher and recitalist, his forte seems to have been improvisation. His actual compositions for organ were few and of less consequence than Brahms's, mostly youthful little *manualiter* pieces and a few short preludes and fugues, only one of which was written after he settled in Vienna.[98]

Brahms did, however, have a nodding acquaintance with a few other Viennese organists such as Rudolf Bibl (1832–1902), who served as organ accompanist in some of Brahms's concerts. Bibl was organist of St. Stephen's Cathedral (1859–1863) and later court organist. His compositions include a concerto for organ and orchestra, some organ sonatas, and Variations and Fugue on the Easter chorale *Christ ist erstanden*. Another Viennese organist with whom Brahms was acquainted was the blind Josef Labor (1842–1924), who had begun his career as a pianist but after 1880 built a reputation as an organ recitalist. Both Brahms and Labor were friends of the music-loving industrialist Karl Wittgenstein, who occasionally hosted gatherings of musicians at his home. Labor's compositions included sonatas and fantasias for the organ, as well as some liturgical works, and he gave occasional recitals on the Ladegast organ of the Vereinsaal. At one of these in 1883, he is said to have played Brahms's *O Traurigkeit* settings; at another, in 1895, he shared a program with a chorus singing excerpts from Brahms's *Triumphlied*. Brahms may have been present at one or both of these concerts.

But on at least one occasion during his tenure as director of the Gesellschaft der Musikfreunde, Brahms engaged not a Viennese organist but Samuel de Lange Jr. (1840–1911) of Rotterdam to take part in a concert that he presented in the Vereinsaal. De Lange, son of the organist of St. Laurens Church in Rotterdam, was noted as a recitalist. He was also a teacher and, like his father, a composer of organ music, including chorale preludes, variations and fantasias, preludes and fugues, pedal exercises, and five organ sonatas (three of which were found in Brahms's library), one of them dedicated to Brahms. De Lange was an admirer of Brahms who may have become acquainted with him on one of his concert tours to the Netherlands. He shared Brahms's interest in earlier music and published editions of works by Bach, Handel, Frescobaldi, and Muffat. It is of interest that Brahms's publisher, Simrock, also published some of the Dutch organist's organ works, perhaps at Brahms's instigation.

Among Brahms's closer friends, the individuals who played or composed for the organ were few indeed. Harry W. Gay, without citing a source, states that Karl Grädener (1812–1883), an old associate from Hamburg who taught at the Vienna Conservatory from 1862 to 1865, was organist for a short time at the Evangelical Church in Vienna.[99] This is not mentioned in any biographical accounts of him, although he did briefly direct the Evangelisches Chor. Possibly Gay confused him with his son Hermann, also an organist, who had studied at the Vienna Conservatory and taught there from 1874 until his death. Among the younger Grädener's compositions is a set of variations for organ, strings, and trumpet. Antonín Dvořák (1841–1904), the Czech composer whose chamber and orchestral music Brahms championed, had been organist of St. Adalbert's Church in Prague during the 1870s, and had even composed a few youthful preludes and fugues, although Brahms may not have known of them.

Theodor Kirchner (1823–1903), a student at Leipzig Conservatory when Mendelssohn was the director, had studied organ with J. G. Schneider of Dresden and was a longtime friend of both Brahms and Clara Schumann. He was employed as an organist between 1843 and 1862 in Winterthur, where Brahms visited him in 1860, and after 1871 he was organist of St. Peter's Church in Zürich. Clara heard him play the organ on a few occasions, and Brahms may have also. A singer as well as an organist and pianist, his compositions—which have not stood the test of time—were primarily songs and piano pieces, some of which Clara Schumann played in recital. But he also wrote some pieces for organ with violin and with cello and, in his later years, some works for organ solo. In 1878, Brahms gave a manuscript copy of O Traurigkeit, O Herzeleid to Elisabet von Herzogenberg, who played it on the piano for Kirchner and reported to Brahms that it had "roused him to great enthusiasm."[100]

Judging from his compositions, Elisabet's husband, Heinrich von Herzogenberg (1843–1900), had some firsthand organ-playing experience. This was, however, quite secondary to a variety of other musical pursuits such as organizing concerts, being a founding member (with Philipp Spitta) of Leipzig's Bachverein and its conductor from 1875, and from 1885, teaching theory and composition at the Hochschule in Berlin. The Herzogenbergs were close friends of Brahms, whom they entertained in their home on numerous occasions. Although an Austrian by birth who had begun his career in Vienna, Heinrich von Herzogenberg was, like Brahms, both a Protestant and an admirer of Bach. He was a fairly prolific composer, counting among his output chamber music and larger choral works, one of which, the Christmas oratorio *Die Geburt Christi,* enjoyed some popularity. Among his published compositions for organ are two extended organ fantasias on *Nun danket alle Gott* (1885) and *Nun komm, der Heiden Heiland* (1883) and six chorale preludes (*Sechs Choräle,* 1890). Brahms owned copies of all of these works, which are written in a rather conservative contrapuntal style that makes frequent use of devices such as canon and *Vorimitation.* Perhaps it is not too far-fetched to surmise, as Otto Biba does, that Herzogenberg's chorale preludes may have at least "partly inspired" Brahms to write or revise some of his own during the 1890s.[101] Although Herzogenberg often sent copies of his compositions to him, Brahms seems to have been generally unimpressed with his friend's work. Any "inspiration" that Herzogenberg's chorale preludes may have provided could conceivably have been by way of making Brahms realize that his own were superior—and just as worthy of publication.

Despite these almost coincidental contacts, however, Brahms's connection with the established "organ world" of his day was at best only peripheral. Wm. A. Little observes that the more noteworthy Teutonic organists, such as Haupt, Hesse, Merkel, Fischer, Lemmens, and the Schneiders, "appear never to have crossed paths with Brahms"[102]—although Brahms did hear Fischer at least once, in the opening concert for the 1872 Ladegast organ in the Vereinsaal. But herein may lie one of the reasons that Brahms was not inspired to write more organ music during the most active part of his career. Most of Brahms's biographers allude to the stimulus often given to the composition of various genres of music by friends and associates whose performance he admired—Clara Schumann for piano works, Joachim for violin and chamber music, Von Bülow for some of the orchestral works, Stockhausen for male voice solos, and, for female voice solos, the various divas with whom Brahms was sporadically infatuated throughout his lifetime. Perhaps the most obvious examples are the works for clarinet, an instrument Brahms had paid scant attention to until, late in his life, he heard and was inspired by the clarinet virtuoso Richard Mühlfeld. Dare we suggest, then, that Brahms simply may never have heard any organ playing—particularly in Vienna—that truly impressed him?

At the time of his death, Brahms's library contained several organ works, largely by German and Netherlands Baroque composers—Bach, Bruhns, Buxtehude (in Spitta's 1876–1877 edition), Marpurg, Muffat, Scheidt, Sweelinck—

plus a few composed by friends and associates, doubtless gifts from the composers.[103] Herzogenberg's chorale fantasias and chorale preludes were there, as well as Samuel de Lange's Organ Sonata no. 5, dedicated to Brahms. Philipp Wolfrum (1854–1919), an organist, choral director, Bach scholar, and hymnologist, composed several chorale preludes and some organ sonatas, the third of which (1863) was also dedicated to Brahms, and in Brahms's library. So were works by Franz Lachner (1803–1890), the Munich music director and friend of Schubert, who had published three organ sonatas and a four-hand work for organ. Max Reger's Suite in E Minor (op. 16), one of his first published organ compositions, was definitely a gift, sent in 1894 by the admiring young composer, who also requested permission to dedicate a composition to Brahms.[104] Although he didn't do so immediately, he did in 1899 dedicate to Brahms's memory two piano works—a turbulent *Rhapsodie* (op. 24, no. 6), "modeled closely on Brahms's Rhapsodies, Op. 79," and *Resignation* (op. 26, no. 5), subtitled with the date of Brahms's death.[105]

With the exception of the Bach organ works, which he may have practiced in the 1850s (and some of which he performed as piano transcriptions, probably directly from the organ score), it is unlikely that Brahms ever actually played much of this music, except perhaps on the piano. In the case of the Baroque works, however, he doubtless studied some of them. Scheidt's *Tabulatura Nova*, published in 1892, was in fact a volume that Brahms himself assisted in editing for the *Denkmaler deutscher Tonkunst*. Possibly this task, in renewing his acquaintance with older forms, also helped to turn Brahms's thoughts toward chorale preludes during the 1890s.

TWO

Bach, Counterpoint, and Chorales

Brahms's interest in playing the organ seems to have burned out rather quickly after only two or three years in the 1850s, never to revive. With the exception of his performance of piano transcriptions of Bach organ works, his interest in organ music, too, appears to have lain largely dormant for nearly four decades. This period did, however, see the publication, in 1864 and 1882, of two earlier organ works that he had gone to some trouble to revise, as well as his occasional provision of organ parts to the orchestral scores of at least two of his own larger choral works, along with works by Bach, Handel, Mozart, and others.

By no means dormant, however, was Brahms's interest in the music of the Baroque period, counterpoint, and the Lutheran chorale. The contrapuntal skills he had honed so conscientiously in the few short months of his exchanges with Joachim in 1856 continued to mature, along with his expertise in orchestration, songwriting, and other facets of his art. Even in his later years, he continued to exhort budding composers to sharpen their skills by diligently studying counterpoint. He teased the young British composer Ethel Smyth for not knowing counterpoint and is said to have told young Hugo Wolf to "go away and study counterpoint"[1]—which was probably not what Wolf wanted to hear. Gustav Jenner, who briefly (and rather informally) studied composition with Brahms in the late 1880s, records that when he first came to Brahms as a young man of twenty-two, he was told to "first find a teacher who will instruct you in strict counterpoint. It is absolutely essential that one see the world through this glass for a long time."[2] Brahms then sent Jenner to his friend Eusebius Mandyczewski to study counterpoint, but he did agree to mentor the young composer in other aspects of composition.

The mature Brahms was speaking of the necessity of counterpoint study from experience, although, with the exception of his early lessons with

Marxsen, his own study had been largely autodidactic in nature. His contact with the Schumanns and Joachim would have made him realize what an important role counterpoint played in formal music study, however. This may have been what Brahms had in mind when, at the beginning of their counterpoint exercises in February 1856, he wrote to Joachim, "Why should not two sensible, earnest people like ourselves be able to teach one another far better than any Pf. [Professor?] could?"[3] Schumann had taught at Mendelssohn's Leipzig Conservatory, and Joachim had been a student there, so he presumably had already experienced some professorial counterpoint, although the main emphasis of his conservatory study appears to have been performance.

Students came from many regions to study in Leipzig—Joachim was from present-day Slovakia—and all were subjected to a heavy dose of counterpoint as taught by Ernst Friedrich Richter, who was a pupil of Bach's pupil J. P. Kirnberger, and Moritz Hauptmann, one of Bach's successors as cantor of the Thomaskirche. Among those students in the late 1850s and early 1860s were a Norwegian, Edvard Grieg, who was to become one of his country's greatest composers, and an American, Dudley Buck, who would return to his homeland to play Bach, compose fugues and chorale preludes (among other things), and help give impetus to the embryonic conservatory movement in the United States.

Grieg kept a notebook, which has survived, in which he inscribed some of his contrapuntal exercises—chorale preludes for Richter and organ fugues for Hauptmann. Some more esoteric efforts include double and triple fugues and a fugue on the surname of the Danish composer Niels Gade, a friend of Mendelssohn and Schumann who had also studied in Leipzig and had conducted the Gewandhaus orchestra for a short time after Mendelssohn's death before returning to his native Copenhagen.[4] Schumann had also written a little piece on Gade's name—which, like Bach's, conveniently utilizes letters of the basic scale—in his *Album für die Jugend*. Although Grieg (unlike Gade) never wrote anything for organ after leaving Leipzig, his conservatory regimen resembles that which Brahms imposed on himself (perhaps with guidance from the Leipzig-trained Joachim) and emphasizes the importance still attached to the organ in the practice of writing contrapuntal music at the midpoint of the nineteenth century.

In the winter of 1855–1856, even before he engaged in the exercises with Joachim, Brahms had acquired three of the major counterpoint treatises then available—Kirnberger's *Die Kunst der reinen Satzes,* Mattheson's *Der Volkommene Kapellmeister,* and Sechter's 1843 edition of Marpurg's *Abhandlung von der Fuge*. Brahms had purchased the first in the fall of 1855; the other two were gifts from Joseph Joachim and Clara Schumann, who were well aware of Brahms's interests and eager to encourage them.[5] Early in 1856, as the counterpoint study got under way, Brahms acquired two more of Mattheson's treatises, his *Kern melodischer Wissenschaft* and, perhaps significantly, his *Organistenprobe*.[6] These books, eventually supplemented by many related ones, remained in Brahms's library to the end of his days.

Musical examples of Brahms's enduring fascination with counterpoint abound. Although this is not the place to examine them in detail, certain ones stand out. Among the earliest are the fugue in the Trio in B Major (op. 8, 1854), possibly inspired by Bach's *Kunst der Fuge*, a copy of which Brahms owned at the time,[7] the Variations and Fugue on a Theme by Handel (op. 24, 1862) for piano, and of course all of the early organ works. The fugal portions of the *Deutsches Requiem* (op. 45, 1861–1869) are familiar to any chorister who has ever sung the work. Counterpoint frequently figures in Brahms's other choral works, among them the *Geistliche Lied* (op. 30, 1856–1864), the motets of Opus 29 (1864) and Opus 74 (1878), the *Drei Geistliche Chor* (op. 37, 1865), and the *Fest und Gedenkspruche* (op. 109, 1890). Less well known are the fugal finale of the Cello Sonata in E Minor (op. 38, 1862–1865), thought to have been inspired by Contrapunctus XIII of Bach's *Kunst der Fuge*,[8] the String Quintet in F (op. 88, 1882), with its contrapuntal final *Allegro-energico* movement, and Brahms's choral/orchestral elegy in memory of the painter Anselm Feuerbach, *Nänie* (op. 82, 1881), in which the choral section opens with three successive fughettas. Other examples of Brahms's use of counterpoint and canon can often be found among the smaller choral works, beginning with some of the pieces he wrote for his Hamburger Frauenchor, which included the set of Thirteen Canons eventually published as Opus 113.

No less than Brahms's love of writing counterpoint was his love of performing it, evident in his inclusion of Renaissance motets and Bach cantatas in his choral programs and transcriptions of Bach organ works in his piano recitals. In 1856—coincidental with his early organ and counterpoint studies—he first performed his piano transcription of Bach's Toccata in F Major (presumably BWV 540) in concerts given in Kiel and Altona. He also included it in his first Viennese solo recital in November 1862. By 1865, when he performed it in a piano recital in Cologne, he had added a transcription of the Prelude and Fugue in A Minor (BWV 543) to his repertoire. The Chromatic Fantasie and Fugue (BWV 903) for harpsichord was also a staple of his piano repertoire.[9] Another contrapuntal organ work that Brahms transcribed for the piano was Schumann's Canon in B Minor from the Opus 56 pedal piano studies, which he first performed in January 1857 at a concert in Leipzig.[10] Brahms may well have played these organ works of Bach and Schumann directly from the score, which would explain why no manuscript or published version of these transcriptions has ever been found. Piano arrangements do exist for two of Bach's solo violin works, however—the *Presto* from the Sonata in G Minor (BWV 1001) and the *Chaconne* from the Partita in D Minor (BWV 1004), a piece that Brahms particularly admired. In 1877, he wrote to

Clara that "the *Chaconne* is in my opinion one of the most wonderful and the most incomprehensible pieces of music," containing "a whole world of the deepest thoughts and most powerful feelings." He transcribed it for left hand alone, saying that playing it this way made him "feel like a violinist."[11]

Brahms's familiarity with Bach's cantatas dates from his early choral associations in Hamburg and in Göttingen, where in 1858 he performed *Christ lag in Todesbanden* (BWV 4) and *Ich hatte viel Bekümmernis* (BWV 21).[12] During his short directorship of the Vienna Singverein in 1863, he performed *Ich hatte viel Bekümmernis* and *Liebster Gott, wann werd' ich sterben* (BWV 8), as well as the Christmas Oratorio (BWV 248). During his tenure as director of the Gesellschaft der Musikfreunde from 1872 to 1875, he conducted performances of *Christ lag in Todesbanden, Nun is der Heil und die Kraft* (BWV 50), *Liebster Gott wann werd' ich sterben,* and *O ewiges Feuer, o ursprung der Liebe* (BWV 34), along with the St. Matthew Passion. Michael Musgrave sees influences of Bach's cantatas—particularly *Ich hatte viel Bekümmernis* and *Wer weiss wie nahe mir mein Ende* (BWV 27)—in Brahms's *Deutsches Requiem*.[13]

Robert Schumann had been one of the founders of the Bach Gesellschaft, which in 1851 began publishing, at the rate of roughly one volume per year, its scholarly edition of Bach's complete works. This serial publication coincided with Brahms's most productive years, and Jan Swafford opines that "those volumes inspired and transformed him, along with the whole of Western music."[14] In 1855, one of Clara Schumann's Christmas gifts to Brahms was the first volume of the set (ten cantatas), and Brahms immediately became a lifelong subscriber to the series. One of the most recent volumes was on the music rack of his piano in his last days. He had been making marginal notations in the score of a motet.[15] Indeed, these marginal notations—evidence of the depth of his immersion in the study of Bach's music—had been a lifelong habit of his, and his annotations are found on many of the organ works.

The *Clavierübung* had been published in 1853, volume 1 of the organ works (trio sonatas, preludes and fugues, toccatas, and the *Passacaglia*) in 1867, volume 2 (*Orgelbüchlein*, Schübler Chorales, Eighteen Chorales) in 1878, volume 3 (preludes, fugues, fantasias, and the concerto transcriptions) in 1885, and volume 4 (miscellaneous chorale preludes, chorale variations) in 1893.[16] What influence these sporadic appearances of new editions of Bach's organ music on Brahms's reading desk might have had in occasionally turning his attention to sketches for the organ is impossible to say. Volume 4, containing as it did some chorale preludes that would probably have been still unfamiliar to him, could have been at least one of the circumstances that again focused his interest on the genre in that late period.

In 1886, Brahms completed his fourth (and last) symphony, in which his love of early music and counterpoint meet in the theme of the final movement. This is thought by many to have been based on the ground bass theme of another final movement, that of Bach's early cantata *Nach dir, Herr, verlanget mich* (BWV 150), although works by Couperin, Buxtehude, and Lully have also been suggested as possible sources.[17] Brahms's ongoing interest in earlier music was surely a factor in the choice of an ostinato form. He admired the final *Chaconne* movement from Bach's violin Partita (BWV 1004), was familiar with François Couperin's *Passacaille* in B minor from having recently coedited that composer's keyboard works, and in 1883 told Elisabet Herzogenberg of his pleasure in discovering Georg Muffat's *Passacaglia* in G Minor for organ.[18] A friend, the Dutch organist Samuel de Lange, may have introduced him to this work from Muffat's *Apparatus musico-organisticus* of 1690. A copy of de Lange's edition of the Muffat collection, published a few years later in 1888, was in Brahms's library.

Brahms's love of the Lutheran chorale parallels his love of the folk song, and he would have encountered both in his early youth. He may have first heard some of the folk songs on the streets of Hamburg or in the taverns where he contributed to his family's meager income by playing the piano as a teenager. We know that Brahms had "learned by heart the catechism according to Luther," no doubt for his confirmation at St. Michael's Church, and "also read the Bible diligently," for he cited these as qualifications for being a fitting godfather to the son of his friend Adolf Schubring.[19] His lifelong study and knowledge of the Bible has been noted by many of his biographers[20] and is evident in his knowledgeable choice of biblical texts in works such as the *Deutsches Requiem, Triumphlied, Vier Ernste Gesänge*, and motets. So, too, would he have been exposed to the wealth of the chorale from an early age, which was eventually reinforced and expanded by his later study (and performance) of the choral and organ works of Bach and his continuing interest in chorales in general. Regarding the reemergence of both chorales and folk songs in Brahms's later work, Malcolm MacDonald observes that the *Elf Choralvorspiele* "constitute a kind of 'high art' counterpart to the 1894 collection of *Deutsche Volkslieder*."[21] But throughout his life both of these elements made periodic appearances in Brahms's choral and instrumental music—the folk songs most prominent, the chorales more in the background.

When Brahms joined the Schumann household in 1854, he assumed the self-appointed task of organizing the Schumanns' extensive collection of books and music, which included considerable amounts of early music and a set of the organ works of Bach as published by Peters in 1844. Even earlier, Robert Schumann had published four of the chorale preludes from Bach's *Orgelbüchlein* in his *Neue Zeitschrift für Musik*. These were *Ich ruf' zu dir, Das alte Jahr vergangen ist, Durch Adams Fall*, and *O Mensch, bewein dein' Sünde gross*.[22] Also in the Schumann library was the 1784 edition of Bach's chorales, which may have triggered Brahms's intentional study of Lutheran chorales early in 1855. In this he was aided by the presence in the library of such (then) recent publications as Gottlieb von Tucher's *Schatz des evangelischen Kirchengesangs im ersten Jahrhundert der Reformation* (1848) and Carl von Winterfeld's three-volume *Der evangelische Kirchengesang* (1843–1848).[23] This study of the chorale predated Brahms's better-known immersion in counterpoint by a year. One unanswered question is whether this, which coincided with the beginnings of his self-propelled organ study, could have resulted in any attempts at composing chorale preludes—attempts or sketches that might have been laid aside because of the more complex demands of his counterpoint studies the following year. What seems certain, though, is that this early study of chorales, like the counterpoint study, continued to exercise sporadic influence on later compositions throughout Brahms's life.

Like Mendelssohn, whom he admired, Brahms was one of the few "mainstream" composers of the nineteenth century to make any significant use of the chorale in his compositions. His *Triumphlied* (op. 55, 1872) incorporates both the then-current German national anthem, "Heil dir im Siegeskranz" (to the same tune as "God Save the King" and also "My Country, 'tis of Thee"), and the chorale *Nun danket alle Gott*. The latter had also been employed by Mendelssohn in his *Lobgesang* (op. 52, 1840, written to commemorate the four hundredth anniversary of Gutenberg's invention of printing by movable type), a work on the same scale as the *Triumphlied*, and a work that Brahms surely knew. Likewise familiar would have been Mendelssohn's oratorio *St. Paul*, where the Advent chorale *Wachet auf! ruft uns die Stimme* appears in the instrumental overture and later, along with *Wer nur den lieben Gott lässt walten*, in the choral parts. It is perhaps not too far-fetched to suggest that Brahms's use of the chorale in his choral works might have been inspired, at least in part, by Mendelssohn's example.

The first of Brahms's *Zwei Motetten* (op. 29, 1864) is quite straightforwardly built around the chorale *Es ist das Heil uns kommen her;* the second appears to be based on an original melody. In the first of the second set of *Zwei Motetten* (op. 74, 1878), the poignant *Warum ist das Licht gegeben dem Mühseligen*, Luther's *Nunc Dimittis* chorale, *Mit Fried' und Freud' ich fahr dahin*, appears at the conclusion, in the manner of the chorales that sometimes conclude Bach's cantatas. The second motet, mentioned as early as 1870 in a letter to Max Bruch,[24] is based on a less familiar chorale, *O Heiland, reiss die Himmel auf*, and is in the form of five variations. Snippets of chorales appear in at least two other vocal works. The unmistakable opening notes of the "Passion Chorale," more familiarly known to Brahms's generation as *Herzlich thut mich verlangen*, appear as the key changes from minor to major toward the conclusion of the song *Auf dem Kirchhofe* (op. 105, no. 4, 1888). A funeral chorale, on the text *Nun lasst uns den Leib begraben*, can be found in the *Begräbnisgesang* (op. 13, 1861), and although Brahms is said to have told his friend Julius Grimm that the melody was original,[25] its opening two measures are in fact identical to the first phrase of *Erhalt' uns, Herr, bei deinem wort* and even bear some resemblance to the opening of a lesser-known chorale set to the same text that Brahms employed in his Opus 13.

Chorale melodies are sometimes suggested in less obvious form in certain of Brahms's other works. Phrases of *Herr Jesu Christ, du höchstes Gut* are suggested by the opening line of the *Geistliches Lied* (op. 30, 1856–1864), and Percy Young discerns the "ghost" of the opening notes of *Vater unser in Himmelreich* at the beginning of the baritone solo in the third movement of the *Requiem*.[26] More than one commentator has seen a resemblance of the motif of the second movement of the *Requiem* to the first line of *Wer nur den lieben Gott lässt walten*, evidently a favorite of Bach, who employed it in eight cantatas and four organ chorale preludes.[27] Michael Musgrave goes so far as to state that this chorale "is quite unmistakable in the funeral march, despite its omission of the upbeat, and modal inflexion."[28] *Freu' dich sehr, O meine Seele* (which opens with a melodic line of similar shape) has also been suggested.[29] Max Kalbeck sees traces of *Ermuntre dich, mein schwacher Geist* in measures 232–236 of the First Symphony (op. 68, 1877),[30] and Robert Haven Schauffler discerns something "very like" *Erhalt' uns, Herr* at the beginning of the *Vier ernste Gesänge* (op. 121)[31]—although this could perhaps also have been a veiled allusion to his own early *Begräbnisgesang*. However, some of these supposed chorale allusions, whether in choral or orchestral music, may have been either subconscious or purely accidental. Unlike Mendelssohn, who based part of his Fifth ("Reformation") Symphony on the full-fledged version of Luther's *Ein feste' Burg* and composed a virtual chorale fantasia on *Gelobet seist du, Jesus Christ* as the final movement of his Piano Trio no. 2 in C Minor (op. 66), Brahms seems to have eschewed overt allusions to Lutheran chorales in his orchestral and chamber works, reserving them for their more natural role in vocal music (and, by extension, chorale preludes). The only fully recognizable vocal music to appear in any of his orchestral works are the lively student songs that provide the thematic material for the Academic Festival Overture (op. 80, 1881).

Chorale preludes and cantatas are generally associated with Bach, Buxtehude, Walther, Pachelbel, and other notable seventeenth- and eighteenth-century composers, but the use of the chorale as thematic material continued unabated throughout the nineteenth century in Germany. Chorale preludes and other chorale-based organ works continued to be written in quantity, although largely by relatively minor composers. Among the better known were the Darmstadt organist J. C. H. Rinck, author of a popular organ tutor; the theorist J. G. Töpfer of Weimar, composer of one of the earliest chorale fantasias; and Adolph Hesse, who, along with many recital pieces, produced several sets of chorale preludes and other chorale-based works. The prolific Gustav Merkel's organ works ran the gamut from fugues to character pieces, and also included chorale preludes and a chorale-based sonata, and August Gottfried Ritter, author of a treatise on organ playing, likewise wrote a number of them. Carl Piutti, organist of the Thomaskirche in Leipzig, published a volume of two hundred chorale preludes at the end of the nineteenth century, and Christian Fink of Esslingen composed several sets of chorale trios. Toward the end of the century, we find Brahms's friends Heinrich von Herzogenberg, who wrote chorale preludes and fantasias, and Samuel de Lange, who based some of his organ sonatas on chorales. And chorale fantasias were written by one of Brahms's earliest biographers, the Berlin organist and music critic Heinrich Reimann.

Among the major nineteenth-century symphonic composers, Schubert, Liszt, Rheinberger, and Bruckner—all of whom were Catholic—left the chorale largely alone, although all wrote some organ music, and Rheinberger and Liszt made significant contributions to the literature. Liszt did, however, include an allusion to *Was Gott tut, das ist wohlgetan* in his organ fantasia *Weinen, Klagen, Sorgen, Sagen* and based a major organ fantasia on the B-A-C-H theme. Despite having incorporated chorales into various symphonic and choral works, Mendelssohn never wrote an actual chorale prelude, although among his lesser-known youthful organ works is a set of variations on the chorale *Wie gross ist des Allmächt'gen Güte*, and numbers 1, 3, 5, and 6 of his six organ sonatas contain a chorale-based movement. Indeed, these sonata movements can easily stand alone as chorale fantasias and were perhaps even originally intended as such. However, Schumann, in whose library Brahms found so much chorale-related music from the Baroque period, seems not to have followed Mendelssohn's example in utilizing chorales. Two of the little pieces in his *Album für die Jugend* (nos. 4 and 42) are based on the chorale *Freu' dich sehr, o meine Seele,* and that seems to be the extent of it. It is possible, though, that chorales could have played a part in a planned but abandoned oratorio to be entitled *Luther*.

Brahms was thus the most prominent nineteenth-century composer to pick up where Mendelssohn left off in his creative use of chorale material, and he went one step further by writing classic chorale preludes for the organ. It is perhaps to be regretted that Brahms never essayed a true chorale fantasia for the organ. It was left for his admirer Max Reger to exploit that medium with the greatest distinction in the early twentieth century.

THREE

Brahms as Revisor

Brahms had written one known chorale prelude, upon *O Traurigkeit, o Herzeleid,* in the 1850s. As he seems rarely to have satisfied himself with only one attempt at any genre, did he also write, or at least sketch out, drafts for any others during this early period? Some fairly well-established facts about Brahms's modus operandi should be examined here. One is that Brahms is known to have subjected his works to extensive revisions, well documented in certain cases, especially with regard to the *Requiem,* the D Minor Piano Concerto, the First Symphony, the Variations Op. 9 and Op. 24, *Rinaldo,* and some of the choral and chamber works. In 1876, George Henschel (1850–1934), then an aspiring young singer and composer, brought some songs for Brahms to critique. Brahms rather kindly opined that some of them suggested that the composer was "too easily satisfied" with the result and that "by actually perfecting *one* piece one gains and learns more than by starting or half-finishing a dozen." He then counseled Henschel to let a piece rest and to "keep going back to it and working it over and over again, until . . . there is not a note too many or too little, not a bar you could improve on."[1] Brahms surely knew what he was talking about, for he was laboring over his First Symphony at the time. Henschel, who remained Brahms's friend, later abandoned both singing and composing to become an internationally known conductor who actively promoted Brahms's music—not only in Germany but also in England and America.

Brahms could never be accused of being too easily satisfied. Virtually everything he ever published, even some relatively short works, seems to have undergone gestation periods of varying length. He is also known to have rearranged and transformed earlier compositions into a quite different mold. A classic example is the Piano Concerto in D minor (op. 15), which began life as a piano duet in 1854. Brahms then unsuccessfully attempted to work it into a symphony before discarding a few tentative movements as it metamorphosed into its ultimate concerto form in 1859.[2] One of the discarded symphonic movement sketches was preserved, however, to eventually provide material for something very different—the second movement of the later *Requiem*, begun in 1861.

When a date appears on one of Brahms's surviving manuscripts, it is simply the date when that particular manuscript (whether an early draft or a later revision) was completed. Although an earlier sketch of this work exists, the inscription "*J. Brahms. Ende Nov. 1861*," found on a manuscript for the Opus 26 Piano Quartet in A Major (now in the Rudolf Serkin collection), seems to make it clear that this is a final revision. This work was first performed a year later and published in 1863. In the case of works revised several times, the date is of the most recent version or revision. It is not necessarily the date of composition, but rather of completion (*Ende*), and in many cases the genesis of a given work can be traced back several years from the completion date. An example, cited elsewhere, is that of the A-flat Minor Fugue. In his own handwritten catalog of published works, he assigns a date of April 1856 to this work, but the earliest known manuscript is dated June 1856, and it was not actually published (with further revisions, the manuscript of which unfortunately no longer exists) until 1864, when he also published some other earlier works. The 1864 version was thus at least the third such, the April 1856 draft having been discarded and the June version surviving only because Clara Schumann had kept a copy.

Much has been made of Kalbeck's account of Brahms having destroyed a quantity of old manuscripts in the 1880s. It appears that Brahms routinely destroyed sketches and early drafts of various completed works and kept only the final one and often only the published version, although in his later years, he seems to have intensified this process, perhaps to winnow out things worth saving. This was true even of other composers' music that he had copied by hand, such as Bach's cantata no. 150, which had provided inspiration for the last movement of his Fourth Symphony. When cantatas 149 and 150 were finally published by the Bach-Gesellschaft in 1884, Brahms immediately discarded his handwritten copy.[3] Robert H. Schauffler tells of Brahms's faithful Viennese landlady, Frau Truxa, finding some torn-up scraps of songs in his wastebasket and carefully pasting them together, thinking them to be unknown works—only to later discover that the songs had in fact already been published.[4]

Once a work was completed and published, Brahms presumably saw no need to clutter up the workroom of his modest three-room apartment in Vienna with earlier attempts—hence the discarded scraps in the wastebasket. Many more probably ended up in the stove. Although a few odds and ends of sketches do survive, the only substantial set of surviving sketches and drafts is of a single work, the Opus 56 Variations on a Theme by Haydn. Donald McCorkle, who made an extensive study of this material, noted three levels of development: a shorthand rough draft (mostly in just two parts—treble and bass), detailed sketches of troublesome spots, and then a relatively complete draft. But Jan Swafford notes that even the earliest and roughest surviving version seems to indicate that Brahms "had already worked out in his mind much of the continuity and general drift of a piece," perhaps during his early-morning walks.[5] The rest was simply a process—often laborious—of "perfecting," as Brahms had explained to George Henschel. There is considerable evidence that Brahms could let some works rest, sometimes for a considerable length of time, before putting the finishing touches on them.

Robert Pascall, one of the editors of the most recent edition of Brahms's complete works, traces in some detail the process by which Brahms revised, corrected, and polished his compositions for publication, as pieced together largely from various surviving sketches, fair copies, engravers' plates, and proof sheets—revisions that sometimes continued even after the first printing.[6] Most of Brahms's own compositions retained in his library were in the printed version only, although even some of these versions contain handwritten corrections or second thoughts. It is said that the only "ready for printing" unpublished compositions found in Brahms's rooms at the time of his death were the Eleven Chorale Preludes (although it could be argued that only seven had really been so prepared) and some four-hand piano arrangements of overtures by his old friends Joachim and Grimm, dated 1854.[7] These latter were probably material that Brahms intended to revise after he was done with the chorale preludes rather than a finished product ready to be printed. It would have been highly uncharacteristic of him to offer anything this early for publication without some fairly extensive updating.

It is of no small significance that most of the surviving earlier versions of works later published posthumously were not found in Brahms's personal library; rather, they were versions given to or copied by friends. Along with the organ fugues, two sarabandes and two gigues dating from the 1850s, as well as thirty-two folk songs, were found in the estate of Clara Schumann, and other early autographs or copies were owned by various other friends, such as Joachim, Grimm, and Stockhausen. Along with discarded drafts, Brahms no doubt did destroy some of his juvenilia and other work he considered unworthy or no longer of any use. But this was probably more in the nature of ongoing routine housekeeping than the great purge it is sometimes made out to be, especially considering the amount of earlier material he is known to have revised and edited for publication after 1890.

There is no dearth of evidence that Brahms retained unpublished things from earlier years that he thought might still be of use, even if not always in their original form. The previously mentioned Piano Concerto in D minor, op. 15, which had its premiere in 1859, continued to undergo innumerable changes and refinements between 1861 and 1874, when Brahms was finally satisfied with it. The *Requiem,* which evolved between 1861 and 1868 from three movements to seven, included in its second movement material from the abandoned symphonic phase of Op. 15.[8] A sarabande, originally part of a "Bachian" suite of piano pieces written in 1855, provided the theme of the slow movement of the String Quintet in F Major (op. 88) of 1882,[9] although this connection would be unknown had Clara not kept a copy of it. Traces of a rejected movement from an uncompleted 1855 Suite in A Minor appear as late as 1892 in an intermezzo (op. 116, no. 2), also in A Minor.[10] The First Cello Sonata in E Minor was begun in 1862 and published in 1866, but a rejected adagio was apparently reworked as part of the F Major Cello Sonata in 1886. A discarded movement from a violin concerto written in 1878 turned up in the Second Piano Concerto (op. 83), completed in 1882.[11]

Sometimes Brahms's penchant for creating forms new to him in twos resulted in his resorting to older material. Having composed the Academic Festival Overture (op. 80, incorporating popular student folk songs) in return for the doctorate granted him by the University of Breslau in 1879, he then produced a companion, the Tragic Overture (op. 81), which Karl Geiringer claims "[made] use of some old sketches."[12] Perhaps the most extreme example of Brahms's revisionism is his Opus 8, the Piano Trio in B Major, which, encouraged by Schumann, Brahms had originally published in 1854. In 1889–1891, he revised it so comprehensively that "it amounted to a recomposition," and, with the exception of the scherzo (improved by a new coda), it was virtually a new work, although retaining the original opus number.[13] Other "recompositions" are found among the forty-nine *Deutsche Volkslieder,* which Brahms published in 1894, but which contained several settings originally written in 1858. Some of these were considerably expanded, set in different keys, and provided with a more sophisticated piano accompaniment. Again, once Brahms had revised them, he had destroyed his own copies of the earlier versions, which we would be unaware of, had he not given twenty-eight of them to the Schumanns.

Among the choral works, the motets of Opus 29, not published in final form until 1864, can be traced back to some contrapuntal studies of 1860 and earlier. The *Geistliche Lied,* originally written in 1856, was also published in 1864, along with *Psalm XIII* and the revised version of the Fugue in A-flat Minor, likewise products of the 1850s. The *Drei Geistliche Chöre* (op. 37) for women's voices, published in 1865, is traceable to 1860 or earlier as well, the first two of these pieces having been found in the part books of the Frauenchor. It is probably no coincidence that 1863–1864 was also when Brahms was directing the Vienna Singakademie and in that context presumably reviewing some of his own earlier choral compositions for revision and publication.

But during his first full year in Vienna, he may also have been encouraged to enhance his name recognition by publishing more of his compositions, for 1864 also saw the publication of his Three Vocal Quartets (op. 31) and a collection of fourteen *Deutsche Volkslieder,* some of which again are traceable to earlier dates. Certain of these were sung in the very first Singakademie concert that Brahms directed.

One of the most interesting instances of the survival (as well as later reworking) of early material is Brahms's so-called *Missa Canonica.* In 1856, during his contrapuntal immersion, he worked some of the canonic exercises into Mass movements—a Kyrie, Sanctus, Benedictus, and Agnus Dei. He thought enough of these movements to send them in 1857 to his friend, the choral director Julius Otto Grimm, hoping for a performance that unfortunately never occurred—apparently because Grimm's chorus couldn't handle it. Between 1856 and 1857, a different Kyrie appears to have been substituted for the original one of the four, and it is the only movement with a continuo accompaniment. In the correspondence with Joachim, a Credo is mentioned, but it seems not to have been completed until the summer of 1861, when he sent a copy of it to Clara.[14] Shortly thereafter, he also sent a copy to Joachim, but both copies of this Credo have unfortunately been lost, along with the original Kyrie. Grimm, fortunately, made a copy of the second Kyrie, which, with the Sanctus, Benedictus, and Agnus Dei, has survived.

Although an isolated autograph of the Benedictus exists, Brahms must have at some point discarded his own manuscript of the full four movements (as well as the Credo) as being of no further use. Only Grimm's copy survives, and this did not turn up until more than a century later, in 1978. In 1984, the four Mass movements were at last published as an entity.[15] However, eighteen years after the Mass movements were originally written, in 1874, Brahms completed the contrapuntal motet *Warum is das Licht gegeben dem Mühseligen* (op. 74, no. 1). Only after the rediscovery of Grimm's copy of the Mass movements was it realized that Brahms had reworked and refined them into this splendid motet. As Robert Pascall describes the transformation, the Agnus Dei, "made more taut then greatly expanded by contrast and variation," became the first movement; the Benedictus, "with a gloriously transformed ending," the second movement, and the Dona Nobis Pacem, "contracted and with a reworked texture," appears in the third movement.[16] One can only wonder whether the lost Credo might not also have been reworked for some later (but as yet unidentified) composition. The manuscript of the two previously mentioned Opus 29 motets is dated July 1860, but they were not published until 1864 (along with other works known to be revisions). These, too, deserve some scrutiny as to their possible origins. The second of the Opus 29 motets, *Schaffe in mir, Gott* (Psalm 51) has four sections: the first and third essentially homophonic, the second and fourth fugal.

Except for key relationship (the second in G Minor, the rest in G Major), these four movements seem to have little in common, and the opening section of the second motet, *Schaffe in mir, Gott,* with its unobtrusive augmentation canon between soprano and bass, has been traced back to one of the exercises Brahms sent to Joachim in March 1856.[17] Most or all of the other three segments could conceivably also have been, at least in part, reworkings of earlier choral and contrapuntal efforts from the 1850s, which are now lost.

The first of the Opus 29 motets raises an even more intriguing question, however. *Es ist das Heil* is a "prelude and fugue" combination in the same way that Brahms's *O Traurigkeit* for organ is, although the first part is simply a reharmonized chorale rather than an actual chorale prelude. The second part, however, rather strikingly resembles Brahms's two chorale fugues for organ—*O Traurigkeit* and *Mein Jesu, der du mich,* the first in the set of *Elf Choralvorspiele* (op. 122). *Es is das Heil* and *Mein Jesu* are *vorimitation* fugues, and both the motet and the two organ pieces feature the chorale melody in augmentation at a low pitch—in the two organ fugues, it is in the pedal; in the choral fugue, it is in the Bass 1 part. In fact, by playing the SATB2 parts on the manual and the B1 part on the pedal (except in the coda, where it joins the B2 part in what is essentially a pedal point), this fugue can with little effort be transformed into an organ piece. Was it actually conceived as one? The composer who could rearrange the original two-piano version of the *St. Antoni* ("Haydn") Variations for full orchestra (op. 56), revise some of his early treble-voice choral works (such as the *Marienlieder*) for SATB, convert a piano sarabande into a string quintet movement and an instrumental movement into part of the *Requiem,* and salvage other bits of early suites, piano pieces, and counterpoint efforts in a variety of ways in later works would hardly have had any trouble transforming an organ work of this kind into a choral work if it suited his purpose. And the purpose, in this case, might simply have been to create some more material for the chorus he was conducting in 1863–1864.

From 1864 on, Brahms's popularity grew, and he was kept increasingly busy conducting, performing, and, above all, composing. The period from the fall of 1872 to the spring of 1875 was occupied, at least in part, by Brahms's activities as director of the concerts at the Gesellschaft der Musikfreunde. Following his resignation from this post, he began devoting himself increasingly to composing larger works and to conducting. His First Symphony was completed in 1877, followed by the Second Symphony a year later, but after this, he seems to have again looked back to some of his earlier drafts for material. The two sets of piano pieces published in 1879 (op. 76) are thought by some to include some earlier works. We know, too, that the *O Traurigkeit* pair of organ pieces, although not published until 1882, were circulated to Brahms's friends Spitta and Herzogenberg in 1873 and 1878, perhaps to solicit their comments before he submitted them for publication. In 1878 also, a second set of motets (op. 74) was published. Here we again find evidence of the reworking of older material.

The first motet, *Warum ist das Licht gegeben dem Mühseligen,* has four movements, seemingly related only by key and the fact that the first three are based on biblical texts; their musical origins in the once "lost" *Missa Canonica* have already been discussed. The final fourth movement, although somewhat textually related to the rest, seems musically quite unrelated—it is simply a reharmonization of the classic Dorian chorale setting of the Song of Simeon, *Mit Fried und Freud ich fahr dahin.* Bach closed several of his cantatas with simple chorales (*Mit Fried und Freud* is the penultimate chorale in his *Trauerode*), but such use in a motet is unusual.

O Heiland, reiss die Himmel auf, the second motet of Opus 74, consists of five strophic verses that comprise a set of variations on another seventeenth-century chorale. In each variation, the melody appears in augmentation in a different voice part, with the exception of the final one, where it is embellished and treated canonically and in inversion, leading to an amen in eighth notes in the same style. Interestingly, this type of variation treatment can be traced back to the organ chorales and Magnificats of Samuel Scheidt, whom Brahms admired as a precursor of Bach, and whose *Tabulatura Nova* (which he later edited) he must have discovered when immersing himself in the Schumann library in the 1850s. Again, we must ask the risky question: Could this choral work have been derived from lost sketches for an organ composition in the style of Scheidt? There is, of course, no way of knowing.

Brahms published a third set of motets (op. 110) in 1890, but these seem very different from the other two sets, not only in form but also in their texts, which, as Brahms wrote von Bülow in 1889, were "intended for days of national celebration and commemoration," citing military victories and the kaiser's coronation.[18] Virginia Hancock suggests that, stylistically, they may have been influenced by Philipp Spitta's edition of the works of Heinrich Schütz, published in 1888 and 1889, which Brahms owned (and annotated).[19] The first motet, set for double SATB choir, alternates contrapuntal sections with essentially homophonic antiphonal elements, and the third is also for double chorus, using a traditional chorale text, *Wenn wir in höchsten Nöten sein,* in an original musical setting. The second is a short and straightforward chorale-like strophic setting. The polychoral format has an antiquarian precedent in works of Schütz, Gabrieli, and others and is thus an expression of Brahms's ongoing interest in early music, but although there are polyphonic and canonic elements, there seems to be little in Opus 110 that is directly suggestive of any connection with the composer's earlier contrapuntal experiments.

In 1890, Brahms, at fifty-seven, seems to have felt he was slowing down and losing his creative drive, although this year also saw the completion of his complex and masterful Opus 111 String Quintet in G Major, unquestionably a mature work. During the preceding decade, he had received honors and, more important, had seen the enthusiastic acceptance of some of his music everywhere—even in Hamburg. Now he was cutting back on his performances and had decided—somewhat prematurely, as it turns out—that he had pretty much said what he wanted to say, although he did leave the door somewhat open by telling his friends that if he did write anything, it would "be for himself." He cleaned house and apparently destroyed some unspecified musical material, but this could have been just to sort out what was worth keeping and possibly revising or reworking. And that is indeed what he set out to do, beginning with a set of six vocal quartets with piano accompaniment (op. 112), begun in 1888 and completed in 1891, and, in the same year, the final revision of his Opus 8 Piano Trio.

Immediately afterward, Brahms reached deeper into his winnowed stack of unpublished compositions to pull out and revise for publication as Opus 113 a collection of thirteen delightful little canons for women's voices, "most of which he had written in the days of the Hamburg ladies' choir."[20] Only the more complex thirteenth canon in six parts, based on a melody from Schubert's *Winterreise* and set to a wistful little verse by Friedrich Rückert, was a later composition.[21] Proof of the earlier existence of at least one of these canons survives in a curious place—an inscription on a photograph given to Frau Ida Flatz (an alto soloist in his Vienna Singverein) in 1864, which includes the theme of *Göttlicher Morpheus*.[22] Had Brahms not collected them for publication, we may never have known that many of these canons had survived; again, earlier drafts do not exist. Possibly he intended some additional sets, for three additional canons for four female voices, probably also written for the Frauenchor, were found and published posthumously in 1908. But these pieces, as well as some previously mentioned examples of his reuse of youthful material, show that Brahms not only had retained some unpublished work going back as far as the 1850s but also held it in favorable regard.

Brahms's first attempt at retirement from composer to revisor was short-lived, however. In 1891, on a visit to Meiningen, he happened to hear the renowned clarinetist Richard Mühlfeld, and the superb playing of this artist rekindled his creative fire. The result was the Trio in A Minor for clarinet, cello, and piano (op. 114) and the Clarinet Quintet in B Minor (op. 115), both written in 1892. The sophisticated complexity of Opus 115 marks the work as fully mature, on a level with the Opus 111 Quintet, with no link to anything earlier. Two sonatas for clarinet and piano followed in 1895 as Opus 120, and here there might have been some reminiscence of Schumann, whose 1849 *Drei Fantastiestücke* (op. 73) for clarinet and piano Brahms surely must have known.

In between the clarinet works came Opp. 116, 117, 118, and 119, all piano works. Brahms had not published anything for piano solo since 1880, but as previously noted, at least one of these late works, Opus 116, contains a reworking of an earlier composition. Geiringer, without being specific, states that "among these [piano works] there were several of an earlier period, which were now marked by the style developed in the last few years,"[23] and Musgrave notes the reappearance of some of the forms used by the composer in earlier years, such as the *Ballade* and *Rhapsody*.[24]

In 1893, Brahms published a set of piano exercises, some of which are known to have originated in the 1850s,[25] and prepared for publication in 1894 a collection of forty-nine *Deutsche Volkslieder* for solo voice and piano, many of them dating from various earlier periods. At least two more collections of these, some dating as far back as 1858, appear to also have been in the process of preparation but were not published until 1926 and 1928. These include the *Volks-Kinderlieder*, believed to have been written for the Schumann children. Clearly Brahms, whatever he may have weeded out previously, had retained a considerable amount of earlier material, largely in the smaller forms, that he deemed worthy of polishing for eventual publication. If nothing else, this knowledge strengthens the probability that many if not all of the Eleven Chorale Preludes (op. 122) may have had their inception at earlier periods in his life. The argument sometimes made that these pieces are too well crafted and mature to be early works simply does not take into account Brahms's lifelong habit of reworking and perfecting older material. It is perhaps not entirely unlikely that the only completely original works written after 1890 were the clarinet pieces and, in 1896, the *Vier ernste Gesänge*.

In the fall of 1894, Brahms, having sent the *Volkslieder* set to his publisher, Fritz Simrock, wrote him a curious letter in which he asks, "Has it struck you that I have clearly said my farewell as a composer?" He notes that the last folk song in the set is the same one that he used as the theme of the second movement in his Opus 1, the Piano Sonata in C Major, published in 1853, and therefore represents "the snake that bites its tail—and thus states with pretty symbolism that the tale is finished." But he qualifies the finality of this by adding, "Even if I write something for my own amusement sometime—I'm renouncing absolutely nothing—I'll take very good care that publishers are not going to be seduced."[26]

Daniel Beller-McKenna has commented meaningfully on the element of "reminiscence" that seems to imbue the piano intermezzi of Opp. 116–119, published in 1892–1893, linking them to both the forty-nine *Volkslieder* and the Eleven Chorale Preludes in this regard.[27] As with folk songs and organ music, the late shorter piano works constituted another return to a medium associated with his younger years and, with the exception of the Opus 76 and Opus 79 pieces (1879 and 1880), laid aside for a long time. David Pacun has drawn parallels between some of Brahms's other published works of the 1890s and his earlier compositions: the last Clarinet Sonata (op. 120, no. 2) containing, like the Opus 1 Sonata, a variation set, and the echo, in the *Vier ernste Gesänge* (op. 121), of the ascending and descending thirds of the Fourth Symphony.[28]

Was the snake biting its tail when Brahms revised the early canons and folk songs for publication? What then of the Eleven Chorale Preludes? Brahms had written at least one chorale prelude (*O Traurigkeit*) in the 1850s, but he seems almost never to have left any musical form alone without experimenting with several examples. Perhaps even *O Traurigkeit* might not have surfaced when it did had Brahms not needed to quickly find a small piece to fulfill a promise of a parting gift to a favorite student. Considering his interest in Lutheran chorales, the organ, and counterpoint during the 1854–1859 period, *O Traurigkeit* could well have been the tip of a modest iceberg of early chorale prelude experiments that, like the canons and some choral works and short piano pieces, he had hoarded over the years. And it might indeed have been the news of Clara Schumann's declining health in early 1896 that finally prompted him to reexamine and polish some of these reminders of their youthful mutual interests—which included the organ—and thus to truly close the circle for good.

PART II

THE MUSIC

FOUR

The Early Works

Brahms in his twentieth year had been thrust into the musical limelight by Robert Schumann's prophetic predictions in his essay "*Neue Bahnen.*" It is greatly to his credit that he seems not to have let it go to his head but rather took it as Schumann surely must have intended it—as strong encouragement to continue pursuing his career as a composer. So earnestly did he try to rise to that challenge that he even temporarily gave up playing piano recitals to devote more time to study and composition. The immediate result was the Piano Sonata in F Minor (op. 5), the Piano Trio in B Major (op. 8), the "Schumann" Variations (op. 9), the *Ballades* (op. 10), some songs and other piano pieces, and the beginnings of some larger works—all this in the space of little more than two years. Yet at the end of this period, in February 1856, he humbly confessed to Clara Schumann that he felt he was "still not a proper musician." At the same time, he nonetheless acknowledged, "I have talent for it, more, probably, than is usual in young people nowadays,"[1] an unusually mature self-assessment for a gifted young man not yet twenty-three years old who had only recently had a rather extravagant encomium laid on him by a highly respected composer and critic. Quite realistically, however, he was aware that talent was something that needed to be refined by diligent practice and continuing study in order to live up to its promise.

When Brahms moved in with the Schumanns in February 1854, he came in contact not only with all of Robert Schumann's compositions (including the pedal piano Studies and Sketches, and the B-A-C-H fugues) but also with the family's extensive collection of musical scores and books, which he eagerly studied. The Schumann library contained much early choral and keyboard music, as well as works by J. S. Bach, including preludes and fugues for harpsichord and organ, the *Orgelbüchlein,* and Mendelssohn's 1846 edition of the Eighteen Chorale Preludes. Also in this collection were organ works by the Viennese composer J. G. Albrechtsberger and C. P. E. Bach's pupil J. G. Vierling. The Schumanns encouraged Brahms to use their resources in self-study, and he soon began to be absorbed in counterpoint. On February 3, 1855, he wrote Clara that he "could now write canons in all possible artistic forms" and was curious to see how he would make out with fugues.[2]

Brahms himself soon acquired some significant additions to what, by the end of his life, would become his own extensive personal library, which he eventually bequeathed to the Gesellschaft der Musikfreunde in Vienna. He was something of a bibliophile and enjoyed frequenting the antiquarian bookshops of Hamburg, where in 1855 he found a copy of Johann Philipp Kirnberger's *Die Kunst der reinen Satzes.* Joseph Joachim and the Schumanns shared and encouraged Brahms's interest in musical theory, and Joachim gave Brahms a copy of Johann Mattheson's *Der vollkommene Capellmeister* as a Christmas present in 1855. Shortly afterward, he also acquired Mattheson's *Organistenprobe,* and a year later Clara presented him with Friedrich Wilhelm Marpurg's *Abhandlung von der Fuge.* These would not be the last theoretical works to find a place on Brahms's bookshelves, but they must have been very welcome acquisitions during Brahms's intensive contrapuntal explorations in 1856 and later. Theoretical works were not the only ones added to Brahms's library in the 1850s, though. In 1856, Karl Grädener gave him Kretzschmer and Zuccamaglio's *Deutsche Volkslieder,* which appealed to a very different aspect of Brahms's interests and from which, over the years, he drew some of the material for his folk song settings.

In February 1856, Brahms and Joachim launched into an intensive exchange of contrapuntal exercises geared to sharpening their understanding and skill in "double counterpoint, canons, fugues, preludes, or whatever it may be."[3] Brahms even set up some rules for the game, requiring a fortnightly exchange with a one-taler fine for tardiness, to be used by the recipient for buying books. On February 26, Brahms wrote to Joachim expressing the expectation that the exchange would "continue for a good long time, until we have both become really clever."[4] Although Brahms seems to have been the more enthusiastic and productive participant, Joachim gamely kept up his end, and in the final analysis, his most important contribution was his criticism and encouragement of Brahms's efforts.

Some of their more recondite exercises included circle canons, canons in inversion and augmentation, canons on the subject of Bach's *Kunst der Fuge,* and fugues on classic subjects such as B-A-C-H and other names and ciphers. We might almost suspect that, in addition to stretching their grasp of practical counterpoint and honing their compositional skills, these two young musicians were also having a certain amount of fun. In June 1856, Brahms received from Joachim a packet of his new exercises, with comments on the fugues and canons that Brahms had previously sent him, and he was so delighted that he replied, "I had to run outdoors, because I didn't want to jump for joy in the room."[5] Brahms was still with the Schumann household at this time, and the activities of these two young enthusiasts probably also offered a welcome distraction to Clara Schumann, as her hopes for Robert's recovery diminished. The early exercises exchanged were either for unspecified media or for voices or strings. Although some of Joachim's survive among his papers, Brahms is presumed to have eventually destroyed many of his with, however, some significant exceptions, which he would later revise or reuse in various ways. As early as the summer of 1854, Clara and Brahms had talked about learning to play the organ, and by November of that year, we know that Brahms had begun practicing on a small organ in Böhme's music store during his visits to Hamburg. He doubtless continued to do this from time to time; in reference to the two fugues he was writing in the spring of 1856, he told Joachim that he had been "practicing on the organ lately."[6]

It was thus perhaps inevitable that by the time Brahms was beginning to feel some real mastery of counterpoint, he should have turned to the organ as a medium for three of the more extensive works sent to Joachim in early June 1856. These were the *Prelude and Fugue in A Minor* (WoO 9), the *Fugue in A-flat Minor* (WoO 8), and the *Geistliches Lied* (op. 30), which combines a sensitive setting of a Paul Flemming text with a masterful canonic melding of voices and organ. Interestingly, he had not sent Joachim anything since late April, from which we can probably deduce that he had been working over these three pieces for about two months. Joachim had not been idle either, having produced some complex canons and a set of piano variations on an Irish melody. The last of this initial intensive round of contrapuntal exchanges between Brahms and Joachim was a commentary by Brahms on the set of variations submitted by Joachim, dated July 22, 1856.[7]

The death of Robert Schumann seven days later and the subsequent geographical dispersal of the "Schumann circle" put an end to this initial phase of contrapuntal exploration, although occasional exchanges appear to have occurred for at least a few more years. One additional organ work, the *Prelude and Fugue in G Minor* (WoO 10), a copy of which Brahms presented to Clara in February 1857, may have been in progress at the time, and perhaps even the chorale prelude on *O Traurigkeit,* although the earliest reference to it does not occur until more than a year later. But with these organ and choral offerings, the exchanges with Joachim had probably accomplished their purpose in making Brahms more confident and facile with regard to contrapuntal composition. That the mastery of (and love for) this discipline had significant influence on some of his future works for a variety of media is unquestioned. But these studies also served to prolong Brahms's acquaintance with the organ on a practical level.

The Fugue in A-flat Minor, WoO 8

In a letter dated June 20, 1856, to Gisela Von Arnim, a mutual friend of both himself and Brahms, Joachim wrote: "You ask for news of Brahms.... Just lately he has sent me some work, among which was a Fugue for Organ that combines depth and tenderness of feeling with a wealth of musical art so nobly that Bach and Beethoven have scarcely excelled it."[8] Clara's response to what she described as a "wonderfully beautiful, heartfelt" fugue was simpler but no less to the point.[9]

The A-flat Minor Fugue is a classic counterfugue, with the answer to the opening subject being its inversion, and its two countersubjects are likewise systematically inverted when they appear. Because of its complexity and sophistication, it appears to be the second organ fugue that Brahms had composed—the more antiquarian and straightforward A Minor Prelude and Fugue being his first attempt. In his own handwritten catalog of published works, Brahms assigned the date of April 1856 to both the A-flat Minor Fugue and the *Geistliches Lied*.[10] He sent a copy of it to Joachim in early June 1856, when he also sent one to Clara Schumann, dated June 8 (Robert Schumann's birthday) and inscribed "*Ganz eigentlich für meine Clara.*" In his letter to Clara, he calls this "the revision of my fugue," so the April date must refer to his initial version, which has not survived. Joachim's copy of the revision also no longer exists, and Clara's copy, handed down by her descendants, came to the attention of scholars only in the 1970s. It must have been made after May 4, as it is written on some special 24-stave paper that Joachim had sent Brahms on that date to facilitate sending exercises by mail.[11] To conserve space, the staves were smaller than usual. To Clara, Brahms wryly noted that "it is horrible to have to write so small."[12]

In 1864, shortly after his move to Vienna, three works from Brahms's earlier period were published, and all involved the organ. Two of these were choral works with independent organ accompaniment, *Psalm XIII* (op. 27) and the *Geistliches Lied* (op. 30), and on July 20 the *Fugue in A-flat Minor*, substantially edited and revised, appeared in the *Allgemeine musikalische Zeitung, neue Folge* 2/29, without opus number. Selmar Bagge, the editor, was an admirer of Brahms who had asked him for a piece of music that he might publish. Possibly because he had nothing new of appropriate size at hand, Brahms decided to submit the hitherto unpublished organ fugue. He requested retention of the copyright, however, in case he might later wish to publish it "together with its born and unborn brothers and sisters"—presumably other organ works.[13] "Born and unborn" suggests both the existence of other unpublished organ pieces and the possibility that Brahms considered writing even more.

Bagge seems to have been a bit disconcerted when he saw the unusual key signature, but Brahms refused to rewrite it in another key, saying that true friends would not be put off by a few "bees." As we know, though, he did take the trouble to make some other significant alterations to it—or perhaps had already made them earlier. The Fugue in A-flat Minor was republished in 1883 as sheet music by Breitkopf & Härtel, but with no change from the 1864 version, and all subsequent imprints are based on this version. Although Brahms did not retain a copy of his manuscript, his personal copies of both these imprints exist (in the archives of the Gesellschaft der Musikfreunde, Vienna) but show no evidence of further alterations or corrections.[14]

Considering the amount of symbolism Brahms managed to weave into this piece, there is probable symbolism behind his choice of the unusual key as well, and thus his unwillingness to change it at the publisher's whim. Brahms admired Beethoven and performed many of his piano sonatas, including the unconventional twelfth, op. 26, in A-flat major. The opening movement of this work is not in the usual sonata form but is a set of variations—a form in which Brahms also cast some of his own works. The second movement, however, is even more off the beaten track. Beethoven had entitled it "Funeral March on the Death of a Hero," and it is in the key of A-flat minor, a key as unusual for Beethoven as it was for Brahms. Young Brahms's "hero"—Robert Schumann—was still living when the fugue was composed, but Brahms, who had several times visited him at the Endenich sanatorium during the spring of 1856, was, along with Schumann's physicians, keenly aware that the composer had not long to live. Brahms gave a copy of the fugue to Clara on Robert's birthday in June, just a little more than a month before his death.

The 1856 version is, of course, of significant scholarly interest, when compared with the later published version, in that it demonstrates Brahms's manner of revising and tightening up his work. It is of interest to performers, however, because it contains some rudimentary performance and registration notations not present in the printed versions. These, like the inscription to "my Clara" and the parenthetical *"Trübe"* following the tempo indication of *Langsam,* appear to have been written in after the completion of the musical portion and could have been inserted as suggestions for Clara's performance of the piece.

Joachim was clearly impressed by this work. He claims to have both played it through several times (presumably on the piano) and "silently immers[ed]" himself in it by simply reading it. "From beginning to end, it is wonderfully deep; I know few pieces that have made such an impression of unity, beauty, and blissful peace on me as this fugue." Calling it a "pure, genuine work of art," Joachim went on to praise the "rich voice leading" and contrapuntal excellence, but he offered a few suggestions as well. Judging from the occasional penciled revisions in Clara's copy, Brahms seems to have heeded at least some of these. In this 1856 version (given as an alternate in George Bozarth's Henle edition of 1988), Brahms gave a tempo indication of "*Langsam (Trübe)*." Joachim objected to the word "*trübe*" (dark, gloomy, or melancholy) as "really not suitable . . . since the mood of sadness and oppression is so greatly dissolved in consolation and hope that it uplifts at the same time."[15] But possibly he made the wrong assumption about *trübe*, a word that could have several meanings; if "dark" was what Brahms meant, it might have referred to the registrational tone color he had in mind. Joachim also took issue with a cross-relationship between a G and a G-sharp, as well as some consecutive fifths near the end; Brahms was reluctant to alter them, however, responding that he found these "at times acceptable."

Concerned by Joachim's comments about sufficiently establishing the tonality, Brahms at one point wrote to him that "A-flat minor will be established by the prelude."[16] But the future tense suggests that a prelude had not yet been written, and it apparently never was, for there is no further mention of it. This may, however, be the reason that Brahms made a small but significant change in the ending of the fugue subject, replacing the F-natural of the penultimate note in the 1856 version with the F-flat that appears in the 1864 revision. Although this seemingly helps to establish key, it also casts the final four notes of the subject in the form of a phrygian cadence—three descending whole steps followed by a half-step. Traditionally, this has the flavor of a half-cadence. In the nineteenth century, it had also come to symbolize grief and sadness, and Brahms uses it thus in other contexts—as in measures 35–36 of the first movement of the *Requiem*, where it gives emphasis to the word "sorrow."

One other small difference in the subject as it appears in the 1856 and 1864 versions deserves mention here. In both versions, Brahms is most meticulous with regard to phrasing slurs, and in general, differences between the two versions are minor. However, in the 1856 version, the slur encompasses all five notes of the third phrase of the subject and its inversions in nearly all entries (an exception being measure 10). In the 1864 version, it includes only the first four notes of this phrase, leaving the fifth note seemingly unconnected, as the slurring does not commence until the following note. This, too, is fairly consistent, although occasionally one finds the fifth note included in the slurring of the next phrase (as in measures 9 and 15), and in measure 48 the slur includes only the first three notes of the phrase, the fourth note unconnected, with the slur for the next phrase beginning on the fifth note. Interestingly, these are passages that occur only in the revised 1864 version. Only in the final pedal statement (measure 54), where the third phrase is expanded to six notes by the addition of a chromatic F-natural, does the slur cover the entire phrase, just as it does in the 1856 version. Was this change in the slurring of the third phrase of the subject meant to denote a slight detachment of the fifth note? Or is it simply to make the slurring more consistent with the altered passages where a new phrase begins on that note? The player must decide.

Susan Testa observes that Clara had at an unknown time returned the manuscript to Brahms for some reason, perhaps because he wanted to revise the fugue and had not retained a copy for himself. On July 19, 1864—just a day before the revised version was published—Clara had written Brahms from Baden-Baden, "Won't you give the A-flat minor fugue, which you intended for me, to Friedchen [Wagner], who will probably be visiting us for a few days?"[17] But on July 31, Brahms himself came to Baden-Baden and probably brought it with him then. Also interesting is Clara's desire to have her copy of this music—presumably the earlier version that she retained—returned while she was in Baden-Baden. Could she have entertained the idea of playing it at one of Pauline Viardot's soirées? The piece would have worked quite nicely on Pauline's *orgue du salon,* a two-manual instrument with an enclosed *Récit* and what was said to be the first thirty-note "German" pedalboard to have been made by Cavaillé-Coll.[18] However, although Brahms's annotations do appear to be performance suggestions of some sort, there is no record of Clara ever having played this piece on any organ, in Baden-Baden or elsewhere.

At the bottom of the first page of Clara's 1856 copy, Brahms has written, "NB: Play the pedal notes only in the deeper Octave. The 2nd manual very gentle (*sanft*), the other good (*gut*)." In view of the *piano* dynamic given at the opening note in both versions, "*gut*" cannot, as some editors suggest, be translated as "full" but rather as simply indicating that a "good" or "suitable" registration for that dynamic should be employed. Just before the pedal entrance in the fifth measure, "*16 fuss*" is written, and again, seven measures from the end, where the theme once more occurs in the pedal in its original form, we find "*bloss 16 fuss*" (16 foot only) immediately preceding the entrance. The meaning seems clear, at least with regard to the final entrance, which comes under serenely ascending half-note chords played pianissimo on Manual II. What is not quite so clear is whether Brahms intends the pedal to be played only at 16' pitch throughout or whether other pitches can be added (or coupled) to the 16' stop up to that final entrance. Considering how many times the left-hand part is crossed by the pedal line (which, particularly as expanded in the 1864 version, sometimes reaches to the highest notes of the standard twenty-seven-note German pedalboard of the period), it seems certain that a 16' basis for the pedal is intended throughout. In the long pedal points under the quiet (Manual II) interludial segments, and in the ascending chromatic half-notes of the final four measures, the right sort of 16' stop—a Violone, perhaps—could sound like an orchestral contrabass.

At the top of the first page of Clara's holograph is written (in parentheses), "Second manual soft stops." Presumably, though, because the subsequent transitions to the softer Manual II (and returns to Manual I) are clearly indicated, the piece should begin on the soft stops of Manual I; the dynamic given is *piano,* and in the organs of the period, the softer stops of Manual I would not have been as soft as those on Manual II. Thus in measure 11, at the beginning of the first, and most lyrical, interlude we find "2nd Man." written, with something in parentheses crossed out immediately after. In the revised 1864 version, this interlude occurs at measure 16 and is marked "Man. II *dolce,*" Brahms having significantly altered the first section by introducing some motivic imitation and expanding it by four measures. Unlike the early version, where the upper voice remains until the entry of the interlude, in the 1864 version it drops out at the end of measure 15, providing a smoother introduction to the manual change—a small but typically Brahmsian refinement. Following this interlude (measure 16 in the holograph, 21 in the 1864 version), another manual change, so marked in both versions, occurs with the reentrance of the fugue subject in the left hand on Manual I. The right-hand obviously also goes to Manual I in the following measure.

From here on, the manual changes are similar in both versions, going to Manual II again with an overlap to the end of the left-hand statement in the right hand at the brief second interlude (end of measure 27, 1864 version), which introduces a new theme in eighth-notes. Here again, we find some major differences between the 1856 and 1864 versions. In the former, a third theme, in chromatic half-notes, comes in over the eighth-note theme, both of which move to Manual I after four measures. In the latter, after only two and a half measures of the eighth-note theme on Manual II, a cadential point occurs, after which this theme is joined by the original fugue subject and the new half-note theme on Manual I. From this point on, a masterful triple fugue unfolds on the main manual, considerably expanded in the 1864 version, and the three themes continue to intertwine in increasing complexity. Suddenly, in measure 49 (1864 version), over an augmented half-note statement of the inversion in the pedal and a thinned-out background, the main fugue subject breaks in alone, detached and off the beat.

Here again is an interesting alteration, in that this offbeat statement occurs in the left-hand voice in the 1856 version but is moved an octave higher to the top of the right-hand voice in the 1864 version. In the 1856 version, the beginning of this section is marked "*dim.,*" which is curious in that the player is still on Manual I, which in all German organs of the period is inexpressive. Possibly it was a sign for a stop reduction (which, only in this earlier version, could have been accomplished with the left hand during a rest), and it is absent from the 1864 version. Following these three brief measures, there is a dramatic pause before both hands go to Manual II (marked *pianissimo* in both versions) for two and a half measures of quiet chords, while the pedal announces the fugue subject at 16' pitch. In the 1856 version, " Man. I" is written just before the entrance of the inverted fugue subject in the left hand, and in the 1864 version (measure 54) this same place is marked "Man. I." But there seems to be no convenient place for the right hand to move smoothly to another manual, and the writing of the right-hand part strongly suggests that it is meant to remain on Manual II to the end in order to allow the single left-hand line to stand out.

The final four measures are similar in both versions, intertwining all three themes cadentially, the only significant difference being the change of the last left-hand note in the penultimate measure from a D-natural to a B-flat. Here again, we find in the 1856 holograph some indications lacking in the 1864 version. At the beginning of the third measure from the end, Brahms writes "*cresc.*" in parentheses, which makes sense only if the right hand has remained on the expressive Manual II. Then, above the fourth beat of the penultimate measure, he writes, "Man. II." There is no slurring in the early version, but there is in the 1864 version, where the "Man. II" indication is missing and the slurring allows no place to change manuals, except possibly before the final slurred phrase in the left hand. A possible explanation is that Brahms meant this final phrase to join the right hand on Manual II, and moving the left hand back to this manual here softens the texture in the last measure, which is marked "*rit.*" in the early version. All of these indications suggest a mildly dramatic buildup in which the left-hand line makes a final solo statement against the countersubjects as the music ascends in both energy and pitch before subsiding in a quiet conclusion.

The notations in Clara's manuscript copy of the A-flat Minor Fugue come as close as anything in Brahms's organ compositions to suggesting the sonorities he had in mind, but not as close as we might like. And even these are, with the exception of the manual changes, lacking in the version he prepared for publication. Also frustrating is the dearth of dynamic markings. Only two are found in either edition—*piano* at the very beginning and *pianissimo* where the fugue subject reenters in the seventh measure from the end. There is no dynamic marking for the Manual I entrances, yet from the directions on Clara's copy, it would seem that some contrast of color was desired. The stringlike texture of the theme, with its separated, "bowed" phrasing, along with the generally broad and open spacing throughout (closely spaced thirds occur only in the last seven measures) suggests an uncomplicated registration of either 8-foot stops alone, or with the softer 4-foot stops, on both the main and secondary manuals—although probably only 8-foot on the latter.

Several theories and observations have been brought forth regarding the source of (or hidden meaning in) the fugue subjects. John Daverio sees the scale letters in Brahms's name—B (B-flat), A (B-double flat), H (C-flat),

S (E-flat is "*es*" in German)—rearranged as H-B-S-A.[19] Hermann Busch suggests a possible connection with Bach's ninth Three-Part Invention in F Minor, where the three detached and off-the-beat phrases of the theme do have a rhythmic if not melodic similarity.[20] Plausible, too, is the resemblance, pointed out by David Brodbeck, of the two opening three-note phrases to a similar passage in Robert Schumann's *Manfred Overture*—a work that had impressed Brahms deeply.[21] Both of the phrases, in quarter-notes, begin on the weak beat and are separated by quarter-rests from each other and the succeeding phrase. Schumann's figure is C-flat, B-flat, F, repeated twice. Brahms's begins the same, with C-flat and B-flat, but the third note drops a whole step lower than Schumann's, to E-flat, and the repetition, while preserving the same intervals, drops them all a whole step. From there, both composers go their separate ways, but the similarity between these two motifs seems more than coincidental, and its relevance is heightened by the tragic scenario of the Manfred story.

One other Schumann connection should not be overlooked, especially in the light of some of the exercises that Brahms and Joachim had set out for themselves, which included the fugal use of the "B-A-C-H" motif (B-flat, A, C, B-natural in non-German notation). In 1845, Schumann wrote his Six Fugues on the Name of BACH "for Organ or Pedal-Pianoforte." In the first fugue (with the tempo marking of *Langsam,* as in Brahms's fugue), the "B-A-C-H" theme is followed by a rising figure strikingly similar to the inversion of Brahms's fugue subject. In the fourth fugue, Schumann spreads the "B-A-C-H" theme out, dropping the "C-H" down an octave, then echoing the first three notes of the four-note theme a whole step down, again creating a pattern very similar (if not quite identical) to the first two phrases of Brahms's fugue. The similarities in this fugue do not end there. In the Schumann fugue, there is a seven-note countersubject in eighth-notes, beginning off the beat (measure 30). Brahms's countersubject, also beginning off the beat (measure 28), consists of six eighth-notes and one quarter-note. Although only slightly similar melodically, they are almost identical rhythmically. Both composers invert their subject, although Brahms does it immediately as a countersubject, in the third measure (in the alto), and Schumann does not do it until the twenty-sixth measure (in the tenor). This "immediate inversion" effect occurs from time to time in other, non-fugal Brahms works, perhaps most familiarly in the opening notes of the Piano Concerto No. 2 (op. 83), the Tragic Overture (op. 81), and the fourth movement of the *Deutsches Requiem.*

Considering these observations, it comes as not too much of a surprise to hear the familiar half-step down, minor third up, half-step down "B-A-C-H" figure in the third and fourth measures of Brahms's fugue, immediately following the first iteration of the fugue subject, but a major third below its usual location (G-flat, F, A-flat, G) and followed by a little "dancing" figure. In the third measure, too, the main theme enters in inversion, and the B-A-C-H figure again follows, also in inversion. As it does, the main theme reenters in the pedal, in exact imitation of its initial entrance, and again followed by the B-A-C-H "coda." However, the next appearance of the fugue subject, in the tenor, leads instead into a brief exposition, concluding with the entrance of the subject in the pedal at the fifth, and transitioning at measure 16 into the next countersubject, a gently flowing rising and falling figure on Manual II over a pedal point. Below its opening phrases, in the tenor, the quasi B-A-C-H figure makes a final appearance in whole and half-notes, but beginning on G-natural instead of G-flat.

Following this brief and rather idyllic episode, entrance upon entrance of the main subject occurs in the next seven measures on Manual I, leading to another short segment on Manual II, again over a pedal point, in which a new countersubject in eighth-notes appears, graced by one brief final appearance of the previous one in diminution. In measure 30, back on Manual I, the key suddenly changes to B minor (perhaps more for notational convenience than anything else), and an additional countersubject, in descending chromatic half-notes, is introduced in measures 30 and 31. Here again we find a possible Schumann reference when, in measures 38 and 39, the descending figure first appears in the pedal line, prefaced by an upward leap of a fourth in almost exact imitation (although a third higher) of the pedal line in measures 35–37 of Schumann's sixth BACH fugue, where it is preceded by the B-A-C-H motif, transposed down a third—as it is in Brahms's fugue.

In measure 30 the key signature changes to B minor, presumably for ease of reading, for until the transition back to the original key signature in measure 39 this segment (not present in the earlier version) is really in the key of C# minor. In measures 32–33, all three subjects invert, and from this point on, the three subjects interweave impressively in both *rectus* and *inversus*. In measure 50, the main subject makes a single appearance in the soprano in a new guise—in detached eighth–notes and off the beat, the final note hanging rather dramatically alone before a pause. Then comes a pianissimo chord on Manual II, with the main theme following alone in the pedal under a chordal accompaniment. The left hand then drops to Manual I, and the two countersubjects return for a four-measure conclusion in which all three subjects participate. But unlike most of his other minor-key works (including motets and chorale preludes), Brahms chooses to close this fugue in minor, rather than with a raised Picardy third. In only a few other instances does Brahms resist this rather standard convention, most notably in the Fourth Symphony and the early Piano Quintet in F Minor (op. 34).

Among recent commentators, Gwilym Beechey aptly describes the A-flat Minor Fugue as "a highly ingenious contrapuntal tour de force,"[22] Jacques van Oortmerssen calls it "one of the most complicated fugues of the 19th century,"[23] Arthur Birkby describes it as "the noblest of all elegaic fugues,"[24] Malcolm MacDonald waxes poetic with "a pearl of particularly rare colouring,"[25] and Günter Hartmann terms it simply a "contrapuntal masterpiece."[26] But it is also what Joachim called "a pure, genuine work of art" and what Clara Schumann simply described as "heartfelt." In varying ways, virtually every other known commentator has agreed with these assessments, a rather dour exception being W. Wright Roberts, who writes it off as "mainly a work of craftsmanship"—although admittedly "no ordinary feat of craft."[27]

The miracle of this composition is that the contrapuntal complexity of the work is surprisingly unobtrusive, never detracting from the seemingly effortless flow or subtle emotional content. It is a measure of Brahms's intellect and genius that he was capable, while still only in his twenties, of so thoroughly assimilating the complexities of counterpoint and subduing them to the service of pure music. Not that it came easily, for we know that Brahms had been working over this fugue during April and May of 1856 (along with the *Geistliches Lied,* an exquisite work of comparable subtle complexity). The copy he gave to Clara in the latter month was already a revision, and Brahms further refined and revised it before its publication in 1864. How many versions he had made and destroyed before the version he gave to Clara we will never know. But as we have learned from Brahms's subsequent history, conscientious reevaluation and revision were behind some of his greatest masterworks, including the First Symphony and the *Deutsches Requiem.*

The Prelude and Fugue in A Minor, WoO 9

On May 7, 1856—his own birthday—Brahms sent a copy of this work to Clara Schumann, who was on tour in England. On the manuscript, he wrote, "So, dear Clara, while away the time on my birthday with this, and perhaps some other time. Write to me about it; is it perhaps rather stiff? Criticize it as you wish; I have another in my bag [presumably the A-flat Minor Fugue, sent shortly afterward] that is better. If you like it, all the better."[28] Clara noted in her diary that she did indeed write to Brahms at length about it, but the actual letter, like many others of hers from the 1854–1857 period, has unfortunately not survived. On June 5, he sent a copy to Joachim, along with the A-flat Minor Fugue and other contrapuntal works, and Joachim responded with some suggestions and corrections. Brahms replied that alterations would be made by the next time Joachim would see it, which suggests that a revised version may have been sent. But despite criticisms, Joachim nonetheless liked the "beautiful prelude" and the "rich theme and even richer working out" of the fugue and observed that "with the proper organ stops it must sound very effective."[29] Joachim's copy no longer exists, but Clara kept hers, inscribed "*Meiner lieben Clara.*"

Because it was never published in Brahms's lifetime, this piece is not cited in the dated list of published compositions he later compiled. Although it is a product of his contrapuntal efforts in the spring of 1856, it probably had its genesis before the A-flat Minor Fugue, with which it was sent to Joachim (along with the *Geistliches Lied* and some other choral material) in June 1856. A possible clue lies in the fact that, although a pedal part is clearly indicated by the stemming (and, in the manuscript, Brahms points out the entrances by writing "Pedal" and "Ped."), this manuscript is written on two staves. Perhaps an earlier version of the A-flat Minor Fugue also began in this form, but in the course of Brahms's organ practice, he must have realized that three staves were more correct form and easier to read. All of his subsequent writing for organ, including the accompaniments to the three choral works with organ, was, with the exception of the *manualiter* chorale preludes, on three staves. In the accompanying letter, Brahms commented, "I have been practicing the organ lately, from which these come"[30]—a significant statement, indicating that, far from being purely abstract conceptions (as the initial contrapuntal exercises appear to have been), at least part of the inspiration for these works came from Brahms's firsthand experience with the organ. Brahms and Joachim ultimately returned each other's contrapuntal compositions with commentary, and Brahms seems to have subsequently destroyed many—but by no means all—of his drafts. So it is indeed fortunate that he gave copies of some of them to Clara.

Despite the fact that it is an ambitious work, the A Minor Prelude and Fugue is less complex and sophisticated than the A-flat Minor Fugue, which suggests that it was probably conceived earlier. It also was presumably never subjected to the kind of extensive revision and polishing that the latter work later received, although a revised version, now lost, may have been sent to Joachim. It is only because Clara Schumann kept her copy of the A Minor Prelude and Fugue that it has survived at all, to be later discovered in the possession of her descendants and finally published (along with the G Minor Prelude and Fugue) in 1927. Some biographers have suggested that the opening five notes of the fugue subject—A-C-B-A-G#—are a variant of Robert Schumann's "Clara" theme, C-B-A-G#-A, with the last note transposed to the beginning.[31] Considering Brahms's inscription "to my dear Clara," the cipher games that he and Joachim were playing in some of their exercises, and the probability that this, rather than the more abstruse A-flat Minor Fugue, was his first serious attempt at an organ fugue, this is not an unreasonable assumption. Four decades later, the "Clara" theme, this time in its original configuration, would be employed again in the accompaniment to "O Death, how bitter art thou," the third of the *Vier Ernste Gesänge* (opus 121), Brahms's final tribute to the woman who was his lifelong muse.

Joachim found the A Minor Prelude and Fugue, while not above criticism, full of "bold, fast-moving life." His criticisms largely concerned a "harsh" passage in measures 14–15, as well the rather too abrupt cadence of the prelude ("not majestic enough for the design, it seems to me") and what he felt was a need for more preparation in transitional aspects of the fugue (especially in measure 42). But by the time he reached measure 57 of the fugue, he was quite ecstatic, if a bit breathless: "That must have an *Ur*-Bachian-Handelian sound on the organ—and especially if the organist can hardly keep calm for joy and just tears loose at the organ, very strong, with four-foot stops, and if the pedal for his part cannot hold out any longer, in the consciousness of his much more powerful voice, but as he was made to do jumps into the middle of the measure, and in the rejoicing fingers with his proud strides, a fine old fellow who isn't bothered about the world and pushes through his own ideas of rhythm."[32] That this enthusiasm was generated simply from reading the score is evident in Joachim's final statement, "How I'll rejoice from the heart to hear that—dear Johannes." It is possible that he did later hear Brahms play it, but if so, it is not recorded.

That the work is "Bachian" in nature is unquestioned. More than one commentator has noted correspondences between Brahms's A Minor Fugue and Bach's (BWV 543), especially in the bravura conclusion of both. But there is perhaps also a nod to some of Mendelssohn's "Bachian" preludes and fugues for piano. Malcolm MacDonald, noting that it was already in Brahms's piano repertoire, cites the Chromatic Fantasia and Fugue as a possible inspiration also.[33] Gwilym Beechey sees suggestions of the fugue subject in the E Minor Fugue of the *Das Wohltemperierte Klavier* and notes the similarity of Brahms's use of triplets to Bach's—although triplet-against-duplet figuration appears in many of Brahms's works.[34] In Bach's Prelude and Fugue in G Minor (BWV 535), the fugue subject is introduced by the pedal during the prelude. Brahms does the same—in this case with a single statement in the pedal in measures 19 and 20, the first six notes of which are marked staccato (which can best be interpreted as detached), perhaps to draw attention to it. In measure 21, the fugue theme appears once more, this time in the soprano, against a reprise of the prelude's opening theme in the tenor, but this would appear to be a purely Brahmsian elaboration.

Only in his earliest (and most Baroque-inspired) keyboard works do we find Brahms employing any ornaments—the Variations and Fugue on a Theme of Handel (op. 24) being one example. Among the organ works, ornamentation occurs significantly only in the Prelude and Fugue in A Minor. A single classic cadential trill appears at the end of both the prelude and the fugue (as also at the conclusion of the G Minor Prelude). Except where it occurs in the pedal, the fugue subject contains a trill at the end of the second measure, just before it breaks into triplets. There seems to be no real consensus as to whether this trill begins on the upper or main note—the player must decide. In the first statement, it is followed by a turn, which probably should be applied to subsequent statements as well, although not so indicated. Ornamentation also occurs in a countersubject that appears in measures 12, 16, and 36.

At its appearance in measure 16, this countersubject is accompanied by triplets in the pedal, leading to a short interlude (measures 18–20) in which triplet figures are punctuated by chords, before the main subject reappears in the pedal at measure 21. When it moves up to the tenor in measure 23, however, the dynamic marking *piano* appears and the pedal drops out, signaling a change to the secondary manual. The indication "*forte, sempre più forte*" at measure 42 indicates a return to the main manual—and possibly even the addition of stops. This coincides with the return of the subject in the tenor, which now also appears in augmentation in the pedal, repeated twice, and followed by an almost verbatim repeat of measures 18–20 at 50–52. Following the last statement at measure 53 of the subject (this time in the major key), a figure nearly identical to that which opens the prelude appears in the pedal at measure 57, repeated six times under detached chords, and leading up to the nine concluding free *stylus fantasticus* bravura measures and Neapolitan conclusion that so impressed Joachim.

The Prelude and Fugue in G Minor, WoO 10

Less is known about the origin of this composition than of any of the other early works. Like the Prelude and Fugue in A Minor, the only known manuscript was found among Clara Schumann's papers, and it likewise received its first publication only in 1927. Although it is surely a by-product of the Brahms-Joachim counterpoint exchange, it must not have been completed by the time the initial exchange concluded near the end of July 1856, and it may have been either a reworking of one of the exercises or the result of some slightly later contrapuntal explorations. In any case, it is tighter and more polished than the A Minor, with a more idiomatic pedal part. The only inscription on the manuscript is "Febr. 57," which would suggest that Brahms had completed the work—or at any rate, this revision of it—between July and February, presenting the finished product to Clara, who already had his holographs of the A minor and A-flat minor pieces. Brahms's correspondence with Clara and Joachim, which sheds so much light on the earlier pieces, gives us no help with this one. Few letters from Brahms to Clara survive from

1857, and none from between New Year's Day and May, nor, in this same period, any from Clara or between Brahms and Joachim.

What is interesting about this manuscript is that although Bozarth describes it as a "fair copy"—suggesting that there had been an even earlier version—it already reveals some further significant revisions, particularly in the fugue, where a small alteration in measure 15 avoids parallel fifths—perhaps in response to a criticism from Clara or Joachim. More significantly, the rhythm of the persistent little figure that first makes its appearance in measure 51 has been changed, the left-hand line in measures 57–58 has been simplified, a line originally in the left-hand part has been moved to the pedal in measures 70–74, and the pedal point from measure 75 to the end dropped down an octave.[35] Robert Pascall suggests that these alterations showed "Brahms rethinking his control of animation, a structural parameter in this piece."[36] The alterations are followed by Bozarth in the Henle edition.

The G Minor Prelude and Fugue, although a reversion to the *stylus fantasticus* matrix of the A Minor Prelude and Fugue, is a more polished and extensive creation, conceived on a broader scale, and the prelude is thematically distinct from the fugue. The two works nonetheless have many characteristics in common, and the fugues are both tonal fugues (unlike the A-flat Minor, which is a counterfugue). Considering Brahms's lifelong penchant for producing works in pairs, the G Minor may have been a second attempt at a classic prelude and fugue produced shortly after the initial exchange with Joachim had ended. The revisions previously cited generally free the G minor of the awkward spots that Joachim (and more recent critics) criticized in the A minor work, and may even have been in response to lost correspondence with Joachim or Clara. Malcolm MacDonald finds the G minor, if anything, even more Bachian and is impressed by the "closely worked counterpoint of the extensive coda that seems to blend [Bach and Brahms] into a single musical personality."[37] In the prelude, Gwilym Beechey again sees a possible influence of two Bach works in the same key—the Prelude (BWV 535) and Fantasia (BWV 542)[38]—yet one could also say that it is almost more Buxtehudian than Bachian.

Although often referred to as "pianistic" (true in a certain sense), the fact remains that the kinds of rhetorical figuration employed in Brahms's prelude can be readily found in the more flamboyant preludes of Bach and some of his North German predecessors such as Buxtehude and Bruhns. Sequential figures and rapid scalar passages figure prominently in Bach's well-known Prelude in D Minor (BWV 565). Buxtehude's preludes abound in similar figures, as well as the jagged broken chords and abrupt changes of tempo that characterize Brahms.. The second of Schumann's B-A-C-H fugues also displays these characteristics, and this piece was certainly known to Brahms. Yet even amid all of this *Sturm und Drang,* Brahms can still slip in a few brief measures of inverted figures (13) and canon (14–15). In the generation preceding Bach, the finest and most characteristic examples of *stylus fantasticus* organ composition emanated almost exclusively from northern Germany. Should we be too surprised, then, to find in the Romantic period another North German successfully applying this old style in a new way?

The fugue, like that in A minor, begins, *forte,* in the traditional manner with the successive introduction of the theme, consisting—somewhat like that of the A-flat Minor Fugue—of three disconnected offbeat phrases, appearing successively in different parts, and culminating with the pedal entrance. Following a chromatic transition, a countersubject enters in measure 31, is joined by the subject, and continues into a manual-only interplay of increasing rhythmic complexity until the main subject enters again in the pedal at measure 41. A short figure, almost too short to be a true countersubject, appears repeatedly in measures 51–56, punctuated by separated chords and pedal notes, and is followed in measures 57 and 58 by a descending chromatic figure in detached eighth notes over a syncopated legato tenor line cadencing in the dominant with a trill.

In measures 60–62, the short figure appears again three times in the left-hand part, echoed in the pedal, and under a right-hand statement of the subject. At a somewhat abrupt break in the manual part in measure 64, the pedal begins its final statement of the fugue subject. In measure 65, at the resumption of the manual parts (and reappearance of the chromatic figure in diminution), the only dynamic change in the fugue appears. The ***mf*** marking would surely seem to indicate a change to a secondary manual following the rest here, perhaps to allow this final statement of the subject to stand out more clearly. *Forte* reappears in measure 70, where the stemming and reappearance of the short figure signal a return to the main manual and what might be called an extended coda. Lively interplay between the various secondary figures culminates in a long cadential descent to the final G major chord of this exuberant work, which is said to have caused the British recitalist Frederick Archer to comment that "a person playing it feels as though he were walking on the ceiling."[39]

The Chorale Prelude and Fugue on *O Traurigkeit, O Herzeleid* WoO 7

Friedchen Wagner was one of Brahms's favorite piano students, as well as a member of his Hamburger Frauenchor. During one of her last lessons before Brahms left for Detmold in 1858, she asked him to write something for her "as a souvenir." She relates in her memoirs that "since I preferably played things by Bach under him, (*Wohltemperierte Klavier,* Suites) he chose a chorale melody, elaborated by him (also for the organ)."[40] This was the chorale prelude on *O Traurigkeit*, based on a Good Friday chorale from the Mainz *Gesangbuch* of 1628 and written in an "*Orgelbüchlein*" style with the slightly ornamented melody in the soprano. Friedchen Wagner's parenthetical "also for the organ" is curious. Did some of the "things by Bach" that she played also include organ chorale preludes, or perhaps piano transcriptions of them? Did she also play the organ? Brahms didn't actually give the piece to her outright at her last lesson but promised that she would soon have it. In fact, he had slyly slipped it under the closed piano lid, where a few days later she discovered "the beautiful gift I had been promised: the marvelous chorale prelude to *O Traurigkeit, O Herzeleid*." Her maid told her that she had seen Brahms put it there.[41]

Unfortunately, Wagner's copy of this piece, said to have been inscribed to her "*zu freundlichen Gedenken*" and dated at Hamburg, July 1858, is no longer extant. But Clara Schumann also was given a copy of the chorale prelude, apparently in June 1858 or earlier, for on July 1 she wrote to Brahms from Wiesbaden, "I showed your Chorale-Prelude to Herr Bogler, [and] we played it."[42] The last comment is interesting ("*we* played it"), for it suggests that it may have been played on the piano as a duet, one person playing the pedal part. It is quite probable that this kind of performance could apply to some of the other instances in which reference is made to playing Brahms's organ pieces on the piano.

Bogler must have admired it, for Clara made a copy of it for him, dated July 1858.[43] Clara's original copy is missing, but Bogler's copy was fortunately preserved, and it reveals some significant differences from the version Brahms eventually published. Later, Brahms is recorded as also having given a copy of the chorale prelude to Elisabet von Herzogenberg, but this, too, has disappeared. In March 1878, she wrote to Brahms to thank him for it and noted that she had already memorized it. "I strummed through it to [Theodor] Kirchner when he was here with Astor, and it roused him to great enthusiasm. I can't get over the way everything is *expression* in this piece. You can sit down and revel in it without ever having enough, and all the art in it seems only designed to heighten the pathos."[44]

There is no mention of a fugue by any of these recipients of the prelude. It thus seems likely that the fugue was written some time after the chorale prelude, and there is one possible clue as to when. It may, of course, also have been something that was begun around the same time as the chorale prelude but put aside and not completed until later. The occurrence of the pedal solo line in the fugue suggests, however, that it was written subsequent to the period when Brahms had been practicing on the little organ in Böhme's music store (with its coupled pedal) and had had a little more exposure to larger organs with independent pedal stops. He may even have been influenced by the new (1872) Ladegast organ in the Musikvereinsaal, which had several solo-quality stops in the pedal.

Of interest is a statement in a letter to Clara written in April 1872. In it, Brahms states, "Over the winter I have very vigorously studied counterpoint! For what purpose? To better know how to put down my pretty things [musical ideas?], as well as [to know] what is not necessary." But he admits to having little hope of learning how to write neater manuscripts.[45] It is thus quite possible that this seemingly sudden return to contrapuntal study was the genesis of the *O Traurigkeit* fugue, as well as perhaps other contrapuntal things that may have surfaced later on, such as the second of the Opus 74 motets and possibly even some of the Opus 122 chorale preludes—especially the first. It may even have been a belated (and contrasting) companion to the A-flat Minor Fugue, for the manual part is likewise a counterfugue—with the added twist of an ostinato-like chorale statement in the Pedal. It is significant that the first actual mention of the *O Traurigkeit* fugue occurs in the summer of 1873, when Brahms presented a copy of it (without the chorale prelude) to his friend, the musicologist and Bach biographer Philipp Spitta. This holograph has survived. Spitta inscribed it "*Choralfantasie 'O Traurigkeit, o Herzeleid' von Johannes Brahms*"[46] and gave the work the ultimate encomium of a Bach scholar, that he found it "worthy of its great Sebastian Bach models in its art and pensiveness, in its warmth" but that it was "by no means a mere imitation, [but] rather a self-sufficient re-creation."[47] Despite Spitta's description, however, the fugue can hardly be characterized as a fantasia, but rather as a kind of hybrid sometimes referred to as a chorale fugue. There is also evidence that in 1878 the conductor Hermann Levi likewise owned a manuscript of the fugue, from which he made a copy for Frau von Herzogenberg, but both of these copies are now lost. Whether Brahms initially intended the two "*O Traurigkeit*" pieces as a pair is unknown, but it was in this form that they were published in July 1882 in E. W. Fritsch's periodical, *Musikalisches Wochenblatt*—perhaps, like the A-flat Minor Fugue, in response to the editor's request for some unpublished work. Brahms had offered the pair to Fritsch a year earlier, with an interesting comment: "One often has things which remain unpublished because there is no appropriate outlet.... I would want it to remain in my copyright in case I wish to make it part of a larger collection."[48] Could Brahms already have been compiling material for what would ultimately become Opus 122? In the same month that it appeared, Brahms gave a copy of the *O Traurigkeit* pair to at least one of his organist friends, Karl Reinthaler, along with a recently published book of his songs. In the accompanying letter, he stated that "the enclosed 'Traurigkeit' commends itself to the great organist, and a book of songs ... to the great baritone-singer!"⁴⁹ Unfortunately, Reinthaler's response is not recorded. Two copies of the published version, with some minor corrections, were found among Brahms's papers after his death, but no manuscript versions.

The copy of the chorale prelude that Clara made for Bogler, like the early version of the A-flat Minor Fugue, again gives insights into Brahms's refining process when it is compared with the revised version published in 1882. The most obvious change occurs right at the beginning. In the 1858 version, the solo soprano line (marked f) and the accompanimental left-hand and pedal parts (marked p) all begin together, rather prosaically, on the first beat. In the 1882 version, Brahms has stretched this out, adding an anticipatory triplet that begins with a single note in the pedal followed by two thirds leading up to the original opening notes of the 1858 version—and thus echoing his treatment of the repeat of this phrase in measure 12, where it begins the six-measure coda. Considering how slight a change this is, the effect is dramatic, lending added poignancy to the first phrase of the melody, which is associated with the words *O Traurigkeit* ("O sadness"). No tempo indication is found in the 1858 version, but the 1882 version is marked *Poco Adagio*. Another noticeable alteration occurs in measure 10, where the final phrase of the chorale enters. It is not improbable that one (or more) of the various people to whom Brahms gave the early version (or versions?) may have complained of the awkwardness of this measure, whether played on the piano or the organ, and measure 10 in the 1882 version is a definite improvement in this regard. Indeed, despite the charm and favorable reception of the earlier version, all of the subsequent revising of this deceptively simple-looking seventeen-measure piece may be seen as an improvement.

It is significant that parts of the pedal line in the 1882 version, especially in measures 2–6, have been rewritten an octave higher. A plausible reason for their having been originally written so low in the 1858 version would be the organ that Brahms practiced on in Böhme's music store, which (as Brahms himself noted to Clara) had only a coupled pedal and thus no independent 16' pedal stop. This in itself might suggest composition prior to 1858. On such an organ, where the pedal played only at the pitch of the manual, the pedal line as revised in 1882 would have crossed with the tenor line in the first few measures, thus confusing the actual bass line unless it was dropped an octave. As rewritten in 1882 (the version followed in all modern editions), it is mandatory that the pedal registration be based on a 16' stop to avoid this. However, the 1858 version, as published as appendix B in the Henle edition, can indeed be played with the pedal simply coupled to the accompanimental manual. The limitations of the organ in Böhme's music store would also explain the generally low range of most of the pedal parts in the A minor and G minor preludes and fugues, as well as Brahms's need to specify a pedal 16' stop in Clara's 1856 version of the A-flat Minor Fugue. There are significant changes in the pedal part of the first dozen or so measures of this piece in its 1864 version, which would not be workable if played on an organ with only a coupled pedal.

There is no question that the chorale prelude requires an organ of two manuals and pedal. The dynamic markings of the soprano and accompanimental parts would indicate this, and in the 1858 version "2 *Manuale*" is written above the first measure. Despite the simple *f* and *p* dynamics indicated (which can also be construed to mean Manual I and Manual II), common sense would dictate that the solo not be so loud nor the accompaniment so soft as to be unbalanced. Both the context and the tonal makeup of the organs Brahms knew would suggest a solo registration that was warm rather than strident. A question of possible dynamic change occurs at measure 12, where the final phrase of the chorale melody ends and a six-measure coda begins. In the 1858 version, the final note of the chorale is marked *sostenuto*, but apparently a slight *ritard* is indicated, too, for the following measure, which begins the coda, is marked *a tempo*. These indications are missing from the 1882 version but are worth noting by the performer. A clear break occurs at this point in both versions, however, and save for the opening phrase of the coda, any pretense of solo line quickly dissolves into the flowing triplets that descend to the close. It would thus seem desirable to conclude the solo voice at the end of the chorale melody (measure 12) and play the coda with both hands on the secondary manual.

The fugue, marked *Adagio*, begins with a subject derived from the first phrase of the chorale, linked with passing notes and with an inverted answer, making it a counterfugue. Because the only pedal activity consists of the four phrases of the chorale melody in half-notes, we might expect from this kind of a beginning a *vorimitation* fugue, but such is not the case. Immediately on the heels of the first subject (measures 2 and 3) comes a countersubject characterized by leaps of a sixth or an octave, which also inverts. The most consistent use of the slur in this composition occurs in the appearances of this leaping countersubject, which suggests that despite the awkwardness of execution it often poses, legato should be especially striven for. A third countersubject in sixteenth-notes, possibly inspired by the rising and falling of the third phrase of the chorale, makes its appearance in measure 5. The interweaving of these motifs that follows could conceivably exist independent of the striding half-note pedal chorale statements, but these serve to effectively bind it all together.

A four-measure sustained tonic underlies the final cadential counterpoint, and, as is characteristic in many of Brahms's minor-keyed works, the final measure of the fugue moves to a conclusion in A Major. Although the manual portion of this fugue is in three parts throughout, some of the wide spreads and the frequent need to divide the middle part between both hands (often occasioned by an appearance of the spread-out countersubject) mandate a need for carefully worked-out fingering and occasionally a hand-stretch of a tenth. Because the pedal has only the chorale melody, these manual parts are especially amenable to being worked out and fingered on the piano.

Coda: Reception

It seems to have taken some time for these early works to become fully appreciated, although Brahms's largely nonorganist friends praised them. We know little of the reception of the two that were published in Brahms's lifetime, although they did not go entirely unnoticed. Without citing his sources, Robert Pascall states that the Fugue in A-flat Minor was performed on April 16, 1873, in the Nikolaikirche in Leipzig by an unidentified organist, and the *O Traurigkeit* pair on December 2, 1882, in the hall of the Gesellschaft der Musikfreunde by the blind Viennese pianist and organist Josef Labor.[50] And at some time or other, Brahms's organist friend Karl Reinthaler presumably performed *O Traurigkeit* from the copy Brahms had given him.

One expatriate British composer, however, may have been influenced by one of these early works. Ethel Smyth (1858–1944) had in her youth spent considerable time in Germany and Austria, studying in Leipzig from 1877 to 1884. Among her teachers were Brahms's friends Heinrich von Herzogenberg and George Henschel, and through them she came into contact with Brahms on several occasions. Her feelings about Brahms, as recorded in her memoirs, were always ambivalent. Her admiration of his music was lifelong, and she thoroughly enjoyed hearing him play the piano, but she found his social roughness and his seeming inability to take a woman composer seriously more than a little annoying at times.

Sometime during or following her Leipzig studies, Smyth composed a set of six chorale preludes. They are generally ascribed to the 1882–1884 period, although not published as a set until 1913. There is at least some probability that some of them may date from the early days of her study at the Leipzig Conservatory in 1877, where the writing of chorale preludes and fugues was part of the counterpoint curriculum, or from her private study with Herzogenberg. Others perhaps originated after 1885, when, back in England, she "became bitten with organ playing" and began taking organ lessons from Sir Walter Parratt, to whom the set is dedicated.[51]

Earlier, at the beginning of her studies, Henschel had given Brahms some songs that Smyth had written, and when she later encountered him, he remarked, "So this is the young lady who writes sonatas and doesn't know counterpoint!"[52] However, in 1878 she began studying that very discipline with Herzogenberg, and it seems clear that she had absorbed her studies quite well by the time she wrote the chorale preludes, which abound in canon, counterpoint, and *vorimitation*. But although neither she nor the Herzogenbergs mention it, it is not improbable that she had seen the holograph of Brahms's *O Traurigkeit* chorale prelude that was treasured by Elisabet von Herzogenberg, or at least the version published in 1882. And Smyth also wrote two settings—a prelude and a fugue—of this chorale. They are very different from Brahms's, to be sure, although more overt Brahms influences can be seen in some of her other chorale preludes, especially the first, *Du, O schönes Weltgebäude!* which, with its accompanimental repeated notes and chained thirds underlying the solo melody in long notes, seems to hint at influences from Brahms's *O Traurigkeit* setting.

When two more Brahms preludes and fugues were discovered and appeared in 1927 in Breitkopf & Härtel's first publication of Brahms's complete organ works, little attention seems to have been initially paid to them, although Alfred Sittard is said to have performed them at the Gedächtniskirche in Berlin on November 15, 1929. When Gerard Alphenaar brought out his American version of the 1927 collection in 1948, T. Scott Buhrman, the acerbic editor of the *American Organist,* dismissed the A minor and G minor fugues as having "themes bad enough to be offered by Guild members for a public improvisation."[53] However, William Lester, reviewing the same edition in the *Diapason,* had a somewhat better opinion, stating that all four "unfamiliar" early works were "well worth study and performance."[54]

The noted modernist Arnold Schoenberg (1874–1951) held an even better opinion of at least one of Brahms's organ works in this period. A budding Viennese composer who had attracted Brahms's attention with some of his early works, he was but twenty-three in the year that Brahms died. Despite the very different direction his music took in his mature years, he is known to have admired Brahms, and, as late as 1931, after he had written some of his more iconoclastic works, he could write that from Brahms he had learnt much about phrasing, plasticity, construction, and "economy, yet richness."[55] In 1933 Schoenberg emigrated to the United States, and by the 1940s he taught at the University of California. Schoenberg wrote little for the organ, his most notable work being the *Variations on a Recitative,* opus 40. Max Miller, then a student, was working on this piece for his master's recital, and was invited to go through it with the composer. The work ends with a classically constructed counterfugue; as Miller recalls, "I had thought all along that he [Schoenberg] had in mind the Brahms A-flat Minor for the final Fugue. And indeed, his first question to me was, 'Why don't organists play the Brahms A-flat Minor Fugue more often? Isn't it a good fugue?' This confirmed it for me."[56] While the 1927 publication of Brahms's complete organ works was well known by the 1940s, one must wonder whether Schoenberg's acquaintance with the A-flat Minor Fugue actually began in Vienna with the

1883 sheet music version—and also whether it was Brahms's early organ works that inspired Schoenberg to write a major work in the genre himself.

To the organ world at large, the appearance of the Breitkopf & Härtel edition of the complete Brahms organ works in 1927 was probably not propitious with regard to timing. A seismic rift was rapidly forming between advocates of the lush, orchestrally oriented early-twentieth-century organ and its antithesis, the spare and spartan instrument inspired by the nascent *Orgelbewegung* movement. Advocates of the former, if they played Brahms at all, preferred transcriptions of his orchestral movements or Hungarian Dances to the more classically oriented organ works. Or if they did play them, it was in the heavy-handed manner in which they often played Bach, with thick registrations and excessive use of the expression pedals. Advocates of the latter type of organ, while recognizing the classical roots of the early organ works, tried to make them even more classical by subverting their obvious Romantic elements with inappropriate registrations and unbendingly metronomic interpretations. Neither approach was calculated to generate much interest at a time when there was more familiar repertoire by Reger and Franck for the romanticists and by Buxtehude and Bach for the classicists. Church organists had, of course, been playing some of the previously published Opus 122 chorale preludes, but, with the exception of the lone *O Traurigkeit* chorale prelude, the early Brahms works published in 1927 were more on the order of recital pieces, and their introduction into the concert repertoire seems to have been slow.

It is also probable that Brahms in his lifetime and immediately thereafter was simply too visible as a symphonist and composer of songs and piano works for much attention to be initially paid to many of his compositions of less universal appeal. Unlike the almost instantaneous acceptance engendered by the accessibility and utility of the posthumous Eleven Chorale Preludes, it seems to have taken the dual appeal of both classicism and romanticism during the second half of the twentieth century to revive interest in Brahms's longer, more contrapuntal, and more technically challenging early works among performers and audiences.

FIVE

The Eleven Chorale Preludes

Brahms's biographers all observe that the period following 1890 was marked by the deaths of some of his closest friends and associates: in 1891, his longtime editor, Robert Keller; in 1892, his sister Elise and Elisabet von Herzogenberg; in 1893, the young singer Hermine Spies, whom Brahms greatly admired; in 1894, the Bach scholar Philipp Spitta, his old traveling companion Theodor Billroth, and one of his greatest interpreters, the conductor Hans von Bülow.[1] But the worst was yet to come. Clara Schumann, his dearest and oldest friend, had been in declining health, and in March 1896 she suffered a serious stroke. It is believed that this was what impelled Brahms to compose the moving *Vier Ernste Gesänge* (op. 121), although the loss of so many old friends had already given him, as he told Richard Heuberger, many opportunities to think about death. According to a letter later written to Clara's daughter Marie, in which Brahms asked her to look upon them as "a real death-offering to your beloved mother," these were completed during the first week of May.[2] Although dedicated to a friend, the artist Max Klinger, Brahms also admitted privately to Heuberger that they had to do with Frau Schumann. The texts, aptly described by Michael Musgrave as an "intense expression of that preoccupation with transience" found earlier in the *Requiem* and some of the songs and motets,[3] are again evidence of Brahms's deep knowledge of the Bible. Karl Geiringer claimed that Brahms was unwilling to ever hear the songs in concert, "fearing that it would move him too deeply."[4] But this may be just another example of urban legend, for Coenraad V. Bos, who accompanied the work in its premiere concert performance later in 1896, claimed that Brahms not only was in attendance but also came to the artists' room afterward to thank the performers and even attended another performance of the songs a few weeks later.[5]

On May 14, Brahms went again to his summer residence in Ischl. Brahms scholar Otto Biba believes that at this time he must have "taken some old organ manuscripts with him" to work on.[6] It would in any case have been quite usual for him to take some work there, for he is known to have often used his summer retreats to put in some intensive time on work in progress, some of which would be sent to his publisher later in the year. The previous year, 1895, would seem to have been an exception, as no new (or revised) works were published after his return from Ischl that year. Jan Swafford wonders if he might have begun working on the set of chorale preludes that summer;[7] indeed, he could even have been sketching out the *Vier Ernste Gesänge* that early, if his comment to Heuberger about "thinking about death" is taken at face value. Clearly, as Biba suggests and Swafford surmises, Brahms had to have been working on the chorale preludes before he went to Ischl in 1896, perhaps even simultaneously with or earlier than the *Vier Ernste Gesänge*. In view of his painstaking work habits and his seeming near obsession for perfecting any composition before offering it for publication, it indeed stretches credulity to think that he could have written (or even revised) seven of them in a single week. However, during that week Brahms apparently did put the finishing touches on a final "fair copy" manuscript of the first seven, inscribing it—in his usual manner—with the date and place of its completion.

On May 20, less than a week after Brahms's arrival in Ischl in 1896, Clara Schumann succumbed to a final deadly stroke. The sad news of her death was sent by telegram to his Vienna address but forwarded by mail to Ischl by his landlady, and it did not reach Brahms until May 22. He immediately set out for Frankfurt am Main, where Clara had died and where he thought the funeral service would be held. Being tired, he slept through his stop, had to backtrack, and arrived in Frankfurt only to discover that the funeral was to be held in Bonn, where Clara would be buried next to Robert in the Alte Friedhof. He then continued his journey without any break, arriving at Bonn as the procession to the cemetery was under way but in time to be among those who threw a symbolic handful of earth into the grave. Grief-stricken and exhausted, he is said to have then leaned on the shoulder of an old friend, Rudolf von der Leyen, and wept uncontrollably. Whether significant or not, it is recorded by several biographers that chorales were sung at the gravesite. This appears to have been a fairly common funeral tradition in the period; it is also recorded that a brass ensemble played chorales at the interment of Robert Schumann, at which Brahms was present as a pallbearer. And in more recent years, having lost some of his close friends in a short span of time, Brahms seems likely to have attended several other funerals. The burial occurred on May 23, and the next day Brahms went to Honnef to rest for a few days—Florence May says "nearly a week"—with the Wehrmanns, relatives of the von Beckeraths and von der Leyens, who were also there, along with other Rhenish friends. To Alwin von Beckerath, he sadly observed, "Now I have nobody left to lose."[8]

While in Honnef, Brahms told his friends that he had brought some new things with him that he would like to play for them. Saying simply, "I wrote them for my birthday" (May 7), he played through the *Vier Ernste Gesänge*, and then, according to May, Brahms "played some new organ preludes."[9] These would have been the first seven of the collection, or at least some of them. In two places "*Ischl. Mai 96*" is inscribed, and thus this particular manuscript must have been finished between May 14, when Brahms went to Ischl, and May 22, when he left for Frankfurt. In Brahms's pocket calendar for May are three short notes referring to the *Vier Ernste Gesänge*, Clara's death, and the seven *Choralvorspiele*. A bracket surrounds them.[10] Its meaning is unclear, but it could perhaps have something to do with completion—of two manuscripts edited for publication, and a treasured life. This would, however, seem to confirm that the final version of the original set of seven chorale preludes, as well as of the four songs, was completed during May.

Brahms returned to Ischl at the end of May and began again to work on his compositions and to take the long walks that he always enjoyed. In the middle of June, he spent a few days in Vienna with his good friends the Fellingers, who were celebrating their silver wedding anniversary. He is said to have played the first and seventh (*Herzlich thut mich erfreuen* in the original order) of the chorale preludes for them and for his friend and editor, Eusebius Mandyczewski, who "wondered at their impersonality."[11] Shortly afterward, Brahms departed again for Ischl. The manuscript of three of the final four chorale preludes is dated "*Juni 96 Ischl*," but these drafts were probably not finished until the very end of the month and seem not to have been actually prepared for publication at that time.

On June 24, Brahms was visited in Ischl by a former pupil, Richard Heuberger, a Viennese choral conductor, music critic, and opera composer. In his diary, Heuberger recorded that on that morning Brahms "played for me his manuscript chorale preludes. Splendid pieces! One, a contrapuntal work, strophe after strophe worked out fugally... soon the chorale enters, and from the developing chorale a theme in the upper fifth follows through. With all its precision this work is splendid music. True Brahms!"[12] Heuberger here seems to be referring to the first of the seven chorale preludes, indeed an impressive contrapuntal essay. Heuberger visited Brahms again on July 5, when he noted that "the package (namely the chorale preludes) must have already been sent away, for today Brahms told me he would show me some new compositions." Unfortunately, Heuberger doesn't say what these were. They might indeed have been more chorale preludes, as some assume, but they could also have been some of the folk song settings Brahms is thought to have also been working on at this time, which were later posthumously published. In either case, they were probably not all new—except, of course, to Heuberger.

Despite his return to seeming normalcy after the emotional and physical stress of the trip to Frankfurt and Bonn, Brahms began to feel increasingly unwell and lacking in his usual stamina, and in July his friends, observing that he was noticeably jaundiced, finally persuaded him to see a physician. He in fact saw several and was at first advised to "take the cure" at Karlsbad, which he did in September. A doctor in Vienna had found Brahms's liver to be enlarged, but apparently it was Dr. Grünberger in Karlsbad who made the fatal diagnosis of cancer of the liver—the same disease that had ended Brahms's father's life.[13] It had probably been developing undetected for some time, for the *Merck Manual,* that classic physician's reference book, states that "jaundice is uncommon early." Even today, after a century of medical progress, the prognosis for advanced hepatic cancer is still poor.

So it was for Brahms. In October, he returned to Vienna noticeably weaker but so determined not to be an invalid that, for at least a while, he continued his daily walks, attended concerts, and socialized with his increasingly concerned friends. In October, too, another distinguished Viennese composer, Anton Bruckner, died, and his funeral was held on the fourteenth of that month at the Karlskirche. Despite the fact that the church was just across the street from his home, Brahms arrived late. As he stood at the back of the church, he is said to have muttered some remark to the effect that it would not be long before his own funeral.[14]

Eventually the walks had to be given up, but Brahms's loyal friends continued to take him for rides and entertain him in their homes, and he spent Christmas with the Fellinger family, whose photographic hobby has provided us with some of the last images of Brahms. In January, he attended a performance by Joseph Joachim's ensemble of his String Quartet in G Major, and in early March, a performance of his Fourth Symphony in the Vereinsaal, at which the audience gave the now gravely ill composer a long and tumultuous ovation. But very shortly thereafter, he became bedridden. On March 30, Heinrich Herzogenberg, who had just sent Brahms a copy of a piano quartet dedicated to him, sadly wrote to Joachim that their dear friend was approaching his end. It came quietly on the morning of April 3, 1897.

Vienna honored her adopted son with a funeral procession worthy of royalty, with a host of friends, students, fellow musicians, and his publisher carrying the funeral torches through the streets, followed by a large crowd of mourners. It began at his residence in the Karlsplatz and crossed the square to the buildings of the Musikverein, where members of the Singverein stood in the entrance to sing Brahms's own choral work, *Fahr wohl.* Then it proceeded to the Lutheran Church in the narrow Dorotheergasse near the city center, where Pastor Zimmerman conducted the funeral service, which included the reading of the scripture text on which Brahms had based the last movement of the *Requiem*.[15] Following this, the procession continued out the long road to the Zentralfriedhof in Vienna's Simmering district. In 1888, a special tree-shaded segment near the main gate of this large landscaped cemetery had been set apart for the city's notable musicians, and the remains of Beethoven and Schubert were moved there. There Brahms also was laid to rest, to be joined two years later by his old friend Johann Strauss Jr., Vienna's beloved "Waltz King," who is buried next to him. It is a hallowed spot for present-day music lovers, as the floral offerings on the graves of the many *Musiker* interred there eloquently attest.

During the summer and early fall of 1896, Brahms had continued to work on his folk song collections and had instructed his copyist, William Kupfer, to prepare a final copy of the first seven of the chorale preludes for publication. This copy was subsequently corrected by Brahms, although it is uncertain just when this was done or how thoroughly. The remaining four chorale preludes, however, were not found until after his death, and it has been speculated that Brahms may have initially intended two sets of seven but was prevented by his deteriorating health from completing the second set. Brahms's friend and subsequent editor, Eusebius Mandyczewski, has been quoted as saying that "it is conceivable that he [Brahms] intended to bring out [*herauszugeben*] two or perhaps more volumes of seven pieces, as he did with the *Kinderliedern*."[16] It is significant that Mandyczewski uses a word that more aptly describes editing, compiling, or publishing than composing (*komponieren*), although this does not necessarily rule out the inclusion of some new compositions in the projected volumes. The reference to the *Volkskinderlieder* is also interesting, as these were published in two sets of seven. Did Mandyczewski know, or at least suspect, that some of the contents of the completed volume of seven chorale preludes were revisions of earlier works—as were the contents of the folk song volumes?

We must also remember that in 1882, when Brahms published the pair of *O Traurigkeit* chorale settings, he had mentioned to the editor "things which remained unpublished" and the possibility of later including these two pieces in a larger collection. It was not the first time he had mentioned the existence of unpublished organ works, for in 1864 he had made a similar comment to the publisher of the Fugue in A-flat Minor, referring to its "born and unborn sisters and brothers." He brought this up again in a letter to Simrock on June 18, 1896, shortly before sending him the completed draft of the first seven chorale preludes, asking that a copy (or perhaps even the holograph) of the two *O Traurigkeit* settings be sent to him.[17] Because these pieces were obviously not included in the first set of seven, Brahms might have been thinking of including them in a hypothetical second set—perhaps with further revisions. If so, this would, with the four found after his death, have brought to six the number of additional chorale preludes, and if Brahms had finished another setting of *Es ist ein Ros' entsprungen* that he had begun to sketch out, the second set of seven would have been complete. Perhaps some future editor may see fit to publish all of Brahms's chorale preludes in two sets of seven, including the *O Traurigkeit* pair and the *Es ist ein Ros'* fragment in the second set.

The concept of at least a second set of seven chorale preludes would certainly not have been incompatible with Brahms's practice, for he sometimes composed or published things in pairs, especially in later years—for example, his only two string quintets (opp. 88 [1882] and 111 [1891]), his only two orchestral overtures (opp. 80 and 81 [1881]), the two Opus 116 sets of fantasias for piano in 1892, and the two Opus 120 sonatas for clarinet and piano in 1895. Ivor Keys notes that "Brahms's essays in new media . . . often come in pairs, as though the way had been cleared for the second by the rigors of the first creative act."[18] Often, too, the second of the pair differs noticeably in character from the first, as with the two overtures—the first joyful and even rollicking, the second somber and serious. Concerning the A major and G minor piano quartets (opp. 25 and 26), Jan Swafford observes a "characteristic pattern" in these pairs for the same medium: "the first looser and more extroverted, the second relatively tighter and more subtle."[19] This could also serve as an apt description of another pair—the two (9th and 10th) chorale preludes based on *Herzlich tut mich verlangen*. The organ was not, of course, a new medium for Brahms, although it was a long-neglected one.

Brahms also had cast several other works in sets of seven: the *Marienlieder* (op. 22), a group of part songs for mixed voices (op. 62), and some sets of solo songs. There are seven stanzas in the *Gesang des Parzen* (op. 89) and seven movements in the *Deutsches Requiem* (op. 45). Fourteen (twice seven) *Deutsche Volkslieder* for four-part chorus were published in 1864, and the forty-nine *Deutsche Volkslieder* for voice and piano published in 1894 are in seven books, each containing seven songs. In the introduction to this collection, Brahms remarked that it "always pleases him to make so sacred a number."[20] Even the posthumously published fourteen *Volkskinderlieder* and twenty-eight additional *Deutsche Volkslieder* are in multiples of seven. We must remember, too, that Brahms's birthday was May 7, the day on which, many years earlier, he had sent the first of his organ preludes and fugues to Clara Schumann, and May was the month when the final draft of the first seven chorale preludes was completed. But finally, Brahms was surely quite aware of the symbolism of the numbers 7 and 14: 14 is the sum of the letters in the name Bach (2 + 1 + 3 + 8), and 7 is the numerical symbol of completion, a symbolism attributed to the biblical Book of Revelation.

The manuscripts of the chorale preludes deserve some discussion here. George S. Bozarth studied them in some detail in preparation for his recent edition of the organ works, published by Henle. Perhaps most interesting, in that it is probably a "fair copy" based on pieces sketched out or revised earlier, is the autograph manuscript of the first seven, consisting of six pages on hand-ruled, ten-stave music paper, although here they are not in the order in which they were eventually published. According to the numbering in the published version (upon which all subsequent editions but one are based), the order of the preludes in this manuscript is 1, 5, 2, 6, 7, 3, 4. Taken in this order, a certain amount of key relationship seems evident, particularly in nos. 1 (in E minor, ending in E major) and 5 (all in E major), numbers 1 and 2 in Brahms's manuscript. These two—in many ways the most "classical" of the set—can be performed effectively as a pair. The next three (2, 6, 7), all beginning in minor and ending in major, are in keys a fifth apart—G, D, A. The last two, 3 and 4, are a sixth apart and in major keys (F and D).

We can only speculate on the implications of the original order in which the chorales were written in this manuscript. The style of the first three (1, 5, 2) rather strongly suggests that they might be revisions of earlier works, in which case the date on the manuscript after the third is only the date of their final revision. There are also some small differences between the first three and the second four in the written details, most noticeably the style of the brackets. Closer scrutiny of some of these differences and comparison with other dated Brahms manuscripts might yield further insights. The inscription "*Ischl. Mai 96*" appears in two places in this manuscript, after the third (no. 2) and seventh (no. 4) preludes. Bozarth notes that the manner in which the first three and the remaining four are grouped in the manuscript might suggest that three were initially entered and dated, perhaps very early in the month, and the final four completed later (but presumably before May 22). He suggests that this "additive" process may have influenced the subsequent change in order.[21] But considering those slight differences in the writing style, the first three could have also been written at an earlier time, leaving some blank pages, which the frugal Brahms then filled in with later work, a possibility that also supports the "additive" theory. The first inscription would then signify only the date when Brahms picked them up again, or perhaps when he put some finishing touches on the third, which, more than the other two, contains a significant amount of corrections, deletions, and insertions. Interestingly, at least one modern recording artist (Ulfert Smidt, for Thorofon) has seen fit to perform the first seven in their original order. The final order, presumably as rearranged (or at least approved) by Brahms himself, was established in the copy made for the publisher Simrock by William Kupfer, which places the two longest and most complex at the beginning and end of the set. This copy of numbers 1–7 contains corrections in Brahms's own hand and thus presumably dates from the summer of 1896, perhaps originating in July, when Brahms told Heuberger that some compositions had been sent to the publisher.

By this time, Brahms had decided either to add to the set of seven or, as seems more likely, to compile another set to go with it. Thus we have a manuscript of nos. 9, 10, and 11, written continuously on newer, printed, fourteen-stave paper and dated in pencil "*Juni 96. Ischl*," and another, of no. 8, written on a single sheet of older, hand-ruled, eight-stave paper and undated. Interestingly, the style of the brackets on the latter closely resembles that of the first entries in manuscript of the first seven, suggesting that this piece could have come from the same period. There are also in existence two undated manuscripts, one of no. 10, on twelve-stave paper, with several corrections, and scratched out—obviously a penultimate draft. What is interesting is that it is entitled *O Welt, ich muss dich lassen*, a text sometimes sung to the same tune as *Herzlich thut mich verlangen*, as well as to the tune that Brahms employs for it. The other is of no. 11, again with some revisions, also written on twelve-stave paper. But this also contains at the end a few tentative measures of an uncompleted canonic setting of *Es ist ein Ros' entsprungen*. The fact that it is canonic might suggest a possible revision of one of the early canonic exercises, but if no. 8 was indeed an earlier work, perhaps another pair was intended, and Brahms was unable to summon the energy to complete it. As his illness worsened, he told Max Kalbeck that his piano remained closed and that his only musical activity—aside from attending occasional concerts with friends—was silently reading through Bach scores.

As can be seen, the order of nos. 9, 10, and 11 is established by their order on a single dated manuscript, but the date and order of no. 8—written in a slightly different style and on a different type of paper—is not. It may have been an earlier draft that Brahms had decided to include in a second group he was assembling, and Mandyczewski may well have had his reasons for placing it where he did. All that these surviving manuscripts can really tell us, however, is that nos. 8–11, never fully prepared for publication by Brahms and found only after his death, were a bit of unfinished business of some kind. And considering that no. 8 is generally viewed as the most popular of the whole collection, we are fortunate to have them at all.

In a letter to Herzogenberg written in June 1896, in reference to the texts of the Four Serious Songs, Brahms had mentioned some "other things not so serious" that were less suitable (or ready) for publication, which Max Kalbeck assumed to be the chorale preludes.[22] But these, it would seem, are just as "serious" as the Four Serious Songs (*Vier Ernste Gesänge*), although the texts are more orthodox. Brahms told Herzogenberg he would like to play the "other things" on the piano for him, and so could as well have been referring to the two "not so serious" early four-hand piano arrangements found with the four additional chorale preludes after his death, which he apparently never got around to revising. If he was in fact referring to the chorale preludes, he might, as Robert Pascall suggests, have been thinking that there might be only a small market for them. In this, though, he would have been very wrong.

Some biographers claim that Brahms took some manuscripts with him to work on when he went to Karlsbad in September 1896, and Kalbeck reported that his landlady saw him writing music there, so perhaps this is where he made a few final corrections to either the chorale preludes or perhaps some folk songs. It must not have been long after this that Brahms's steadily deteriorating health, the concomitant fatigue, and his growing awareness of what it meant finally made it impossible for him to continue any composition or revision.

There are certain stylistic differences between the last four and the previous set of seven that are noteworthy. Although all four might be said, like the first seven, to be "*Orgelbüchlein*-inspired," there seems less overt contrapuntalism in any of them. Except for no. 9, which has much in common with no. 2, the others are markedly different in significant ways. In no. 8, the chorale melody is so obscured as to be almost undetectable; no. 10, while displaying Bachian influence, is structurally very different from the other two chorale preludes in which the melody is carried by the pedal; and the echo effects in no. 11 are unique and rather un-Bachian.

Most different, however, are the cadences. In each of the first seven (as well as in the *O Traurigkeit* fugue), we find, in some form, a prolongation of the final tonic note of the chorale. Save in the first (where the melody is in the pedal) and in the third, it is doubled in the bass—and twice in the tenor as well—and accompanied by flowing eighth-notes, often in thirds and in contrary motion. In the last four, with the exception of no. 8, the concluding note of the chorale is more perfunctory, never more than a full measure in length, and with no particular change in the nature of the accompaniment. Still another difference between the first seven and the final four has to do with the use of the alto clef. In the original manuscripts (and earliest publications), it crops up somewhere in every one of the first seven but is entirely absent in the last four. It is also absent in the four early works. Was its presence only in the first seven chorale preludes the result of the final revision, to eliminate the need for ledger lines in the printed version, or has it something to do with chronology?

And there is one other, rather curious, difference that must also be considered. With the exception of two notes in measure 16 of no. 3 (which may have been the result of a later revision), the pedal part of every one of the first seven can be played on an organ with a twenty-note pedalboard, and none of the manual parts exceeds the compass of fifty-one notes. These shorter compasses were often found in German organs of the late eighteenth or early nineteenth centuries, particularly in smaller organs, but organs built in the latter part of the nineteenth century had larger manual and pedal compasses. Two earlier organs that Brahms could have known—at very different times in his life—were the 1755 König organ in St. Maximilan's Church in Düsseldorf (which, despite its size, had only a twenty-note pedalboard) and the 1808 Deutschmann organ in the Lutheran Church in Vienna (recorded in two sources as having had a twenty-two-note pedal). Both had a manual compass of fifty-one notes. Regarding the last four chorale preludes, whereas no. 8 (like three of the first seven) is on two staves and no. 11 (which pairs with no. 3) has a pedal part that does not exceed twenty notes, the other pair—nos. 9 and 10—requires at least a twenty-five-note pedalboard. Do some of these differences also have any significance in the chronology of the pieces? As with many other aspects of these works, the temptation to speculate is great, but there are—at least at present—no clear answers, and, as Little observes, Opus 122 "remains in many ways as much an enigma today as when it was first published."[23]

The problem with regard to the manual and pedal compasses is that although Brahms and Clara may have had some familiarity with the Düsseldorf organ in the period just preceding the counterpoint study with Joachim, and Brahms may have had some contact with the Vienna organ in later life, there is no actual proof of either. And there is always the possibility of contact with organs in other places, such as Ischl, of which there is no record. Nor is there any other satisfactory answer to the question of why Brahms would write for organs with a restricted and old-fashioned compass, when in Hamburg—as well as in Bremen, Vienna, and probably elsewhere—he had experienced organs with the more modern compasses early on. The pedal parts of the four early works are written to the limit of the standard twenty-seven-note German pedalboard of the second half of the nineteenth century, and in a few places the Prelude and Fugue in G Minor requires the similarly standard fifty-six-note manual compass. These were the compasses of the Wolfsteller organ in St. Peter's Church and the Hildebrandt organ in St. Michael's. They were presumably also the compasses of the anonymous music store organ on which Brahms occasionally practiced in the 1850s when the early works were written, because despite its small size, it was apparently intended as a practice instrument for organists playing larger church organs.

As to whether any or all of the Eleven Chorale Preludes were revisions of earlier drafts, definite proof is lacking, but circumstantial evidence—including some of the discrepancies cited here—is strong. Max Kalbeck, Brahms's friend and biographer, opines that "exterior and interior evidence makes it probable that several of Brahms's posthumous chorale preludes originated at that time [1855–1856] and were only revised in 1896."[24] Others have expressed similar opinions. Harry W. Gay notes the "shadows of the studies of the older masters" and thinks that these pieces "could well be the reflections of earlier years."[25] Wm. A. Little finds suggestive the fact that early copies in Brahms's hand exist of the melodies on which four of the preludes were based: *Herzliebster Jesu, Herzlich thut much verlangen, O Welt ich muss dich lassen* (also known as *Innsbruck*), and *Mein G'müth ist mir verwirret* (the early folk dance version of *Innsbruck*).[26] Michael Musgrave sums up the general thinking on this matter when he states that "Kalbeck's assertion that they are drawn from a wide period seems ... perfectly reasonable, and can be supported on grounds of style and formal relationship to the early works."[27]

Indeed, the "wide period" hypothesis might be the most logical, considering Brahms's history of periodically returning to counterpoint and chorales at different times in his life, as well as references he made at different times to the possible existence of unpublished organ works. One must also, as Otto Biba does, take seriously into account the improbability that a composer so prone to taking his time to revise and perfect his work, even when in the best of health, could have dashed off such polished little masterpieces from scratch in just a few weeks.[28] And in the spring and summer of 1896, Brahms was, as we know, already seriously ill. On the other hand, Robert Pascall sees "the contrapuntal control of discord, the motivic intricacy and complexity, and the masterly integration of Baroque techniques with a rich, essentially romantic chromaticism" as indications of a later dating.[29] Yet, as we have seen, Brahms in his mature years was no stranger to the process of updating and polishing earlier works to this level of sophistication. Witness his documented improvements to the *O Traurigkeit* prelude and the A-flat Minor Fugue in the 1870s and 1880s, the reworking of the early Mass movements into the masterly *Warum?* motet, and the late-period transformation of his youthful Opus 8, to cite but a few of the known examples.

As with *O Traurigkeit* and the chorale-based motets, Brahms chose classic Lutheran chorale melodies from the sixteenth and seventeenth centuries as the basis for all eleven chorale preludes in this collection. Four of these melodies (set in 3, 4, 8, 9, 10, and 11), all dating from the sixteenth century, have their roots in secular folk songs. Three (2, 5, and 6) are by the seventeenth-century composer Johann Crüger, and the remainder are anonymous chorales from seventeenth-century *Gesangbücher*. All but 1, 4, and 8 can be found in the late-eighteenth-century collection of Bach's 371 chorale harmonizations, a copy of which was in the Schumann library.[30] Andreas Schröder calls the *Elf Choralvorspiele* an "*Orgelbüchlein* in the language of the late romantic."[31] And it is hard to deny the influence of Bach's collection of smaller chorale preludes, especially in Brahms's settings where the melody is continuous (nos. 2, 5, 6, 8, 9) rather than broken up or gapped. As in Bach's *Orgelbüchlein*, too, we find Brahms using motifs derived from the melodies in their accompaniment. However, unlike Bach's *Orgelbüchlein*, there seems to be no particular liturgical significance to either the original or revised order of Brahms's chorale preludes., One must conclude that these settings are based purely on the composer's personal choices, which seem to have been at least partly influenced by the chorale texts. Like the biblical texts Brahms chose for the *Requiem,* the motets, and the *Vier Ernste Gesänge,* the texts of the chosen chorales tend to deal broadly with hope, trust, compassion, and a loving God.

Lorene Banta, noting the "strange impression which many have" that the Eleven Chorale Preludes are "preoccupied with grief," is of the opinion that "this is certainly not the case."[32] Another commentator, Harry W. Gay, sees Opus 122 as "eleven small sketches of a serene assurance expressing the elemental sacraments of life."[33] Yet far too many other writers have commented indiscriminately on the supposed "funereal" nature of all of Brahms's chorale choices. Hans Joachim Moser dismisses them in a short paragraph as "Bachian technical studies" and Brahms's "funeral music for himself."[34] Karl Geiringer, while making possible exceptions for nos. 4 and 8, rather flatly states that "the whole atmosphere of this collection is that of profoundest grief."[35] Statements of this sort have influenced many players to perform all of Brahms's chorale preludes in a dreary and dirgelike manner.

Such a blanket interpretation is not supported by scrutiny of the texts. Of the first seven, no. 1 sings praise to Christ, who grants salvation; no. 2 is a Passiontide chorale, relating to Christ's condemnation by Pilate; no. 3 does deal with life's end, commending the soul to God's love; no. 4, with its roots in a secular springtime carol, is an allegorical vision of eternity, suitable for the post-Easter season or Rogation days; no. 5 was, and still is, a classic Communion hymn; no. 6 is concerned with departed souls, but again in the context of eternal life, and is associated with All Saints' Day; and no. 7 belongs in Trinity season and is a hymn to God, the source of all good—but also a prayer for a sound body and soul. Of the final four, no. 8 expresses the hopefulness of Advent and Christmas, and only the nos. 9 and 10 pair (based on the same chorale) and no. 11 (based on the same chorale as no. 3) can be said to have any funereal associations. And we should not overlook the fact that all eleven, whether written in major or minor keys, end in the major in Brahms's manuscripts—although the Picardy third of no. 10 was for some reason not reproduced in the earliest printed editions. This is rather interesting in view of Wilfrid Mellers's observation that the reverse was true of "several of the piano pieces of Brahms's last years [which] invert classical precedent by beginning in the major and ending in the minor."[36]

Many of the older and best-loved Lutheran hymns, especially of the Pietist tradition, do in fact deal in some way with death but generally in the context of eternal life for the faithful, which signifies hope and rescues them from morbidity. And indeed, hope is an element in many of the texts Brahms chose for some of his more solemn utterances. Unlike Bach, Brahms was never a church musician, nor even much of a churchgoer, and he has been rather unfairly called an agnostic or unbeliever by some who seem not to have discerned his very real—if perhaps unorthodox and transcendentalist—spirituality. As R. W. S. Mendl expresses it, "For him, either in the background or the foreground of his thoughts, there was the presence of a loving God."[37] There is in any case little question that the Lutheran catechism, liturgy, and chorales were, along with Luther's translation of the Bible, deeply embedded in Brahms's North German cultural heritage. He not only fully understood these things in their historic, aesthetic, and liturgical context but also throughout his life found creative ways to express his own love and respect for them through his music.

(1) *Mein Jesu, der du mich*

Ivor Keys states that at first sight, this chorale prelude, based on a chorale melody of 1697, is "the most antiquarian" of the set, but that "the chromaticisms and the subtle variety of the textures bring it into a world where 'ancient' and 'modern' lose much of their relevance."[38] The same could easily have been said of Brahms's other contrapuntal works, of course, particularly the A-flat Minor Fugue, but the use of "antiquarian" forms is much less characteristic of Brahms's late works than of his youthful ones. Michael Musgrave harbors no doubt that it is one of the latter, calling it "an obvious example of earlier composition."[39]

This piece, accurately described by Eileen Coggin in her detailed analysis of it as "the most intricately woven" of the set,[40] stands apart from all but one of the others in its length and stands alone in its contrapuntal complexity. In his memoirs, Richard Heuberger recalled the occasion when Brahms had played through some of the chorale preludes for him in June 1896 in Ischl. Concerning *Mein Jesu,* he related that Brahms had told him: "Such work is actually enormously hard to do, but I am very interested in it, apart from the technicalities involved, especially for the sake of enhancing and beautifying the melody."[41] This does not, of course, indicate whether the piece was new or an older one he had revised, although it would provide a convincing rationale for his having preserved and improved an older piece on which he had expended so much hard work. And as we know, Brahms had been very interested in the "enormously hard" work of elegant counterpoint throughout his entire career. It is indeed difficult not to believe that this chorale prelude is in actuality a polished final revision of an earlier composition, for although it has no counterpart among Brahms's later music, it has a strong kinship with two earlier works—the *O Traurigkeit* fugue and the first of the

Opus 29 motets, *Es ist das Heil uns kommen her*. These works are also characterized by the appearance of the chorale in unadorned long notes against a complex contrapuntal background.

Such chorale preludes fall into two general types: that in which the essentially seamless fugal part has little or no connection with the melody, and the *vorimitation* chorale, in which each statement of a phrase is preceded by a fugal peroration based on the opening notes of that phrase. The chorale melody can appear in any part, but in some of the most characteristic examples, it occurs in the pedal. Pachelbel wrote a number of chorale preludes of this type, although its roots are even earlier, in sixteenth-century motets and the works of Scheidt. But it was Bach who brought the form to its highest perfection, especially in some of the *Eighteen Chorales*. A particularly notable example of a contrapuntal *vorimitation* fugue of the type employed by Brahms is no. 15, *Jesus Christus unser Heiland* (BWV 665); another occurs in Bach's variations on *Vom Himmel hoch*. Surely it was Bach, at least as much as Pachelbel, from whom Brahms drew his inspiration for these particular works.

In the *O Traurigkeit* fugue, the main subject is derived from the opening notes of the chorale, but the fugal part continues throughout in developing this subject quite independently of the pedal chorale statements. *Mein Jesu, der du mich,* on the other hand, is a classic *vorimitation* chorale, like the Opus 29 motet, *Es ist der Heil uns kommen her,* and could possibly have originated in the same period. Such compositions can be broken down into a series of fughettas, each based on the chorale phrase that follows, and linked to the next by a brief episode. *Mein Jesu* consists of six such fughettas, the subjects of which enter alternately in the soprano and tenor lines. Brahms varies the treatment of each subject. The first is fairly straightforward and in eighth-notes, the second (measures 10–11) more rhythmically complex, the third (measures 18–19) even more so, and the fourth (measures 26–27) somewhat less. The fifth (measure 34) begins in direct imitation of the chorale phrase, then suddenly breaks into an arpeggiated figure, and the final sixth (measure 42) comes in boldly and as straightforwardly as the first, leading to what Vernon Gotwals calls "a heart-warming climax"[42] that Wilfrid Mellers describes as "at once quintessential Bach and high romanticism."[43]

The manual texture in the *O Traurigkeit* fugue never exceeds three parts, but in *Mein Jesu* it is more varied. Although largely in three-part texture throughout, the arpeggiated episode (measures 34–41) in the fifth fughetta is mostly of two-part texture, and the fughetta to the sixth and final phrase begins almost immediately in four parts. Here, in measure 42, the descending theme in the left-hand part is followed at the space of only a single beat by its inversion in the right-hand part. The counterpoint then weaves in contrary motion until it climbs upward in rich harmony against the descending final phrase that leads to the cadence. Bach and romanticism indeed seem to entwine in Brahms's treatment of the text of the last two phrases, a literal translation of which is "The great Bridegroom's praise, thus gladly tell."[44] W. Wright Roberts writes admiringly of this piece, with its "feeling of noble urgency," feeling that "the grasp of the organ is bigger than in the other preludes, the end superb in its clinching power."[45] Although the key signature of the piece is E minor, Brahms intermittently flirts with E major throughout, concluding affirmatively in that key.

In his discussion of the manuscripts used in preparing his new edition of Brahms's organ works, George Bozarth states that with regard to the Eleven Chorale Preludes "neither the full autograph manuscript nor the Kupfer copy presents entirely accurate readings, for Brahms's notation of his autograph and his proofreading of the Kupfer copy were not always done carefully."[46] With regard to *Mein Jesu*, he notes that "Brahms did not enter the slurs fully and carefully in the autograph," and that although Kupfer, in his copy for Simrock, omitted even some of those that Brahms did enter, Brahms did not replace them when he corrected Kupfer's manuscript. What this suggests is that the ailing Brahms simply had not the energy to do as thorough a job of editing as he might have done when in better health, and that other small things may have slipped through the cracks as well.

Manual changes seem to be clearly implied by the dynamic changes that occur at most of the entries, but certain inconsistencies suggest that here, too, there may have been a bit of carelessness on the part of Brahms, which could easily have been overlooked by subsequent editors. The opening dynamic in the manuscript was originally *mezzo forte* but later changed to the somewhat more ambiguous *forte ma dolce* by Brahms, and one can assume that the piece begins on Manual II. Then, in measure 10, *più forte* appears, significantly placed below the tenor entrance of the second fughetta subject rather than between the staves. This would suggest to an organist not the addition of stops (which would be incompatible with the overlap of the first subject in the right hand) but the transfer of the left hand to the louder Manual I at this point and the picking up of the alto entrance at the end of measure 11 with the left hand. Both hands would then come to this manual with the soprano entrance of the subject in measure 13. The *piano* marking directly below the soprano entrance of the third subject in measure 18 clearly would indicate the removal of the right hand to a softer manual. But *piano* is softer than *forte ma dolce* (or *mezzo forte*), so a stop reduction seems also indicated here—and Brahms actually provides a convenient rest in which to retire a stop or two.

Another problem arises with the tenor entry of the fourth subject in measure 26. This entry overlaps the close of the preceding section, and Brahms's notation (and beaming) suggest strongly that the left hand should go to

Manual I here while the right-hand alto line finishes up the overlap before joining it. There is no corresponding dynamic marking as in all the other entries, and an omission must be strongly suspected. Puzzling too is the use of the *forte* marking at both the fifth and sixth entries (measures 34 and 42). However, if the *forte* mark is moved from the fifth to the fourth entrance and replaced by a *piano* mark, seemingly more suited to this arpeggiated and thin-textured segment, the manual changes begin to make more sense. The tenor entrances, all of which overlap endings, are thus now announced on the louder manual; the soprano entrances, which do not overlap, occur on the softer manual; and the climactic four-part concluding section is highlighted by contrast. If Brahms was somewhat careless in the matter of slurs, he could have overlooked the misplacement of a few dynamic marks, too. And Eusebius Mandyczewski, who ultimately edited the Eleven Chorale Preludes for their posthumous publication, was not an organist and thus could have either also overlooked these inconsistencies or assumed them to be correct.

It will be seen from this and subsequent chorale preludes that Brahms often did not indicate manual changes as such or, if he did, was not consistent. Usually he simply indicated them by *forte* and *piano* markings, but always at places where the musical context plainly suggests a change. In general, it makes the best sense to interpret the *f* and *p* markings as *mezzo forte* and *mezzo piano,* thus avoiding extreme contrasts, which are foreign to the nature of the music. And in this particular prelude (as in no. 10), the pedal should be registered, possibly only at 8' pitch, so that the chorale stands out clearly but subtly against both Manual I and Manual II.

(2) *Herzliebster Jesu*

Among Brahms's Eleven Chorale Preludes, this work is distinguished as one of only two to which the composer gave a tempo marking (*Adagio*), and it is the only one where Brahms himself overlaid the text of the chorale. In fact, he did this not once but twice, in his original dated holograph and in his amendments to the copy made by Kupfer. Why he should do so with this fairly familiar text and no other is just another of the many questions raised by Opus 122. Possibly it was only to point out the melody notes in the somewhat ornamented treble line, although he seems not to have found this necessary elsewhere except perhaps in no. 7, where he calls attention to the meandering entrances of the melody by simply writing "*Choral*" over the first note. Nonetheless, for the first published edition of 1902, Mandyczewski, who did the final posthumous editing, saw fit to follow suit by inserting the text in the other ten chorale preludes, a practice that was continued by several subsequent editors. The Passiontide chorale on which this prelude is based has enjoyed long popularity and appears in many present-day hymnals, substantially as harmonized by Johann Crüger in the *Newes vollkömliches Gesangbuch* published in 1640 in Berlin. It has been used as the basis of numerous chorale preludes from the Baroque period to the present day, and it appears in J. S. Bach's St. Matthew Passion as well as in his St. John Passion. Brahms conducted the St. Matthew Passion (which also contains the chorale melodies on which chorale preludes 3, 9, 10, and 11 are based) at a concert given for the Gesellschaft der Musikfreunde in March 1875, shortly before his resignation as director.

Several commentators have called this chorale prelude one of the "most Bachian" of the collection and compared it with some of the *Orgelbüchlein* chorale preludes such as *Jesu, meine Freude, In dich hab' ich gehoffet,* and *Durch Adams Fall*. Bachian, too, is Brahms's apparent use of symbolic motifs. The broken descending figure at the end of each phrase is reminiscent of figuration in Bach's *Nun komm, der Heiden Heiland,* which opens the *Orgelbüchlein,* and suggests what Albert Schweitzer calls the "cross motif." The three-note ascending and descending "sighing" figures in the accompaniment at the beginning and end are usually thought to symbolize grief, and Niemann makes note of the "faltering, diminished fifths in the delicate fretted accompaniment" that appear to him to allude to the sufferings of Jesus.[47] Roberts feels that "no other prelude of the series assimilates Bach's music so completely; no other is such perfect organ music."[48] The seemingly strong Bach connections might hint that this piece, the third in the original manuscript, could also have had its origins earlier in Brahms's career, either when he was actively studying Bach's own chorale preludes or when he was conducting Bach's cantatas and passions. But the flowing lines and expressive chromaticism make it clear that this is no pale imitation; this ability to successfully cast new music in old forms was a unique aspect of Brahms's genius.

For dynamic markings, we find again the usual *f* and *p*, the former at the beginning, the latter at measure 16. As Bozarth observed, the autograph has a single *forte* mark below the first (soprano) note, but Brahms wrote in additional *forte* marks below the other parts when he corrected the Kupfer copy, which makes it very clear that all parts were to be played on the same manual, presumably Manual I.[49] The *piano* mark at measure 16 (as well as the musical context) suggests a change to Manual II, and it is indeed necessary to move to an expressive division to observe the crescendo required in measure 19. The descending left-hand fifths in measures 16–18 transfer to the pedal at this point. However, another manual change is suggested at measure 24, where the final phrase begins, overlapping the end of the previous one, and it is probable that we have here another missing dynamic marking, of *forte*. This restores the logic of moving to an expressive division with the box closed at measure 16 and gradually opening it from measure 19 to 23 in preparation for moving back to Manual I at measure 24. It would also suggest that the registration of the expressive manual with the box open should be only slightly softer than that of Manual I, and of similar color, and that the pedal, which reenters at the beginning of the crescendo, should either be coupled to Manual II or registered independently of either manual.

In the space of only thirty measures, Brahms has constructed a work of expressive delicacy. The melody appears throughout in the treble and in a lightly embellished form that in no way obscures it. The temptation to be avoided is to try to "lift out" the melody on a solo stop. For one thing, this is so awkward in many places, even for a player with large hands and a penchant for "thumbing," that it should be plain that this was not what Brahms intended, and the emphasis of the three *forte* marks at the beginning would surely confirm this. Countering the argument that the melody needs to be brought out more prominently, Max Miller observes that "it is hard to imagine its not being perceived. In this composition the extraction of the melody on another color tears the fabric of the whole."[50] And this piece is indeed a closely woven fabric into which the melody is artfully threaded. The player needs only to be always conscious of the melody, as well as everything that undergirds it, including the strategically placed rests that often allow the long notes of the melody to stand out from the accompaniment, with no need for help from a solo stop.

(3) *O Welt, ich muss dich lassen*

The melody of this chorale has a long history, appearing in a setting by Heinrich Isaac with the secular text "*Innsbruck, ich muss dich lassen*" in Georg Forster's *Ein Auszug guter alter und neuer Liedlein*, published 1539 in Nürnberg.[51] According to Kalbeck, it was sung with the "Innsbruck" text by Brahms's Frauenchor in 1860, on an occasion when the singers were joined by Clara Schumann, and was later included in one of Brahms's concerts with the Vienna Singakademie.[52] For the chorale prelude, however, Brahms gives it the title of the sacred text with which it had been associated in Lutheran hymnals since 1598. The tune, generally called "Innsbruck" and divested by Bach and his contemporaries of its original irregular rhythmic structure (which Brahms, however, preserves), still appears in many English-language hymnals, although usually set to a translation of *Nun ruhen alle Wälder,* and has been utilized as a chorale prelude subject by numerous other composers.

The chorale melody appears in Bach's St. Matthew Passion and parallels have been drawn between the structure of this chorale prelude and that of the final chorus of Part 1 of that work. Even closer is the texture (and key) of *O Lamm Gottes* in Bach's *Orgelbüchlein*. Closer still, however, is its relationship to the opening section of the final movement of Brahms's own *Deutsches Requiem*, with its texture of rising and falling eighth-note repercussions (frequently in contrary motion) underlying a melodic line in slower note values. It is even in the same key (F major) and could conceivably have had its origins in the same period or even earlier. If earlier, could it possibly have been the inspiration for that movement? It would hardly have been the only instance in which Brahms derived something new from earlier material. Even the general musical shape of *Selig sind die Toten* seems to somewhat mirror that of the first phrase of the chorale, although there is almost no actual note-for-note correlation. Another instance of Brahms's use of this kind of slurred repeated eighth-note accompanimental figuration occurs in the second (*Poco adagio*) movement of the Piano Quartet no. 2 in A (op. 26), completed in 1862, where the strings accompany the soaring piano melody. Although *O Welt, ich muss dich lassen* has no tempo indication, the tempi of both the *Requiem* movement (*feierlich*, or solemn) and the second movement of the Piano Quartet are suggestive more of a simple *adagio* rather than of the somewhat ambiguous *larghetto* assigned to this chorale prelude by editors such as West and Biggs.

As to the dynamics, we find here the same *forte ma dolce* indication seen at the opening of the first chorale prelude. The opening of the seventh movement of the *Requiem* is marked *forte* but is scored initially for strings, with occasional subsequent supplementation by woodwinds. It is certainly not a "full orchestra" *forte* and perhaps a clue to the enigmatic *forte ma dolce* level of intensity. Some editors have seen the rather noticeable break in measure 13 as a suggestion to either move to a softer manual or (because a rest there provides a momentary silence) retire a stop or two on the same manual. No dynamic change is indicated in the manuscript, however. Although one might again suspect a missing dynamic mark (and the text, "commit to God's kind hand," could also suggest a dynamic reduction), this piece seems equally effective whether played throughout on the same registration or slightly reduced at measure 13.

This is a work of calm serenity. As in *Herzliebster Jesu*, the melody is in the soprano and ornamented—indeed, even more so—and, as Max Miller observes, "the ornamentation is at one with the whole texture."[53] Symbolism, too, is there, as in the sighing motif in measures 5 and 6, foreshadowing the ensuing third phrase of the chorale. Although the first two phrases of the melody repeat, there is subtle variation of the harmony in the second statement. As in nos. 2, 6, and 7, the final tonic note of the chorale is sustained by the soprano and bass, between which eighth-note figures in thirds flow in contrary motion.

Each phrase is preceded by hints of *vorimitation* and floats in and out of the constantly moving eighth-note-based counterpoint that continually shifts from duple to triple time and back again—no less than ten changes of time signature in a mere nineteen measures. In this regard, it is unique among the Eleven Chorale Preludes, although not entirely without precedent among Brahms's other works, notably the third movement of the Piano Trio in C Minor (op. 101, 1887), which also shifts back and forth between duple and triple time signatures. The result is a piece in which the somewhat irregular phrases, linked by the ongoing accompaniment, determine the flow, as in Isaac's original unmeasured setting of the "Innsbruck" text. The player must thus never lose awareness of the chorale melody or the phrasing that is in part determined by the shifting time signatures.

(4) *Herzlich thut mich erfreuen*

In this joyously bittersweet prelude, singled out by Vernon Gotwals as "one of the most wonderful of the organ pieces of Brahms,"[54] the composer's love of the chorale and the folk song intersect. Indeed, although this melody is occasionally found in hymnals, it is more likely to be encountered in folk song collections, where its several verses are a paean to May and the coming "joyous summertime," full of references to birdsong, flowers, and pretty girls.[55] Like "Innsbruck," the melody dates from the sixteenth century, traceable back to Georg Rhaw's *Bicinia Vitibergae* of 1545 in its folk song form and to the *Wittemburg Gesangbuch* of 1552 with its sacred text. The text of the first line of the first verse is virtually identical in both versions: "My heart rejoices in the joyous (lovely) summertime." But there the resemblance ends, for the first verse of the sacred text treats the allusion to spring and summer as an allegory for eternity, when God will make a new heaven and earth and, as the last phrase states, "all creation shall be wholly splendid, fair, and bright." W. Wright Roberts calls Brahms's setting a "signal triumph over depression," in which the composer "attunes his mind to the blithe melody and the hearty swing of a chorale that started life as a folk-song telling of the joys of summer."[56] The original positioning of this particular prelude at the conclusion of the first set of seven may not be accidental. Although this setting might be said to be wistfully retrospective, it can never be called sad. Ann Bond calls it "the sprightliest of the set," and this suggests the spirit in which it should be played.

Again, however, one might suspect that this chorale prelude has earlier origins. Although Brahms's love of folk song continued throughout his life, his earliest folk song arrangements date back to the 1850s. He obviously encountered *Herzlich thut mich erfreuen* in both its secular and sacred forms fairly early on, for it is one of a group of four melodies young Brahms copied out during his Düsseldorf days—copies that he preserved until the end of his life. The somewhat pianistic broken-chord accompaniment has often been commented on, and here again we might discern some reflection, perhaps only coincidental, of an earlier chamber work—the beautiful and familiar broken-chord opening *Allegro non troppo* melody of the F Minor Piano Quintet (op. 34) and its subsequent permutations. This, too, was one of Brahms's many revisions, begun as a string quintet, revised as a two-piano work, and reaching its final form in 1865. In the chorale prelude, however, the dancing broken-chord figuration bridges the gap between pianism and the usage of Bach in his *Orgelbüchlein* chorale prelude, *Ich ruf' zu dir*. Indeed, it goes a step further, becoming a *vorimitation* vehicle to introduce the first three long phrases of the chorale melody.

Here again we find some apparent examples of careless editing by Brahms. Bozarth notes more examples of missing or misplaced slurs.[57] But of equal importance are the missing upper stems, both in the manuscript and in Kupfer's copy, on some of the notes that outline the melody in parts of the *vorimitation* introductions and interludes (measures 2, 3, 4, and 19) by doubling the value of these notes. This omission is indeed so obvious that Bozarth in his edition has added the missing stems in editorial parentheses, although not every previous editor seems to have noticed their absence. In performance, these doubled note values must be brought out with care, sufficiently to make them noticeable but not at the expense of the free-flowing movement that underlies them. Most certainly, one should not stoop to anything as ludicrous as attempting to accent the doubled notes with the swell pedal, recommended with perfect seriousness by Archibald Farmer in 1931.[58]

The first two *vorimitation* introductions consist of a single tenor line in the dominant with the melody outlined in a detached manner by the upper-stemmed notes. But the third, while maintaining the prolonged-note melodic emphasis in the tenor line (also in the dominant), complements it with an alto line in contrary motion. Although no prolonged notes are found in this part, a little imitation at the octave can be discerned in measures 16–19. The introduction to the final phrase, in the subdominant, breaks the pattern with the melodic phrases outlined by legato slurs in the upper line. Here the broken-chord accompanimental material, with its skipping, off-the-beat tenor part and rests under most of the strong beats, serves to further emphasize the melodic line, and the eighth-note figuration resumes as the final phrase enters in measure 28, continuing to the end.

Although Brahms gives no manual indications, the positioning of the dynamic marks under the beginnings of the introductions and the main chorale phrase statements makes it clear that two manuals (and possibly three) are required, and that the introduction to each phrase is meant to begin on the secondary manual. The first introduction is marked *mezzo forte dolce,* the second *mezzo forte* (but, considering its similarity to the first, probably with no change of registration), and the third and fourth *piano*. This change could mean either a stop reduction, closing of a swell box, or moving to a softer third manual for these—any of which would appear to serve Brahms's purpose and could easily be accomplished without distorting the lines. In contrast, the main chorale statements are uniformly marked *forte* and are the only places where the pedal is employed, which would thus presume a 16' Pedal stop and coupling to the *forte* manual (Manual I, Great).

If the practices of the period are observed, the *forte* manual should be registered with principals—up to 4' and possibly even 2', with flutes at 8' and 4' or perhaps lighter principals at 8' and 4' on the secondary manual. Farmer suggests a string celeste, which, although possibly appropriate in certain of the other preludes, would hopelessly blur the clarity that the figuration asks for in this one. The pedal part is important in the *forte* passages, for it generally follows the legato half-note and quarter-note texture of the soprano melodic line, while the alto and tenor lines, in continuation of the interludes, flow along in eighth-notes between them. Brahms's slurring should be carefully heeded throughout. The slur at the end of the last phrase is missing, but it can be safely assumed.

(5) *Schmücke dich, o liebe Seele*

This well-loved Communion chorale, still found in a number of modern hymnals, first appeared in Johann Crüger's *Geistliche kirchen Melodien,* published 1649 in Berlin. Bach wrote an exquisite chorale prelude on it (BWV 654) that was greatly admired by both Mendelssohn and Schumann. Although, like many of the early chorales, it has a rhythmic version, Brahms bases his chorale prelude on the more straightforward isometric version in the collection of 371 Bach chorales, but with fewer passing notes. In the original order of the first seven chorale preludes, this was number two and could easily be termed as "antiquarian" as the first. The technique of writing *manualiter* pieces in which the melody stands out in long notes over a two-part contrapuntal accompaniment moving in shorter note values is indeed antiquarian, going back to Scheidt and Pachelbel, and is used by Bach in some of his chorale partitas, as well as in single chorale preludes such as *Allein Gott in der Höh sei Ehr* (BWV 717). In this regard, it can be said to be similar in concept to *Jesu, meine Freude* in Bach's *Orgelbüchlein,* the main difference being that here the contrapuntal background to the long-note cantus firmus is in three parts, rather than two, which puts the bass line in the pedal.

Ann Bond calls this gently flowing chorale prelude an "idealized essay in fifth species counterpoint,"[59] and perhaps it even had its origins during or immediately following the early counterpoint exercises. The use of diminution in the two lower parts is evident throughout, although it never detracts from the lyrical flow. The first seven (occasionally eight) notes of the chorale appear in sixteenth-notes in the middle part right after the second quarter-note of the chorale, again in the bottom part in the second measure, and back to the middle part, both *recte* and *inversus,* in the third measure. This activity continues throughout the piece as the diminution continues to crop up in various guises, right to the end, where it leads to the final note of the chorale, and is echoed in inversion leading down to the tonic at the very end. Roberts observed these same complexities but aptly distilled their essence when he described the piece as "a miniature for manuals, with the plain tune floating uninterrupted, in resigned joy, over two parts blithely busy with a diminished version of the first line."[60]

Schmücke dich, along with the following similar *manualiter* chorale, *O wie selig* (no. 6), is meant to be played on a single manual, without pedal (save for the cadential pedal point in the latter). Yet few others of the set have been subjected to the amount of well-meant tampering as these two. In their editions of the Eleven Chorale Preludes, E. Power Biggs, along with Walter Buszin and Paul Bunjes, append versions of these that variously transpose the melody to the pedal or place it on a separate manual in the treble and transpose the lower accompanimental line to the pedal. Jack C. Goode even suggests that no. 5 be played as a kind of trio sonata, with a "neo-Baroque" registration of Gemshorn 8' and flute 4' in the left hand, flutes 8' and 2 2/3' (alto part) in the right hand, and the melody in the pedal on a 4' "reed or other bright stop."[61] Max Miller notes that, indeed, "many [organists] prefer to take the chorale on the Pedal with a 4' stop."[62] But while the piece (like some of Bach's) is in fact a trio, a pedal solo is not what Brahms intended in nos. 5 and 6, or he would have written these pieces that way, as he did in nos. 1 and 10. What is required, however, is the player's strong consciousness of the melody and fingering that guarantees that each phrase sings through smoothly to its end, where the fermata signals not a hold but a slight breathing place, as in many of Bach's chorale preludes.

Although it makes no appearance in most of the editions (including George Bozarth's), Brahms's extensive use in his manuscript of awkward-looking upward stemming and diagonal beaming (largely in octave leaps) in the bass line strikes editor Bozarth as having "musical relevance." He notes that the bass line alternates between pure harmonic bass function (mostly in eighth-notes) and contrapuntal imitation (mostly in sixteenth-notes) and that the diagonal beaming in the former and frequent use of upward stems in the latter may thus suggest that Brahms wished to call attention to the "double function" of this bass line.[63]

There is no tempo indication, although various editors presume to supply it, generally in the catchall *andante* range. In spite of this, some performers tend to drag this chorale out almost *molto largo,* thus not only misinterpreting its text but also compromising its marvelously fluid quality and making it disagreeably (and boringly) "notey." Brahms's only clue to performance is his "*piano dolce*" indication at the beginning. Registrationally, this, plus the inherent texture, would suggest quiet simplicity, and a single carefully selected light 8' flute, perhaps even in conjunction with a mild string, will often suffice, especially if there is a slight rise in intensity in the treble to emphasize the legato chorale melody.

(6) *O wie selig seid ihr doch, ihr Frommen*

This prelude, no. 4 in the original manuscript, bears so many superficial similarities to *Schmücke dich* that the probability is strong that this stylistically contrasting pair had their origins in the same period. Both are based on Johann Crüger melodies of 1649, *O wie selig* being a hymn to the departed faithful, and as such often associated with All Saints' Day. Interestingly, the number of measures in both (twenty-one and fourteen) are multiples of Brahms's "sacred number," 7. The structure of this prelude, especially as regards the use of thirds in triplets against a melody in longer notes, is reminiscent of *O Traurigkeit,* particularly in its earlier version, a major difference being in the ending—perfunctory in *O Traurigkeit,* prolonged in *O wie selig.*

With the exception of the brief cadential pedal point, this is, again like no. 5, intended for performance on a single manual, and both have the dynamic marking of *dolce.* Numbers 5 and 6 are also the only two pieces in the entire set in which Brahms provides no slurring in his manuscript, and the only two to employ the fermata sign as Bach does in the *Orgelbüchlein*—not as a hold, but simply to indicate a vocal breathing place. Unlike no. 5, however, no. 6 has a tempo marking—*Molto moderato*—added to the autograph by Brahms in pencil, seemingly as an afterthought, and perhaps suggesting that it be played slightly slower than no. 5. Like its predecessor, this chorale prelude has also been subjected to heavy-handed and unnecessary rearrangement intended to solo out the melody on either the pedal or another manual. Properly played, and on a carefully chosen registration, the melody will stand out perfectly well as originally written.

O wie selig is the shortest piece in the entire collection, but, as Max Miller observes, "that so much of musical interest can be packed into a scant fourteen bars is a marvel."[64] Into this brief space, and within a quite stable tonality, Brahms manages to introduce a rather surprising amount of expressive chromaticism. Crüger's chorale is in duple time, but Brahms casts his setting in 12/8 time, making use of hemiola to shape it to the irregular melody and giving it what Ann Bond calls a "timeless, trancelike atmosphere."[65] The only slightly ornamented melody floats serenely over an accompaniment of gentle rising and falling triplets in which a six-note pattern and its inversion repeatedly occur. It is the melody line, rather than the bar lines, that should determine the flow in this piece.

From measure 11 to the end, the hemiola pattern emerges to give motion to the ascending melodic line of the final phrase and the drawn-out cadential note with its rising and falling thirds. In measure 11 also, Brahms indicates the beginning of a crescendo, which culminates in a *forte* on the final melodic note. This alone would indicate that the piece be played on a secondary enclosed division, beginning with the swell shades completely closed. Whatever registration is used should probably not exceed 8' (or at most, gentle 8' and 4') pitch but be capable of properly outlining the soprano cantus firmus—possibly a flute and string combination, or even a "hybrid" color such as a Geigen Diapason or Gemshorn if of agreeable quality.

As in the preceding five preludes, the final note of the melody is sustained over the continuously moving accompaniment, which provides a kind of second cadence. And as in nos. 2 and 3, it is accompanied by a double tonic pedal point. Probably the only reason that Brahms indicates a parenthetical "pedal" direction here is the extreme awkwardness of trying to play the inner parts between the sustained octaves smoothly with the left hand. The pedal should thus simply be coupled to the manual, without a 16' stop, so as not to suddenly add a foreign heaviness to the texture.

(7) *O Gott, du frommer Gott*

Kees van Houten, while acknowledging its Bachian inspiration, designates this eloquent prelude as "a romantic organ-poem of the first rank,"[66] and Vernon Gotwals sees it as "perhaps the greatest of the eleven and perhaps the most controversial."[67] Number 5 in the original manuscript (but the last of the set of seven as rearranged), it is one of the more complex and extended pieces in the set and is rich in the contrapuntal devices of imitation, diminution, and inversion. It is based on an anonymous chorale from a Hannover *Gesangbuch* of 1646—a chorale also utilized several times by J. S. Bach. The text dates from a 1630 Breslau collection, in which it is called "A Daily Prayer." The piece is *manualiter* and largely in three-part texture up to measure 51, where it thickens into predominantly four-part texture. In the concluding five measures the pedal appears in half-notes to ground the half-note soprano melody and thus provide a harmonic framework for the moving four-part chordal material in between. The dynamic indications alternate between *f* and *p*, and by writing "Manual II" over the first *piano* entrance in Kupfer's copy, Brahms makes it clear that two manuals are required throughout, the stronger introduction and interludes being played on Manual I.

This prelude is unique in that the unadorned long-note phrases of the chorale melody migrate from soprano to tenor and back—a practice that again tempts editors and players to "lift them out" in various ways on a stronger registration. Both Biggs and Bunjes provide an alternate arrangement to facilitate this in their editions. Interestingly, Brahms felt it necessary to point out these shifting phrase appearances by writing "*Choral*" above each entry—the only instance in which he does this. It is not unlikely that Brahms was aware of the use of this same kind of melodic migration in the seventh movement of Bach's Partita (BWV 767), which is based on the same chorale melody. Certainly the player must be keenly aware of the chorale melody wherever it occurs if it is to be communicated to the listener—which is perhaps why Brahms felt it necessary to point out its entrances.

It seems possible that the structure of this chorale prelude could have been inspired by the practice, common in Bach's day and still followed by many Lutheran organists in Brahms's day, of playing an introduction and interludes to the phrases of the chorale melody sung by the congregation. It is not improbable to suggest that the young Brahms would have heard the organist of St. Michael's Church, and perhaps also his friend Armbrust, the organist of St. Peter's Church, engaging in this practice. Such introductions and interludes, making use of material from the chorale melody, were often improvised but were also included in some chorale collections and in didactic publications such as J. C. Kittel's *Der angehende praktische Organist*, published 1801–1808, and the later organ tutor by Kittel's pupil J. C. H. Rinck. This practice might explain the somewhat enigmatic *piano* dynamic of Brahms's chorale phrases—the congregation singing between the organ interludes. Interestingly, Mendelssohn, in the first movement of his Organ Sonata No. 1, also employed the device of alternating louder interludes with quieter chorale statements, although in a more dramatic manner than did Brahms.

An extended introduction, based on the first four notes of the chorale melody and interspersed with a "sigh" motif, occurs first *forte* and is then echoed *piano*. The first phrase of the chorale in the soprano, still on the softer manual, follows. The second phrase is treated similarly, and as in the chorale, this pair of phrases is repeated. The second ending, however, swoops upward to return to the *forte* manual, and the flowing eighth-note texture with its recurrent "sigh" motif is suddenly interrupted by the opening measures of the next introduction, announced in chords reminiscent of the trombone entrances in the finale of Brahms's First Symphony and the slow movement of his Third Symphony. This is as brief as it is startling, for the eighth-notes subsequently resume, rising into the treble register and creating a sense of mystery as they move in measure 26 onto the softer manual for the echo section that precedes the third chorale phrase, now occurring in the tenor, with the text "A sound body grant me." This flows into the introduction of the fourth chorale phrase, based on its opening notes, with the actual chorale melody again in the tenor. The fifth chorale phrase is identical to the first, and its introduction begins like that of the first, although soon taking on a different and more agitated character, as does the background of the melody, again in the soprano.

The "sigh" motif reappears in measure 51, where it introduces the final phrase in measure 54. Its last two measures, before the final statement appears in measure 58, are marked pianissimo, suggesting either a stop reduction, change to a third manual, or simply the closing of a swell box—any of which could be accomplished during the rests that precede these measures. A hesitant, off-the-beat figure of eighth-notes—strongly resembling that at the opening of Brahms's *Rhapsodie,* op. 79, no. 1 (1880)—also makes its appearance here in the lower parts, continuing into the statement of the final chorale phrase, where, as in the *Rhapsodie,* it lends emphasis to a melodic line in half-notes. Unlike the other chorale phrases, however, this final phrase statement is assigned to the *forte* manual (Manual I) and accompanied by a pedal bass—undoubtedly coupled, although, considering its low range, possibly without a 16' stop (or with only a very mild one). Wijnand van de Pol suggests that this treatment could be Brahms's way of emphasizing the text of this phrase—a prayer for a clear conscience.[68]

(8) *Es ist ein Ros' entsprungen*

This chorale prelude is both an anomaly and an enigma. Among Brahms's surviving manuscripts, it stands alone, undated, and on a sheet of eight-stave manuscript paper different from that used for either the first seven or the last three. Some of the calligraphic characteristics, however, are similar to those in the manuscript of the first three of the set of seven. Whereas Otto Biba considers the possibility that no. 8 may be a late work, perhaps even the last, Max Kalbeck believes it to be an early work. Some others tend to concur with Kalbeck, including Kees van Houten, who then goes so far as to surmise that "perhaps Clara had a special love for this melody."[69] Hans Bertram, who seems to regard the Eleven Chorale Preludes as having all originated in 1896, fantasizes even further by suggesting that the melody could have been sung by Brahms's parents or was perhaps inspired by a "recollection of Clara and Robert Schumann."[70] But all such suppositions are mere guesswork. Although they might make charming folklore, they can be neither confirmed nor denied by available evidence and, in any case, are of no help in determining the period of composition. The melody would surely have been long familiar to Brahms anyway, due in part to his interest in earlier music. Said to be based on a Rhenish folk song, it first appeared in the *Alte Katholische Kirchengesang* of 1599. The Singverein had included the well-known 1609 Praetorius setting in some of their concerts during the early years of Brahms's residence in Vienna, and later his friend Herzogenberg incorporated the melody into his Christmas oratorio, *Die Geburt Christi*, which Brahms presumably knew.

One characteristic, however, does suggest possible early origins for this piece. Although written on two staves, it probably was meant to be played on an organ with pedals—coupled pedals. The broad stretches in some places are usually dismissed as the work of a pianist with large hands, but, with the exception of the *O Traurigkeit* fugue, such stretches do not occur in any of Brahms's other organ works nor in any of the other chorale preludes. What is almost certainly the very earliest of the existing organ manuscripts, that of the Prelude and Fugue in A Minor, while very clearly marked as demanding the use of pedals, was, like *Es ist ein Ros'*, written on two staves. It can still be found this way in the Breitkopf & Härtel edition, although more recent editors, including Bozarth, have laid it out on three staves for easier part recognition. Manuscripts of subsequent early organ compositions requiring pedals are all on three staves, perhaps reflecting Brahms's growing knowledge of organ playing and organ music. If Brahms wrote *Es ist ein Ros'* while he was practicing on the little music store organ with its coupled pedal, he could have conveniently played some of the bass notes, particularly the tonic half-notes that appear at cadential points, on the pedal, which would have facilitated smooth phrasing. If nowhere else, in the last two measures, where the texture goes to five parts, the use of the coupled pedal would seem clearly indicated, as it is at the conclusion of nos. 6 and 7, where it doubles the tonic in otherwise *manualiter* settings.

Like most Germans, Brahms seems to have had a fondness for Christmas and enjoyed spending this holiday with friends. Brahms's vocal and choral music occasionally touches on Christmas themes, including some of the *Marienlieder* and folk song settings and perhaps most notably the gently lyrical *Geistliches Wiegenlied* (op. 91, no. 2, 1884), built around the old Christmas folk song *Josef, lieber Josef mein* (also known as *Resonet in Laudibus*), but *Es ist ein Ros'* is his only purely instrumental Christmas offering. Moreover, if this chorale prelude is in fact an early work, it may well be the earliest example of an organ prelude based on this well-loved sixteenth-century melody. Many have been composed since, but for Brahms to have chosen it when he did, alongside the more "standard" chorale prelude subjects that he set, only adds to its mystery.

Like the final three, this chorale prelude was not discovered until after the composer's death, and the manuscript shows no sign of having been edited for publication. That task was carried out in 1901 by Brahms's friend Eusebius Mandyczewski (1857–1929), archivist of the Gesellschaft der Musikfreunde and professor at the Vienna Conservatory, who is responsible for its placement as no. 8 in the set of eleven. However, George Bozarth points out that Mandyczewski has, apparently in the interest of consistency, somewhat altered Brahms's slurring at the ends of phrases, and this was usually followed in subsequent editions. In the recent Henle edition, Bozarth reverts to the original manuscript in this regard. Indeed, slurring appears more consistently in this prelude than in any other and seems to invite a very subtle rubato that shapes the phrases and slightly stretches (but does not break) the rhythm. In any case, the slurring is an important element of which the performer should be particularly aware if Brahms's intentions for this deceptively understated composition are to be carried out.

Robert Jordahl calls this the "most happily inspired and original of Brahms's chorale settings for organ,"[71] and J. A. Fuller-Maitland sees in it "some of the artless charm of the folk-songs which were so near to Brahms's heart."[72] It differs from the preceding seven in that it is essentially homophonic. In its construction, Brahms deviates from the arrangement of the original melody, in which the first line is repeated, but the second is not. Brahms not only provides a different, inner-voice setting for the first repeat but also repeats the second line in this manner, closing with what could almost be construed as an "Amen." In addition, he breaks up the long phrases into smaller segments, each ending in a gentle, undulating motif that cadences in the home key. Although in some of his other preludes Brahms ornaments the melodies to a greater or lesser extent, they are always fairly clearly discernible. Here, however, the melodic notes are completely enveloped—indeed, virtually obscured—in what is essentially a new melody, or, as Hermann Busch puts it, a "mysterious melisma."[73] They are there, but rhythmically altered and frequently off the beat, which reduces their significance further. Yet with this somewhat radical treatment, which Michael Musgrave observes as belonging "entirely to Brahms's time,"[74] Brahms has somehow distilled the essence not only of the melody but also of the text, and the tranquil and hopeful poetic symbolism that it expresses.

The only dynamic marking given is *piano dolce* right at the beginning, but Brahms has indicated manual changes. This suggests that the registrations should differ more in color than in intensity. Although not specifically marked, the piece obviously begins on Manual I, moving to Manual II at the end of measure 4, where the repeat of the first phrase in the tenor and alto begins. Somewhat confusing is "Manual I" in parentheses at the end of measure 6, where the melodic line finally climbs up from the tenor and alto to the soprano again. "Manual I" again occurs (without parentheses) at the end of measure 8, where the repeat ends and the second long phrase begins. Bozarth thinks the parenthetical marking may be an alternate to this, but this is rather doubtful; it occurs in the middle of the repeated phrase, and Brahms has crossed out a similar manual change at a corresponding place (measure 16) in the second repeat. Manual II is indicated at the end of measure 14, where the melodic line repeats in the tenor, and because of the crossed-out "Manual I" at measure 16, we must assume that Brahms intended the piece to end on Manual II. While Brahms may initially have considered returning to Manual I when the melody of the repeats returned to the soprano, he must have thought the better of it. If the piece does in fact date from an early period, Brahms may have even tried it out on an organ, which could account for these changes. And the logic of the piece does seem to be best served by playing the echolike repeats of the two long phrases on Manual II throughout.

Such details as these are, however, indicative of some unfinished editing on Brahms's part. But if Brahms had not completely put the finishing touches on this piece, his careful provision of phrasing slurs would indicate that he was very close to it. Many organists (including the writer) have found *Es ist ein Ros'* quite perfect as it stands. However, others have subjected it to the same kind of tinkering that has been applied to nos. 5, 6, and 7. In 1935, John Holler published an arrangement in which Brahms's manual changes are ignored, a pedal part added, and thematic material "lifted out" on a separate manual in measures 4–6, 8–10, 15–17, and the penultimate measure. In a footnote, Holler explains that the changes were made "in order to help the performer intensify the salient parts of the piece."[75] A performer who has thoroughly studied the structure of the piece and pays attention to Brahms's careful slurring will find that the "salient parts" will come through quite nicely without any such artifice.

(9) *Herzlich tut mich verlangen*

Numbers 9 and 10 are based on the same melody, the well-loved "Passion Chorale," used by Bach five times in his St. Matthew Passion and found in most modern hymnals set to the text "O Sacred Head, now wounded." First appearing in 1601 as a secular folk song, *Mein G'muth ist mir verwirret*, it became associated with the sacred text *Herzlich tut mich verlangen* in 1613 and was later also occasionally set to the texts *Ach Herr, mich armen Sünder* and *O Welt, ich muss dich lassen*, becoming associated with Paulus Gerhardt's *O Haupt voll Blut und Wunden* in 1656. As with many other early chorale melodies, it has both a rhythmic (the earliest) and an isometric version, the latter being most commonly used today. Interestingly, Brahms employs the isometric version for no. 9 and the rhythmic version for no. 10.

In the manuscript, the final three preludes in the collection—the first two based on the same chorale and the third on a chorale that appeared in the first seven (no. 3)—are all written on four consecutive pages of fourteen-stave music paper. "*Juni 96. Ischl.*" is inscribed at the end, indicating that they had reached what one must presume to be a final state about a month after the first seven. It seems probable that nos. 9 and 10 were conceived as a pair—although a deliberately contrasting pair—and thus may both date from the same period. Some confirmation of this is in the fact that they are also the only ones in the entire eleven with pedal parts that exceed a twenty-note compass.

Of the two, no. 9 makes the greatest use of contrapuntal devices. It is marked *forte* at the opening although this could be only an 8' *forte*, or 8' and 4' at the most. Beginning in duple time, the first notes of the poignantly ornamented melody lead immediately into motivic imitation between soprano and tenor in the first half of the first melodic line, the tenor being inverted. In the second half, it is between the soprano and alto, but the alto is not inverted. This same pattern obtains in the reharmonized repeat of the first line, but the pattern changes—along with a change in time signature (triple), dynamic (*piano*), and manual (II)—at the beginning of measure 9. This lyrical phrase is set for manual only, with a predominance of thirds and sixths in the accompaniment. Even here, though, there is a hint of imitation, at least rhythmically, between the melody line and the three lower parts. The final line, back to duple time, returns to the Manual I and canon at the subdominant between soprano and alto, cadencing with a held note over rising sixths.

Although hints of A major regularly occur throughout the entire piece, the major mode becomes gradually more predominant in the final phrase, working toward the closing Picardy third. This major-key flavoring, along with some seemingly symbolic usage of rising figures, gives this setting a brighter and more optimistic feeling than the more somber no. 10 and heightens the contrast between the two. It is of some interest that this is the only one of the set that concludes with a hold over the rest that follows the final eighth-note chord, rather than over the chord itself. This would suggest that although some *ritard* is in order, these final notes should be held no longer than their value allows. The only other of Brahms's chorale preludes that ends this abruptly (although minus the hold) is O *Traurigkeit*.

There would seem to be some stylistic correlations between no. 9 and no. 2. Both begin with the first note of the melody standing alone, both ornament the melody, and both change to a softer manual and somewhat different structure for the third phrase. Number 2 also contains several instances of direct inversion, usually between soprano and tenor. Perhaps the most noticeable resemblance is in the pedal lines, with the frequent occurrences of off-the-beat two-note punctuations separated by rests—although in no. 2 these consist of the drop of a fifth, whereas in no. 9 they are usually a rise of a minor (occasionally major) second.

Although Brahms gives clear directions for manual changes in nos. 10 and 11, he does not do so in no. 9. Yet here (as in the similar context in no. 2) a manual change from I to II is indicated by the arrival of the third phrase in measure 9, with the alteration in time, texture, and dynamic and the dropping out of the pedal—an indication that the pedal is to be coupled to Manual I. Indeed, this alone would suggest a manual change rather than a sudden *diminuendo* on an expressive manual. At the pickup to phrases 1 and 5, the *forte* marking is at the first note of the phrase; at the pickup to the third phrase, the *piano* marking is placed under the second note of the phrase, at the beginning of measure 9. Bozarth questions this, leaving it where it appears in the autograph in his edition but noting that "the new dynamic level should probably begin with the anacrusis"[76]—which seems indeed logical. But the question then arises as to where to play the accompanimental notes of the fourth beat of measure 8. To leave them on the *forte* manual would obscure the pickup note. The dropping out of the pedal and soprano at the fourth beat might, however, suggest that the alto and tenor notes of this beat should also be transferred—as smoothly as possible—to the secondary manual and the seemingly misplaced *piano* marking moved back one beat. It can be argued that this leaves a cadence unresolved on the preceding beat, yet these notes do flow comfortably into measure 9. The player should explore the options before deciding which course to follow. The return to the Manual I at the end of measure 12 could not be clearer, however, as Brahms marks with a *forte* both the overlapping soprano pickup note and the ensuing harmony in measure 13 and returns to the same texture and rhythm as at the beginning as it moves gently toward the conclusion.

(10) *Herzlich tut mich verlangen*

Max Kalbeck is of the opinion that nos. 9 and 10 "belong together like two stanzas, like the beginning and ending of a poem,"[77] and some characteristics do suggest this. Rather than stanzas of a poem, however, the complementary opposites of yin and yang might better describe these two. Stylistically, no. 10 is quite different from no. 9, but perhaps intentionally so. As previously noted, Brahms sets the isometric version in no. 9, but the older rhythmic version in no. 10. And in no. 9 the melody is in the soprano and ornamented, whereas in no. 10 it is played by the pedal in long notes. Yet there are similarities, too, for here again the third line of the melody is given different treatment from the first two and last, and Max Miller is struck by the fact that rhythmically, "what is duple in the first [setting] is triple in the second, and vice versa."[78] Thus no. 10 begins in triple time, going to duple time for the third melodic phrase, and returning to triple for the final phrase.

Although some commentators like to find "funereal" connotations in virtually every one of the Eleven Chorale Preludes, it is only the two of which Brahms made double settings (3 and 11, 9 and 10) that are based on chorales dealing specifically with the ending of life. And it is in no. 10 that one finds the most musical symbolism in this regard. Most prominent are the incessant repeated bass notes that drop out only briefly in measures 13–16. These would seem to represent the *Totentrommel*—the drumbeat that for centuries set the pace for German funeral processions. Bach employs this device in the sonatina that begins his *Actus Tragicus* (BWV 106), and Brahms uses it in the opening movement of his *Requiem*. In both, it is played by the strings; in the *Requiem*, it is assigned to the contrabass and doubled by the organ. It also appears in Brahms's *Gesang des Parzen* and certain symphonic works. The restlessness of the upper manual parts might be said to express longing (*verlangen*), and the descending figures of measure 16 and the closing ritardando measures, finality. Even though the major key begins to make some tentative incursions in the last phrase, which closes with a Picardy third, there seems to be some further symbolism in the final adagio measure, where two broken chords hang suspended over a dominant E in the bass until the pedal drops to the tonic in the final, bell-like chord—the "passing bell"?

On only two other occasions does Brahms assign the chorale melody to the pedal, in the *O Traurigkeit* fugue and the first of the Eleven Chorale Preludes, *Mein Jesu, der du mich*, where the manual parts are likewise fugal. In no. 10, however, the manual part is not fugal and only occasionally contrapuntal. Many commentators have noted the similarity of its texture to that of *Ich ruf' zu dir* in Bach's *Orgelbüchlein*—a similarity impossible to ignore. In this regard, John Butt cites this setting as "perhaps one of the most beautiful homages to Bach."[79] Bach's chorale prelude, however, is structurally simpler, being in three parts throughout with the melody as a solo in the soprano, but its sixteenth-note broken chords in the left hand and relentless repeated eighth-notes of the pedal seem to set the parameters for Brahms's more complex chorale setting.

Unlike Bach's example, where the melody enters right at the beginning, Brahms prefaces the entry of the melody with an almost subliminal *vorimitation* similar to that which opens no. 4, but with the notes of the first phrase more obscured. From the beginning, the manual portion is in three parts, but its middle part is in long notes until the entry of the pedal solo, suddenly going to sixteenth-notes in contrary motion to the upper line at measure 3. At measure 5, a fourth part briefly enters, predominantly in thirds and sixths, before the repeat of the first line. Unlike no. 9, where the repeat is reharmonized, this repeat is note-for-note identical to the first statement until the transition into the duple-time middle section on the secondary manual at the end of measure 11. Here the texture thins, and after a brief transition, the repeated bass notes temporarily drop out as the upper parts ascend into the treble register, floating along in little separated four-note figures, with an echo of the pedal melody at the fourth making a fleeting appearance from the last beat of measure 13. As the pedal statement concludes in measure 16, it is accompanied by a dramatic chromatic chordal descent, not unlike that which concludes the second verse of *O Lamm Gottes* (BWV 656) in Bach's *Eighteen Chorale Preludes*. This is followed by a return to the same type of figuration found at the beginning, accompanying the statement of the final phrase, where the broken chords give way to dramatic scalar passages over the words "O Jesus, come quickly" before reverting to broken chords in the final (*adagio*) measure.

Of all of the eleven, this piece contains the most detailed performance directions. Although the manual on which it begins is not indicated, it is obviously Manual I, as "Man. II" is indicated at the beginning of the middle section on the last beat of measure 11, and on the last beat of measure 16, where the pattern of the first section recommences, a return to "Man. I" is indicated. Although the "Man. I" indication at the end of measure 16 coincides quite logically with the change in texture, the conclusion of the third pedal solo phrase, and the resumption of the repeated-note bass line, Brahms at some point revised his slurring to carry over to the end of measure 16. George Bozarth suggests that despite the manual change, "it would seem that Brahms wanted bar 16 to flow on to its end without any articulation and bar 17 to begin after a slight pause."[80] Vernon Gotwals, however, believes that in measure 16 "it is clear, upon reflection, that the R. H. must stay where it is [on Man. II] until the new measure [17], while the L. H. may and probably should switch for the last beat of m. 16."[81] The player should experiment with both options and decide which works most smoothly with his or her chosen registration. In any case, a smooth and subtle transition is what is required here, not a jarringly obvious change.

The pedal part, with the chorale melody, is marked "*8 fuss*" (8') at its first entry. As it is written in the extreme upper range of the typical German twenty-seven-note pedalboard, never descending below tenor C except at the very end, it generally sounds above the left-hand bass notes except where they drop out in the middle section. It is evident that Brahms intends both manuals to be of reasonably similar intensity (although presumably of slightly different color), for both at the beginning (for Manual I) and at the change to Manual II, the dynamic is given as piano. At the return to Manual I, Brahms writes "*piu dolce sempre.*" One sometimes hears this piece performed with a change of pedal registration in the middle section, something that would be awkward on an organ of Brahms's day. This, and the *piano* dynamic given for both Manual I and Manual II, would suggest that the pedal remains the same throughout, perhaps with only a single flue stop such as an 8' principal, and both manuals registered to make them slightly subordinate to this.

Other directions written in the manuscript are also significant. At the very beginning, Brahms writes *molto legato,* and the long slurs would seem to reinforce this. More unusual is his indication of *rit. sempre* in measure 19, at the beginning of the last phrase of the last line, and then, at the beginning of the final measure with its two partially sustained broken chords, he writes *Adagio.* Although no tempo indication is given at the beginning, this gradual (and somewhat unusual)—deceleration of the last five measures suggests the need for more motion in the preceding portions of the piece than is often given them.

(11) *O Welt, ich muss dich lassen*

Based on the same chorale melody as no. 3, this is the last of the three in the autograph dated July 1896. As such, it is described by many writers as Brahms's "swan song"—and possibly it is. Two autographs of this prelude survive, differing somewhat in calligraphy. One, apparently the earlier of the two, is undated and written on a single sheet of paper, showing a number of alterations and/or corrections. This would appear to be an earlier draft for no. 11, but whether it predates the June 1896 autograph (upon which all published editions are based) by years, months, or merely weeks, it is impossible to say. It does not have the manual indications found in the final version, and following its conclusion are a few measures of an abandoned canonic setting of *Es ist ein Ros' entsprungen.* With the alterations, this version of no. 11 is not significantly different from the final version, written on the same paper as nos. 9 and 10, dated July 1896, and displaying only one significant correction.

This chorale prelude is unique to the set in that it is clearly laid out for a three-manual organ, although this is simply to facilitate the diminishing double echoes that close each phrase. Each begins on Manual I, marked with Brahms's familiar *forte ma dolce* at the beginning, with Manual II at *piano* and Manual III at *pianissimo.* Brahms only writes "Man. II" and "Man. III" over the two echoes of the first phrase, but the dynamic markings at the end of the ensuing phrases leave no doubt that the same manual changes apply there. It is, of course, perfectly possible to play this piece on a two-manual organ by retiring a stop or closing the swell box of Manual II for the Manual III echo.

Brahms seems to have been quite precise as to his placement of these dynamic markings and, until measures 20 and 22, even breaks the stemming at these transitions. Because this piece exists only in a manuscript that was never fully edited by Brahms for publication, this lack of breaks in these later measures could tempt the player to change manuals on the note before the dynamic mark, although the slur that extends to the note that precedes it clearly indicates that this is the concluding note of the previous phrase and should be played on the corresponding manual. At measure 26, the break is there, yet despite the existence of three half-notes that must be held for a full half-measure on Manual I, the temptation to change manuals before the third beat is great, and the whole situation here is complicated by the fact that a phrasing slur over the alto line (which echoes the preceding soprano line) begins at the first note of the measure, before the break and dynamic mark. Although its phrasing slur is missing, the tenor echo that begins in measure 28 begins similarly, and the often overlooked quarter-note on B-flat again suggests that the manual change should occur at the dynamic mark on the third beat. Brahms's phrasing slurs in the final five measures may thus simply serve to tell the player that the legato continuity of the phrase must be carefully preserved through the manual change.

Although Wilfrid Mellers believes that the Manual I statements should open "resonantly on full organ,"[82] this interpretation of *forte ma dolce* is doubtful indeed, and rather at odds with the contemplative nature of the writing. It is more suitable to register all three manuals in descending levels of unison (8' or 8' and 4') sound, with no mutations, mixtures, or reeds, and the dynamic differences between them should not be so great as to make each change jarring. As used here by Brahms, the manual changes are a perfectly normal organist's procedure for effecting a stepwise decrescendo without using a swell box. And as it is absent in the echoes, the pedal should be coupled to Manual I throughout.

The texture of this piece is largely homophonic but not without some contrapuntalism in the inner voices. Chromatic eighth-note countermelodies, slightly reminiscent of those in no. 8, intermingle, appearing in different parts, including (in measure 23) the pedal. Brahms's treatment of the seemingly artless echoes is, upon closer inspection, somewhat complex. The melodic motif, taken from the final notes of the phrase, is first echoed in the same range as the initial statement and then, in the second echo, an octave lower. In the first three phrases, this occurs in an inner voice; in phrases four and five, the whole texture drops lower, and the echoed melody appears in the top line of the second echo. The countermelody—slightly different in each echo—likewise shifts around. Brahms generally identifies these with a slur, as if to bring the player's attention to them. Sometimes a slur is missing but implicit, as in the tenor part in measures 9–10.

The echoes of the sixth and final phrase are longer, stretched out by hemiola. The slurs encompassing these long echo phrases are an open invitation to disregard bar lines and allow the phrases to flow as a whole; a similar slur, although left out in Brahms's incomplete editing, is implicit when the echo phrase enters in the tenor at measures 28–30. The texture in these softly concluding measures changes and thickens, with chords appearing below the echoed line in the first echo and both above and below in the concluding one.

Here again, various editors and players sometimes suggest "lifting out" the concluding echoed tenor-line melody on the pedal, but this is quite unnecessary, for here (as in other instances) Brahms detaches some of the chords to let the echoed line stand out without need of any help. The nature of the chords is such that they will be slightly detached even when there are no rests between them, and if a conscious, connected legato for the tenor line is observed, it will stand out perfectly well. As with all of Brahms's chorale preludes (and indeed much of his work in general), a study of the subtleties of phrasing will reward both player and listener and make such subterfuges unnecessary.

Coda: Reception

"After the fireworks of Liszt and the 'majestic constancy' of Reubke, we come in conclusion to the deep, still waters of the *recueillement* of Johannes Brahms ... the Eleven Chorale Preludes of the master come as a fitting summary to the whole of his work in the vast field of musical art, an act of supreme homage from a musical poet to the sacred poetry of the canticles."[83] Thus wrote (somewhat effusively) the British organist A. C. Delacour de Brisay three decades after the initial publication of Brahms's Opus 122. By this time, although performers and editors were still tempted to rearrange and transcribe these pieces, their intrinsic worth as real organ music and a small but significant part of Brahms's oeuvre was gradually beginning to be recognized.

Brahms's friends were warm in their approval of the early organ works that were given to them in manuscript, but of the two that were eventually published in his lifetime, we hear little or nothing of their reception by the musical world at large. Ironically, the opposite is true of the posthumous *Elf Choralvorspiele*, op. 122. Although the first seven had been prepared for publication by Brahms's copyist in the summer of 1896, and apparently even sent to his publisher, Fritz Simrock, they were not published until five years after the composer's death, following a certain amount of litigation with regard to Brahms's estate. By this time, four additional chorale preludes had been discovered among Brahms's papers and edited by Eusebius Mandyczewski to accompany the first seven. Was the immediate publication of the first seven delayed because Brahms had promised a second set of seven? Until new documentary evidence may emerge, this remains one of the many unanswered questions relative to these pieces.

The Simrock firm devoted a full-page advertisement in the Leipzig musical periodical *Signale* for March 26, 1902, to their publication of the "last work of Johannes Brahms"—the Eleven Chorale Preludes—which was to appear in fourteen days. The advertisement further stated that "this work was composed in Ischl in May and June of 1896, [and] comprises the only musical legacy of the master," and that according to the last wishes of the composer, it was given to the Simrock firm. We know, however, that other pieces began to surface and to be published as early as 1908, and others appeared before the publication of the complete works in 1927. Thus the Eleven Chorale Preludes were not, strictly speaking, Brahms's "only musical legacy," although they are the only ones given an opus number. Interestingly, this same advertisement cites that in preparation were editions for piano two hands, piano four hands, harmonium, and harmonium and piano. Simrock was apparently desirous of making the most of Brahms's legacy.

In the same issue of *Signale* is an extensive article by Ludwig Karpath, who rather confidently asserted that the chorale preludes "surely stem from an earlier period" and are proof that Brahms did not destroy all of his unpublished work, as some would believe. Other proof would soon be found in folk song settings and other material, also to be eventually published. Karpath quoted Ernst von Dohnanyi, who, after studying the chorale preludes, had pronounced them "a noble enrichment of the literature." He also reported that "Simrock has orders right now from America and England alone for 5000 (five thousand) copies of the chorale preludes, which will hopefully be even better received in Germany."[84] They were not long in reaching America, for in July 1902 the American periodical *Church Music Review* published a review of them by the composer Daniel Gregory Mason. Although Mason found in the chorale preludes "the characteristic touch of Brahms" in mannerisms "such as cross-rhythms and momentary displacements of accent," he also discerned "Bach's ever-springing melodic fancy and Beethoven's august solidity of structure" and predicted that these works "will immediately take their place . . . among the world's masterpieces for the organ."[85]

One of the American purchasers was the noted organ recitalist Clarence Eddy, who lost little time in putting some of the chorale preludes to use. In November and December 1902, Eddy was concertizing in the British Isles, and on his programs there were three of the op. 122 pieces, described as "new."[86] Ivor Atkins, the organist of Worcester Cathedral and editor of Novello's 1916 edition of Bach's *Orgelbüchlein,* was an early British purchaser. He is recorded as having played some of Brahms's chorale preludes in the cathedral services soon after their appearance; indeed, a photograph of Atkins published in 1908 shows him seated at the cathedral console, with a copy of the Eleven Chorale Preludes plainly visible on the music rack.[87]

As Karpath predicted, German organists also lost no time in performing the newly published chorale preludes. Almost immediately after their publication, on April 24, 1902, Heinrich Reimann, organist of the Kaiser-Wilhelm-Gedächtniskirche in Berlin (and also one of Brahms's earliest biographers), performed all eleven in a recital there. Several reviews of the collection were published in German periodicals following its publication. In addition to the Karpath article in *Signale,* Andreas Stock wrote a review for the same periodical a few issues later, in which he discerned the "tone-painting and contrapuntal craft" of the passacaglia-based last movement of the Fourth Symphony reappearing within the "small framework" of the chorale prelude form.[88] In September 1902, Eugen Segnitz wrote glowingly in the *Musicalisches Wochenblatt* of this "new, lustrous example of the admirable musical work of the great master" that exerts a "mysterious and mystical attraction to the hearer."[89] Other favorable commentaries followed in various European periodicals.

Chorale preludes were, of course, no novelty in Germany after Bach, although during the nineteenth century, they were largely the work of minor (if often prolific) composers who, with the possible exception of J. C. H. Rinck (1770–1846), were largely unknown outside the country. Hymn-based organ music was not, however, a significant part of the organ music tradition in English-speaking countries, nor a part of historic liturgical usage there. But by the end of the nineteenth century, German chorale tunes were entering English-language hymnals (if often with very different texts), and organists in England and America were becoming acquainted with Bach's chorale preludes. Chorale preludes by someone as well known to musicians and music lovers as Brahms thus found an eager and ready market in all Protestant countries by the turn of the century—at least as far as organists were concerned.

Not all shared the depth of appreciation displayed by reviewers such as Stock, Segnitz, and Mason. Writing in 1925, British organist R. Walker Robson more cautiously described Brahms's Chorale Preludes as "beautiful examples of this form of composition which are difficult for the lay mind to understand. They should be given in small doses, and should be prefaced by some explanation."[90] In 1920, the American organist Latham True praised Brahms for bringing to the organ "such maturity of technique and musical conception" while at the same time opining that many of the chorale preludes "are seemingly better adapted to [the] piano" and even suggesting, as did J. A. Fuller-Maitland in 1911, that no. 10 could just as well be played on the piano with a baritone singing the melody.[91]

In many quarters, though, the turn-of-the-century taste in organ music ran to large-scale recital pieces, and chorale preludes (excepting Bach's) were still generally viewed as little more than church organists' *Gebrauchsmusik,* thus not to be taken very seriously. Brahms had not only taken them quite seriously but also, at least in the eyes of many of his contemporaries, elevated them to the level of art music. The noted musicologist Carl Dahlhaus has observed, "In Brahms's hands, not only the *lied* but its instrumental counterpart, the lyrical piano piece, underwent a process of ever-increasing sophistication in musical logic."[92] He could well have included the chorale prelude—also a small form, and combining vocal and keyboard idioms—in this evaluation.

One result of the interest generated by Opus 122 was an almost immediate spate of transcriptions, in what was presumably meant as an effort to make this music more accessible to the world outside the confines of the organ loft. Simrock wasted no time in making good his advertised promise of transcriptions, which indeed must have been in the works even before the publication of the original version. Later in 1902, Simrock's firm issued the set as arranged for piano by Paul Juon, for harmonium by August Reinhard, and as piano duets arranged by Mandyczewski. In addition to these fairly straightforward transcriptions, selected numbers were more drastically treated in "concert arrangements" for piano and harmonium by Reinhard, and piano arrangements by Ferruccio Busoni that were full of splashy octaves and added dynamic directions, with a new introduction for no. 8 and a virtuosic coda for no. 9. These latter were unquestionably intended for recital use and, as Vernon Gotwals archly observes, are "masterful, if a shade imaginative."[93] Edwin Evans, in his 1912 *Handbook to the Pianoforte Works of Brahms,* includes as "organ works applicable to pianoforte solo" all Eleven Chorale Preludes plus the *O Traurigkeit* prelude and fugue.

Various editors have subsequently arranged some of the Eleven Chorale Preludes for strings, brass ensemble, and orchestra. As recently as 2001, an Australian, Peter Billam, posted on his Web site his transcriptions for recorder quartet of the entire set. Virgil Thomson, in his role as music critic, had at one time disparagingly voiced the opinion that of the eleven, only two (not specified) were "genuinely inspired, though neither of these is particularly well conceived for the instrument."[94] However, Thomson must have later altered his opinion of Opus 122, for in 1956 he transcribed seven of the chorale preludes for symphony orchestra, and in this form they were premiered by the Juilliard Orchestra on November 8, 1957. Perhaps he had also by this time changed his opinion of the instrument for which Opus 122 was written, for in 1954 he published some organ "chorale preludes" of his own—actually a set of variations on Sunday school hymns. While hardly Brahms-inspired, some of them do contain a fugal movement.

Another result of the popularity of Opus 122 was that sincerest form of flattery, imitation—or at least emulation. Heinrich Reimann (1850–1906), an early biographer of Schumann and a devotee of Bach, is thought by Gotthold Frotscher to have been influenced by Brahms, although his chorale-based organ works are all in the longer chorale fantasia form and were mostly written before 1902. Max Reger (1873–1916), on the other hand, was a student of the historian and theorist Hugo Riemann (1849–1919), another promoter of Brahms's music, and his interest in (and even adulation of) Brahms has been acknowledged by many, sometimes in a negative way. In April 1896, the young Reger sent the older composer a copy of one of his earliest organ compositions, the *Suite in E Minor* (op. 16, dedicated "to the spirit of Bach"), and requested permission to dedicate one of his compositions to Brahms. Brahms replied quite cordially and in good humor, thanking Reger for his "warm and most friendly words," and the offer of "the beautiful present of a dedication." Permission was not necessary, said Brahms, but "I had to smile when you asked me for that, while including a work whose all too bold dedication [to a deceased composer] frightens me! Therefore you may certainly go ahead and add the name of your respectfully humble J. Brahms."[95] Brahms corresponded again with Reger a few months later, in June—after the crisis of Clara's death, and the completion of the manuscript of the first seven chorale preludes—but this letter, in which he enclosed a photograph of himself, has unfortunately been lost. In it, Brahms is thought to have expressed interest in meeting Reger, but if any meeting did occur, it is unrecorded. Brahms had returned to Ischl in June. Later in the summer he was beginning to feel unwell, and he went to Karlsbad in September, where the fatal nature of his illness was diagnosed. As his health declined steadily thereafter, it is very probable that the meeting, which Reger had greatly desired, never occurred.

Reger was devastated by the news of Brahms's death the following spring and seems to have expressed his grief by throwing himself into the composition of some decidedly "Brahmsian" works. Antonius Bittmann notes that these pieces, written in 1897 and 1898, "are saturated with Brahmsian substances, characteristic compositional techniques, as well as references to specific models by the older master."[96] One of these, the *Rhapsodie* (op. 24, no. 6), composed in 1898, is dedicated—in the exact wording of the Bach dedication that had frightened Brahms—"to the spirit of J. Brahms."

Although a lifelong Roman Catholic, Reger was in the early part of his career influenced by Bach and Mendelssohn as well as Brahms, and during his lifetime he wrote a large number of choral and organ works based on Lutheran chorales. Best known for the monumental chorale fantasies beloved of present-day organ recitalists, he also wrote a quantity of shorter chorale preludes. Most significant is the three-volume set of fifty-two chorale preludes (op. 67) published by Bote & Bock in 1903, followed by the thirteen chorale preludes (op. 79b) published by Beyer a year later, and the set of thirty short chorale preludes (op. 135a) published by Peters in 1915.

Reger's fifty-two chorale preludes were published but a year after the posthumous appearance of Brahms's eleven in the spring of 1902, and there are some correspondences so striking that it is hard not to think that at least a few of Reger's chorale preludes were influenced by Brahms's. Nonetheless, Reger would later, despite his own admiration of Brahms, plead ignorance of the Opus 122 chorale preludes, at least prior to his own compositions in the genre. In this, he was probably encouraged by his most ardent supporter, the organist Karl Straube who, in a review of the Reger compositions in *Die Musik*, took no small pains to distance Reger from Brahms. To Straube, Reger's chorale preludes descended directly from Pachelbel and Bach, with no influence from anyone in between, most particularly Brahms, whose chorale preludes he dismissed as "religious studies of a secular mind," while Reger's proceeded "from a feeling for the Church."[97] This rather lame comparison sounds suspiciously like a not very subtle sales pitch to church organists for the Reger product. Paradoxically, Straube is recorded as having played nearly all of the Brahms chorale preludes at the Thomaskirche during 1903 and 1904, although in his teaching at the Leipzig conservatory, he ignored Brahms and (with the exception of Liszt) most other organ composers between Bach and Reger, including Mendelssohn and Rheinberger.[98]

Among Reger's Opus 67 chorale preludes, one might cite nos. 33 and 34 in Volume II of the collection as possible examples of Brahmsian influence. Both are based on chorales set by Brahms (*O Welt, ich muss dich lassen* and *Schmücke dich, o liebe Seele*), and although their harmonic component is unquestionably Reger, each follows the structural pattern of its Opus 122 counterpart. Like Brahms's no. 11, Reger's *O Welt, ich muss dich lassen* is in five parts and gives the melody in quarter-notes, with the accompanimental material mostly in eighth-notes, each phrase being followed by a single echo, melodically an octave lower. And like Brahms's no. 5, Reger's *Schmücke dich* has the melody in quarter-notes over a running sixteenth-note accompaniment (breaking for a few measures into triplets). Like Brahms's, too, neither of the Reger settings places the soprano melody as a solo on a separate manual, although manual and pedal solos appear in many other Reger chorale preludes. It is true that Reger utilized similar structures in others (echo effects, a fairly common improvisational device, appear even in the *30 Kleine Choralvorspiele*), but his use of them in setting these two particular chorale melodies invites speculation that, Reger's denials notwithstanding, this is more than coincidence.

Brahms's Eleven Chorale Preludes appear to have also influenced certain English composers. Brahms had many devotees in the British Isles, and they repeatedly encouraged him to come there to perform as conductor or pianist, even tempting him with an honorary Cambridge degree. His unwillingness to cross the English Channel has been laid to various reasons, from seasickness to inability to speak English, although none of these things seemed to daunt his friends Clara Schumann and Joseph Joachim from concertizing there. And Brahms's continued absence from their shores never dampened the ardor of his British admirers, who actively promoted performances of his compositions both during his lifetime and after his death.

Most conspicuous among these admirers was C. Hubert H. Parry (1848–1918), a major British "mainstream" composer of the period, who, while in his twenties, aspired (unsuccessfully) to study with Brahms. Although the two composers never met, Parry shared many personal characteristics with Brahms, including painstaking work habits and a love of earlier music, especially Bach. As a conductor and pedagogue, Parry was a lifelong advocate of Brahms's music. Like Reger, he regarded Brahms's death in 1897 as signaling the end of an era, and he commemorated the event with a poignant orchestral *Elegy for Brahms.* Jeremy Dibble, Parry's biographer, asserts that Brahms "epitomized Parry's ideal of all that was artistically sincere, single-minded, and intellectually honest."[99]

Parry shared one other characteristic with Brahms. Although he was an accomplished organist who had written two substantial contrapuntal works for organ in his younger years, Parry did not turn to composing for the organ again until the last decade of his life. And what he wrote, with the exception of a brief *Elegy* and a substantial *Toccata and Fugue in G,* were chorale preludes. Two sets of seven and three ambitious chorale fantasias were published between 1912 and 1916. Dibble opines that "the Bachian tradition of Brahms's preludes, published posthumously in 1902, was undoubtedly a central impetus to Parry's own treatment of well-known tunes from hymns, psalms, or plainsong."[100]

Although Parry called his two sets "chorale" preludes, they were in fact all based on familiar British hymn tunes rather than Lutheran chorales. And as Reger's chorale preludes were in his own harmonic language, so, too, were Parry's. Yet it is not hard to discern the shades of both Bach and Brahms in both. Parry's "Old 104th" for instance, is an extended *vorimitation* chorale with the melody in the pedal, and this device is used in several other pieces, such as "Croft's 136th," in which imitation and figures in thirds and sixths also appear. "Rockingham" is possibly the most "Brahmsian" harmonically; others explore more dramatic Reger and Karg-Elert territory. There is no question that Parry knew Brahms's chorale preludes—and it is quite probable that he knew Reger's, too. But one must wonder if he also knew that the first seven of Brahms's had initially been edited as a set and had intentionally published his own in two sets of seven (in 1912 and 1916) as his homage to Brahms.

Charles Villiers Stanford (1852–1924), another British Brahms devotee and friend of Parry, also published two sets of chorale preludes, along with several larger organ works. When Parry died in 1918, Stanford and several others of Parry's associates composed a set of short organ pieces in tribute, which were played at his funeral in St. Paul's Cathedral and later published. Only two in the set of thirteen are chorale preludes—one (on a tune by Parry) by Stanford, the other by Ivor Atkins, on the old English hymn tune "Worcester."[101] Both pieces seem to hint of Brahms as well as Parry. This English school of hymn-prelude writing continued after Parry's death with younger composers such as Healey Willan (1880–1968), a prolific writer of hymn-preludes and likewise an admirer of Brahms, who emigrated to Canada in 1913 and exerted no small influence on North American organ composers in his day.

The foregoing should not be taken to suggest that Brahms was by any means the only influence on the Anglo-American chorale prelude revival. Bach was undoubtedly the initial inspiration, and Britons and Americans had already written some chorale preludes before Brahms's were published. Nor should the considerable popularity in English-speaking countries of Sigfrid Karg-Elert's six sets of chorale preludes, published in the early years of the twentieth century, be discounted. But for those who, like Parry, Stanford, Atkins, and Willan, were admirers of Brahms's music, the publication of the Opus 122 Chorale Preludes may very well have given added impetus to their own subsequent compositions in the genre.

SIX

Interpretation

Registration

Unlike their French and English counterparts, German composers were never noted for giving detailed registration directions in their music prior to the twentieth century. Buxtehude and Bach, like most of their contemporaries (with the notable exception of Georg Friedrich Kaufmann) left us very little in the way of registrational hints beyond dynamic markings, manual changes, and an occasional indication of pitch.[1] Nineteenth-century German composers were little better in this regard. Therefore, an understanding of German registrational practices of the seventeenth, eighteenth, and nineteenth centuries depends largely on a few treatises, the occasional mention of stops or pitches in some scores, and a knowledge of the organs that the composers played. This approach works fairly well with everyone from Scheidt to Reger because all were church organists, recitalists, or both, and we know not only what kind of organs they played but also specific instruments associated with them. With Brahms (as with Schumann), it becomes more tenuous. Although Brahms was familiar with the organ music of other composers and is known to have dabbled in organ playing sufficiently in his youth to know how to write for the instrument, it is impossible—urban myths to the contrary—to connect him directly with any particular instrument beyond the anonymous little music store organ he occasionally practiced on in Hamburg and possibly the organs in St. Michael's Church and St. Peter's Church in that city.

We must thus consider a somewhat wider range of organs that Brahms is known or believed to have heard during his lifetime. These include, during his early career, the two Hamburg organs and very possibly some in Düsseldorf's churches. Later, he would have heard the Schulze organ in the Bremen Cathedral during an early performance of his *Requiem* and certainly the

Ladegast concert hall organ of the Gesellschaft der Musikfreunde during concerts he directed or attended there. Perhaps Madame Viardot's salon organ in Baden-Baden and the organ in Vienna's Lutheran Church can be included, as well as possibly even the organ in the parish church of Ischl. What these organs have in common is that they were all built after the death of Bach, most of them at various times during the nineteenth century. This fact alone makes misleading—indeed, rather irresponsible—the registrations recommended by Walter E. Buszin and Paul G. Bunjes in their 1964 edition of the Opus 122 Chorale Preludes, predicated as they were on a small, two-manual, "neo-Baroque" stoplist with no 8' principal, no strings, and no enclosed division. In no. 7, for example, a registration of 16', 8', 4', and 2' is given for the pedal entry in the last five measures, completely overbalancing the melodic line assigned to 8' and 4' stops in the manual. To be fair, it should be said that other writers of this period also promulgated similar misconceptions regarding the registration of Brahms's music. But Brahms—his love of earlier music notwithstanding—did not conduct "period" orchestras or play Bach on the harpsichord, and would probably have regarded the thin-sounding, top-heavy, and inexpressive organ described in the 1964 Peters edition as something of a curiosity at best.

One of the older organs Brahms would have heard (and possibly even played on one occasion) was the large 1768 Hildebrandt instrument in St. Michael's Church in Hamburg—the church that his family attended and in which he was confirmed. The work of a progressive Central German builder, it was already very different tonally from the organs of Arp Schnitger and the older North German school. Each of its three manuals, while possessing a complete principal chorus from 8' through multiple mixtures (as well as various mutations and reeds), also had a 16' stop and no fewer than five 8' stops. The pedal stoplist ranged from two 32' stops to a mixture. The full organ sound of this organ (no longer extant) surely had brilliance, but it also had plenty of gravity; in short, it was well balanced. Its 8' and 4' stops included (in addition to principals) stopped, open, chimneyed, and tapered flutes, Gemshorns, a Quintatön, a Gamba, and an Unda Maris. Thus it also had much color, variety, and shades of dynamic at the 8' and 4' level. The oldest organs Brahms may have heard in Düsseldorf, likewise built in the second half of the eighteenth century, were similarly progressive in their tonal design, and in addition, one of them—the 1755 König organ in St. Maximilian's Church—had a small enclosed division as its third manual.

The rest of the organs Brahms is known to have encountered were built at various times in the nineteenth century and included the 1848 Wolfsteller organ in St. Peter's Church, Hamburg, and the 1849 Schulze organ in Bremen Cathedral. The largest of these, the 1872 Ladegast belonging to the Gesellschaft der Musikfreunde in Vienna, was, on paper at least, rather surprisingly similar to that of a century earlier in St. Michael's with regard to the extent and variety of its stops, fourteen of which were of 8' pitch. This organ, however, also possessed a substantial enclosed *Oberwerk* (Manual III). Thus we can generalize with some safety that the organs Brahms knew were tonally well balanced, with full but brilliant choruses and ample foundation work, as well as a variety of softer and solo-quality stops at 8' and 4' pitch—and that nearly all of them had one expressive division. It should also be noted that in the nineteenth century, the manuals of a Germanic organ were numbered in order of their dynamic hierarchy: Manual I being the main (*Hauptwerk*) division; Manual II the secondary division, usually enclosed (*Echowerk/Schwellwerk*) in two-manual organs and unenclosed (*Oberwerk*) in three-manual organs; and Manual III the enclosed (*Echowerk*) division in three-manual organs. Except when part of reused older casework, *Ruckpositivs* were virtually nonexistent, all divisions being housed behind what was essentially only a façade.

These generalizations are probably the closest we can come to describing a "Brahms organ," but they can in fact give us some assistance in the registration of Brahms's music. The type of organ familiar to Brahms was, after all, the same kind of organ also known to his contemporaries, who do provide us with some good basic ground rules. But we must also keep in mind that although it can legitimately be called a "Romantic" organ, the mid-nineteenth-century German organ was tonally and mechanically quite different from the more orchestrally oriented "Romantic" organ of the early twentieth century, with its greater extremes of dynamics and color.

Brahms, like many of his contemporaries, usually gives the player two very general kinds of suggestions in his organ music, one being dynamic markings and the other (where applicable) being manual changes. Interestingly, it is only in the very last of the chorale preludes that three manuals are specifically called for, although some editors have suggested that a third manual might be useful in other instances. In two of the chorale preludes, Brahms also includes expression indications. In only two instances does he specify pitch—the tenth chorale prelude, and the early version of the A-flat Minor Fugue. In this latter, he comes as close as he ever does in suggesting stops—and this is only for "soft stops" on Manual II. More enigmatically, although the entrance on Manual I is marked *p*, Brahms parenthetically says it should be "good" [*gut*] while Manual II should be "very soft" [*sehr sanft*]. Manual II is not given an actual dynamic marking until near the end, where it is marked *pp*. In the later version, Manual II is marked *dolce* at its first entrance in measure 16. The only piece with no dynamic markings at all is the *O Traurigkeit* fugue.

In both the early works and the chorale preludes, there are (with one exception) only three dynamic markings specified: *f, p,* and *pp*. The exception is *mf dolce,* which appears in the fourth chorale prelude. In this piece, as in some others, no manual changes are marked, although the context as well as the dynamic change clearly indicates such. Conversely, in no. 8, manual changes are marked, but the only dynamic indication is *p dolce* at the very beginning. Here we should perhaps bear in mind Mendelssohn's caution, in the preface to the German edition of his Organ Sonatas, that when two manuals are employed, they should differ in tone color but not contrast greatly in dynamic.[2] Finally, there is Brahms's enigmatic *forte ma dolce,* found at the opening of chorale preludes no. 1 (where Brahms changed it from *mezzo forte* in the editing process), 3, and 11. This may indeed simply be Brahms's *mf,* the "dolce" perhaps limiting it to 8' stops and the "forte" signifying Manual I, on which these particular preludes presumably begin. The softer stops of the main manual of a nineteenth-century German organ (usually Gedeckt, Gamba, and Gemshorn) are by no means as reticent as those of the secondary manuals.

However, the chorale preludes are not the only works in which Brahms employs the *forte ma dolce* dynamic. For example, a section of the middle movement of the Sonata for Clarinet and Piano in E-flat Major (op. 120, no. 2) is marked "*forte ma dolce e ben cantando.*" "Well sung" could indeed be something to also keep in mind for the chorale preludes and other Brahms instrumental works in which a "singing" melodic line is important.

How, then, does one translate Brahms's dynamic markings into the registration conventions of the period? Various nineteenth-century composers give some general suggestions. In the preface to the 1845 German edition of his Organ Sonatas, Felix Mendelssohn gives the following table:

ff = full organ
f = full organ, without some of the strongest stops
p = more soft 8-foot stops together
pp = a soft 8-foot stop alone
Pedal: 16' and 8' tone, "unless otherwise indicated."

A little later, Mendelssohn's contemporary, Adolf Friedrich Hesse (1809–1863), expands the table slightly to include *fff*:

fff = with full organ
ff = with full organ, but without the "screamy" [*schreiende*] stops
f = with powerful stops
mf = with strong stops
p = with softer stops
pp = with gentlest stops

Brahms's Viennese contemporary, Rudolf Bibl (1832–1902), in a footnote to his *Sechs Characterstücke,* published in 1890, repeats essentially the same formula:

ff = full organ
f = the same, without the strongest stops
mf = various 8' and soft 4' stops, or on smaller organs the full Manual II
p = two or three soft stops
pp = Salicional or Aeoline 8' alone
"The Pedal speaks at the same strength as the manual. Any exceptions from these you will find indicated."

Joseph Rheinberger (1839–1901), in a footnote to his Organ Sonata op. 88, provides what by this time would seem to be a fairly standard table:

ff = full organ
f = full organ without mixtures
mf = soft and medium-strong stops on Manual I
p = soft 8' and 4' stops on Manual II (also on Manual I)
pp = one soft stop on Manual II

For his Eighth Sonata, op. 132, and *Phantasie*, op. 154, he is somewhat more specific:

ff = full organ on Manual I
f = the same, without mixtures
mf = Principal 8' on Manual I, or full Manual II
p = two or three soft stops (or a pair of soft 8' and 4' stops)
pp = Salicional or Aeoline 8'

In eleven Rheinberger works surveyed, from op. 65 to op. 196, there is very little variation from these formulae. In all, *ff* and *f* are identical. Minor variations occur in the softer levels. In *Praeludium*, op. 196, *mf* on Manual I is Principal 8' and Octave 4', and *p* is Salicional 8' and Dolce 4'. In the Fifth Sonata, op. 111, *mf* is Principal 8' [Man. I] or 8' and 4' stops on Manual II, and *p* is Gamba or Salicional 8' and Dolce 4'.

Similar registrations are found in the Variations, op. 45 of Gustav Merkel (1827–1885), and works by Louis Rebbeling (mid-nineteenth century), as well as in J. C. H. Rinck's (1770–1846) *Praktische Orgelschule*. Rinck, in his op. 108 *Introduction, Variations and Finale on a Theme of Corelli* (a late work), gives some general registration suggestions for its movements: "with soft stops," "with strong stops," "with Principal and Gedackt 8'," "with Gedackt and Gamba 8'," and, for the Finale, "for full organ." Rinck's registrations contain no surprises but rather confirmation that already in the earlier part of the nineteenth century, organists were expected to combine 8' stops to achieve a desired color. The only mention of reeds is by Rebbeling, in his op. 28 *Pedal-Etude*, where he cites the usual Manual II 8' and 4' stops for *mf*, "but without reeds." It seems clear that there were certain "givens" in this period with regard to dynamic levels, as well as the association of Manual I with *ff*, *f*, and *mf* levels, and Manual II with *mf, p,* and *pp* levels; Manual III, when indicated, is almost always *p* or *pp*. Organists were expected to use the dynamic levels as a guide to registration and to adapt these guidelines to their specific instruments.

Brahms's contemporary Carl Piutti (1846–1902) was, despite his Italianate surname, German-born, a graduate of the Leipzig Conservatory (where he later taught), and from 1880, organist of the Thomaskirche in Leipzig. In 1900, he published, as his op. 34, his *Zweihundert Choralvorspiele,* in which we find much confirmation that, excepting specific "full organ" indications, chorale prelude registrations in this period still consisted largely of 8' and 4' stops (occasionally with a 16' stop), either singly or in a variety of combinations. Some of his combinations—all indicative of the variety of colors available to him on the large Sauer organ then in the Thomaskirche—can be translated as follows:

Soft 8' and 4' stops
Soft, bright 8' and 4' stops
Soft 8' and 16' stops
Soft, dark stops
Soft string stops
Flute or Gedackt
Weak and strong flutes (presumably 8' only)
Salicional alone
Rohrflöte 8', Quintatön 8', Harmonica 8' (a free reed)
Aeoline and Voix Celeste (Swell)
Voix Celeste and Gedackt 8' (Swell)
Soft string stops, Salicional 8' and Quintatön 8' (Man. II)
Aeoline 8' and Gedackt 8'
8' and 4' flutes
Bright 8' stops, Salicional 16' and Flute 4'
Strong, serious registration
Strong 8', 16', and perhaps also 4' stops
The strongest flute in the organ, plus Gedeckt 8' (Man. I)
Full organ excepting the sharpest mixture stops (Man. I)

Catechisms and organ tutors corroborate (and sometimes amplify) some of the registrations given by the various composers. Johann Georg Herzog (1822–1909), Rheinberger's teacher, published an *Orgelschule* in 1841 giving registrations that relate not only to Rheinberger's but also to Piutti's of a half century later.

For a "soft, stringy sound": Salicional 8' alone or with Lieblich Gedeckt 8', or Gamba and Gedeckt 8', with Subbass 16' and Violoncello 8' in the pedal.

For a "clear, bright sound": Gedeckt and Flute 8' with either Flute 4' or Principal 8' and Octave 4', and Subbass and Violonbass 16' and Oktavbass 8' in pedal.

For a "dull [or gloomy] sound": Gedeckt and Gamba 8' with Bourdon 16 and Gedeckt 4' or Gamba and Hohlflöte 8' with Quintatön 16' and a soft 4' stop, with Subbass and Violonbass 16' in the pedal.

For a "full, serious sound": more than one 8' stop, including the Gamba, plus Bourdon 16' and one 4' stop, with Subbass and Violonbass 16', Violoncello and Flötenbass 8', and Posaune 16' in the pedal. [N.B.: The 16' pedal reed in a nineteenth-century German organ is usually darker and less prominent than most modern examples.]

For a "full, brilliant sound": Both manuals coupled, with Geigenprinzipal, Gamba, Salicional, and Rohrflöte 8', Trompete, Fagott, and Clarinett 8', Fugara and Spitzflöte 4', Bourdon 16', Superoktav 2' and Cornet 8' (when full compass), plus Subbass, Violonbass and Posaune 16', Oktavbass 8' and Clarino 4' in the Pedal—but no pedal coupler.[3]

A catechism for organists by E. F. Richter of the Leipzig Conservatory, originally written in 1868 and reprinted in 1896, gives several guidelines, summarized here:

1. A "strong" [*starke*] combination can include principals and other flue stops at pitches from 16' to 2', with lower-pitched mutations, secondary compound stops, and free reeds, but without higher pitched mixtures and strong reeds. But it can be modified by omission of all reeds, mutations, and mixtures and, for a clearer sound, omission of the 16' and 8' flutes and strings.
2. Most 8' flue stops can be used alone, including the Gamba if it is prompt-speaking, but the Quintatön should always be combined with another 8' stop.
3. Soft reeds are good for solos, alone or (preferably) with an 8' flute stop.
4. The best registrations combine stops of the same pitch but different scale (e.g., flute and string). Combining stops of similar scale is the exception but may be done to achieve a particular effect.
5. The 8' combinations can be enriched by adding a soft 4' stop (an example given being flutes at 8' and 4' to accompany a solo played on the Gamba or Clarinet stops).
6. The 8' Principal can be added to these combinations to make them more open and clear.
7. Softer reeds can be combined with various 8' stops. Strong reeds are not effective in chordal textures, however, but are better used for solo lines.[4]

In 1888, the theoretician Hugo Riemann, in his *Katechismus der Orgel*, propounded a similar list of guidelines for registration. The most pertinent ones can be summarized as follows:

1. All 8' stops can be used alone for solo purposes, but the organist must choose which one best suits the musical purpose.
2. With a few exceptions (some 16' and 4' stops), stops of other than 8' pitch should not be used alone and only when combined with 8' stops.
3. A soft 8' flue stop can be strengthened by the addition of one, two, or three more 8' stops, then a Principal 8', Octave 4, 16' Flute, and finally higher pitched stops.
4. No gapped combinations (e.g., 8' and 2') are to be used except when specified by the composer. Mutations should be added in sequence, without gaps.
5. For a noble, mild, and dignified sound, use 16' and 8' stops without 4', 2,' or mutations; adding these will make the tone bright and sharp. Adding reeds makes it pompous and brilliant.
6. Open flutes are soft and lovely; stopped flutes dark and sad; principals fresh and cheerful.
7. A cantus firmus can be played on a suitable reed stop, or if none is available, a Gamba or Gemshorn. [N.B.: In nineteenth-century German organs, the Gamba, usually found on Manual I, can be quite a strong-sounding stop.]
8. The Tremulant should be used only with soft and weak stops, never strong ones.
9. When a composer says "with soft stops," soft 8' flute stops are meant; "with strong stops" means more stops, especially principals, foundations, and flutes, with some reeds; "with full organ" means all the stops, except in large organs, where softer stops should be omitted. However, enormous masses of sound should be used only for short passages, never for a whole piece.[5]

In the same year that Riemann's *Katechismus* appeared, an English translation of Carl Locher's treatise on organ stops was published. "The organist," he writes, "must first make himself acquainted with the 8-ft. tone on his organ, which is the basis of all stops," and, like the others, Locher advocates combinations of principals, gedackts, flutes, and gambas at 8', or 8' and 4' pitch, adding higher pitched stops and reeds for "brilliancy and acuteness." The Salicional—stronger in nineteenth-century German organs than the often thin-toned or wispy stops of that name found in twentieth-century organs—he considers a good blending stop that can be used with flutes at both 8' and 4' pitches. Like some of the previously cited composers, he reserves the mixtures for *ff* passages.[6]

In 1896, the young Max Reger presented Brahms with a copy of his Opus 16, a four-movement suite for organ, dedicated to Bach. In it are the predictable dynamic markings, but in many cases these are coupled to specific manuals and pitches. Full organ is, as usual, *ff* (in one instance, *fff*), but most other dynamics—as in Piutti's chorale preludes—require only 8' or 8' and 4' combinations and in a few instances 8', 4', and 2'. The indication *pp* can be 8' and 4' on Manual II or 8' only on Manual I; *p*, usually on Manual II, is either 8' or 8' and 4', and in one instance it is 8' and 4' on Manual I. Like Brahms, Reger dispenses with *mf*, but his *f* can be either 8' and 4' or 8', 4', and 2' on either manual. Registration changes in the course of the music are minimal, consisting mostly of the adding or removing of 4' or 2' stops. It must be always borne in mind that the organs that all of these composers were familiar with—even the smaller ones—had multiple 8' and 4' stops, and the difference between a *piano* 8' and 4' and a *forte* 8' and 4' depends on the dynamic of the stops themselves, as well as the number of 8' and 4' stops to be utilized and the manual designated.

On comparing Brahms's organ scores with those of his contemporaries such as Hesse, Richter, Rheinberger, and Piutti (as well as Bibl and Herzogenberg, with whom Brahms was personally acquainted), we see that they are in general conformity with the usages of these composers, showing that Brahms was familiar with the conventions of dynamic-related registration and manual changes. Schumann presumably was, too, although in the six B-A-C-H fugues, only one organ-related direction occurs—*mit sanften Stimmen* [with soft stops] at the opening of Fugue 3, where it simply confirms his dynamic marking of *piano*. Only when there are exceptions (as Bibl, Riemann, and others suggest) is anything more than mere dynamics and manual changes specified in the score. An example is Herzogenberg's third chorale prelude, *Aus tiefer Not schrei ich zu dir*, where he specifies 8' and 4' pitches for Manual II (R.H.), 16' and 8' pitches for Manual I (L.H.), and 4' Trompete for the pedal. A similar arrangement occurs in the fifth, *Komm her zu mir, spricht Gottes Sohn*, except that the pedal is at 8' pitch (no stop cited, possibly suggesting use of a flue rather than reed stop). The rest of the set of six have only the usual manual and dynamic indications. Thus, too, we have Brahms specifying 8' pitch for the pedal in the tenth chorale prelude and pedal 16' alone near the end of the A-flat Minor Fugue in its earlier version. We must assume, therefore, that in all instances where no such exceptions are cited, the general conventions of the corroborative dynamic tables set down by various nineteenth-century composers, as well as the recommendations in the various "catechisms," are just as applicable to Brahms as to other composers of his era.

It will be noticed that nowhere in any of Brahms's organ works does *ff* occur. The one instance where this—the full organ with mixtures—might be applicable would be the G Minor Prelude, where Brahms simply writes *f* at the beginning and, to make sure that the player understands that this applies to the whole prelude, adds *sempre f* at measure 7, where the time changes from triple to duple. The free *stylus fantasticus* rhetoric of the prelude would suggest a full and brilliant sound for this movement. The accompanying fugue, however, is thinner textured, marked *f*, and it should probably be played without the "strongest stops"—the mixtures. This, too, would seem best for the more reserved and thinner textured A Minor Prelude and Fugue, especially in that measures 23–41 are marked *p* and should obviously be played on Manual II, returning to Manual I at measure 42, marked "*forte, sempre più forte.*" This may suggest the addition of mixtures here, particularly in view of the fact that the writing becomes increasingly brilliant as the conclusion is approached. If, on the other hand, the piece is begun on an 8' *forte* (not an impossibility, considering some of the suggestions in the catechisms), then *forte* 4' stops would be added here, making some sense of Joachim's enigmatic comment about letting loose with "very strong 4' registers" at this point.[7] Otto Biba observes that such strong 8' and 4' registrations were quite characteristic of the practices of the period.[8] Carl Piutti may have had something similar in mind when he specified for his prelude on *Wir glauben all an Einen Gott, Vater* a "bright, strong registration (predominantly eight- and four-foot tone)" [*Helle, kräftige Registrierung (vorweigend Acht- und Vierfussston)*].[9]

The A-flat Minor Fugue is in decided contrast. Although it requires two manuals, dynamic markings occur only at the beginning (*p*) and seven measures before the end (*pp*), although Brahms writes *dolce* the first time that the music moves to Manual II. If we go by the generally accepted guidelines, a registration of softer stops of either 8' or 8' and 4' pitch is the only option for both manuals. The stringlike nature of the fugue subjects suggests that string-toned stops could be part of the mix, but flutes should probably also be present for clarity. The *pp* passage on Manual II near the end should almost certainly be on a single soft stop—a string, according to Rheinberger, Bibl, and others—and the texture indeed would support this choice. The "ideal" registration for this piece will of necessity vary from organ to organ but should always be chosen sensitively so as not to blur the subtleties of the counterpoint.

The chorale preludes are still another matter. None are of the brilliant or extroverted character sometimes practiced by later composers such as Max Reger or Sigfrid Karg-Elert in the early decades of the twentieth century. Their inspiration comes from an earlier era, even as they represent the ultimate culmination of that earlier, more introspective, and less self-conscious style. In this, they pick up where Bach's *Orgelbüchlein* leaves off more than a century previous. For these works, the player must largely explore the possibilities—abundant in even modestly sized nineteenth-century German and Austrian organs (as well as some nineteenth-century British and American ones) of the 8' and 4' stops, with perhaps the occasional addition of a 2' stop or even a soft 16' stop. An organ with as few as three 8' stops per manual will invite some experimentation, but fewer will be limiting and more will provide a broader dynamic range, as well as a greater variety of color.

It is interesting that, with the exception of O Traurigkeit, Brahms left us with no chorale preludes of one prominent *Orgelbüchlein* type—that having a soprano solo played on a separate manual. In Brahms's only example, a strong 8' flute, or perhaps a mild reed such as a Clarinet, with a softer 8' flute, will suffice for the solo. Three, however—the O Traurigkeit fugue and numbers 1 and 10 of the *Elf Choralvorspiele*—place the melody in long notes in the pedal, a type used by Bach in some of the *Eighteen Chorales*. Of these three, the dynamic level should dictate the character of the solo stop, and a good, warm 8' principal is probably a better choice than a reed, especially in no. 10. Of the remaining chorale preludes, the melody is generally in the soprano part, sometimes unadorned, sometimes lightly or extensively ornamented, but always on the same manual as its accompaniment. In no. 7, it begins and ends in the soprano, but wanders into the alto and tenor in the middle. One object of registration for all the chorale preludes should be to choose, in whatever dynamic range Brahms prescribes, a combination that allows the chorale melody to sing out most clearly.

Tempo

Brahms's tempo markings, especially in his ensemble music, could be quite detailed and specific at times, although they are somewhat less so in his solo music. For the four longer early organ works, however, Brahms consistently provided tempo indications. The A Minor Prelude and Fugue is marked *Allegro* at the beginning, which presumably obtains throughout. The Fugue in A-flat Minor also has but a single tempo indication, *Langsam,* which every player seems to interpret differently, and the *O Traurigkeit* chorale prelude is marked *Poco adagio,* while the fugue is simply *adagio.* Brahms becomes more specific only in the G Minor Prelude and Fugue. The prelude is marked *Allegro di molto,* and there is a *poco ritard* at measure 16, which is cadential and presumes an *a tempo* as the texture changes in the following measure. The last two measures are marked *più lento,* and the fugue that follows is *Tempo giusto.* Of all his organ works, this is the one in which Brahms appears to have been most carefully conscious of matters of tempo.

Of the Opus 122 chorale preludes, only two have any tempo marking: no. 2 (*Adagio*) and no. 6 (*Molto moderato*). Outside of the fact that these were originally nos. 3 and 4 in the original autograph (and thus may have originally been written or revised at around the same time?), there seems no particular reason for these to have tempo indications while the rest do not, unless it is because Brahms wanted them played a bit slower. Indeed, long before Brahms's time, it was quite customary not to provide tempos for chorale preludes. There are none at all in Bach's *Eighteen Chorale Preludes,* and only four appear in the entire *Orgelbüchlein*—all of them slow (*adagio, largo*), suggesting that such tempi are the exception to the rule. Bach's contemporaries and pupils likewise rarely gave tempi for chorale preludes. As the nineteenth century progressed, however, some composers were beginning to use tempo markings on their chorale preludes. Although Rinck, in the early part of the century, hardly ever employed them, Reger, at the opening of the twentieth century, consistently did, and a superficial survey of chorale preludes written in between reveals a rather wide range of usage (or nonusage, as in the case of Brahms's friend Herzogenberg). That they are rare in Brahms's preludes may simply reflect the fact that his source of inspiration was not his contemporaries but rather his predecessors, particularly Bach.

Some students of Baroque organ music believe that unless otherwise specified, Bach's chorale preludes were meant to be played at *tempo ordinario* (or *tempo giusto*)—singing tempo or "pulse tempo."[10] This is applicable to Bach's contemporaries and successors as well and is one probable reason for the general scarcity of tempo markings in the genre as a whole prior to the beginning of the twentieth century. Some confirmation of this is found in the previously mentioned collection of chorale preludes published in 1900 by one of Bach's nineteenth-century Leipzig successors, Carl Piutti. Several of these do have tempo markings—invariably faster (*Allegro, Animato*) or slower (*Lento, Langsam, Ruhig*) than singing tempo, which would seem to indicate that they are exceptions to the unwritten rule. The majority, however, are simply marked "The quarter-note in chorale tempo" [*Die Viertel im Choraltempo*], although one calls for "solemn chorale tempo" and one is simply marked "chorale-like" [*choraliter*]. In general, the chorale melody in these compositions is in quarter-notes, although "chorale tempo" is assigned to the half-note in an example where the melody appears in half-notes. The only possible interpretation of "chorale tempo" would be the tempo at which the chorales were generally sung. It is noteworthy, though, that even today chorales are usually sung somewhat more slowly in Europe than in America.

Bach lived before the invention of the metronome; Brahms of course did not but seems to have held the little machine in some contempt. In response to a question from George Henschel regarding the strictness of his tempo indications in the *Requiem,* Brahms responded, "I think that here as well as with all other music the metronome is of no value." He goes on to say that although he had occasionally been talked into putting metronome marks in some of his own music (including the *Requiem*), by performers or publishers,

"I myself have never believed that my blood [pulse] and a mechanical device go well together." He then adds that so-called elastic tempo is "not a new invention" and that "*con discrezione*" should be "added to that, as to so many other things."[11] In correspondence with conductor Otto Dessoff concerning the performance of one of his symphonies, Brahms suggested that even his verbal tempo suggestions were "superfluous indications" and that a good performer familiar with the style could indeed use his own discretion in certain places, provided that he really felt it that way.[12] This does not mean, of course, that Brahms condoned extravagant liberties with his or anyone else's music, but rather that a good performer well versed in a particular genre or style could be trusted to interpret a piece of music in an individual way without distorting it.

With regard to Brahms's total output, Stephen May observes that although the majority of his published compositions do in fact have tempo markings of the standard sort, there are significant exceptions. One is dance-based music (gigue, sarabande, minuet, waltz), where the title essentially signifies the tempo, and the other is chorale-based music, including some of the choral works.[13] Here, too, the title would suggest the tempo. Interestingly, some of the posthumously published songs also lack tempo markings. Because these were never prepared by Brahms for publication, it might seem that tempo markings (at least in such smaller vocal works) could have been almost an afterthought with Brahms, added only after a piece was virtually complete—and perhaps at the request of the publisher.

Chorale preludes are, of course, rooted in vocal music—the chorale itself. Brahms, himself a sensitive and prolific composer of choral music and songs, was as surely aware of this as Bach was. Max Miller observes that "Brahms's love of folk song, here the religious folk song of the chorales, is the foundation for all of Opus 122; this vocal base must not be forgotten at any time."[14] The vocal element is evident not only in the chorale melodies but also in the long phrases so often incorporated into the contrapuntal texture of these pieces. Some performers seem to have bought so strongly into the idea of the "funereal" with regard to the Eleven Chorale Preludes that they drag the tempo of all of them in a static, plodding manner, as though playing a dirge, not a hymn. But hymns and chorales are in fact vocal music, and a reasonable tempo for chorale preludes not otherwise designated is still the singing, breathing *tempo giusto*. They are not dead and stagnant; they are alive and have a strong heartbeat.

Performance Practice

Although Brahms began his career as a performer on the piano, it was not long after his arrival in Vienna that he began to curtail this activity in favor of conducting and composing. By the early 1880s, he was appearing more rarely as a performer, and then usually only in his own compositions. Eventually, he gave up even that, practiced less, and ultimately played the piano mostly in informal situations or to accompany his own songs. Fanny Davies, one of Clara Schumann's pupils who had heard Brahms play on many occasions, noted that "in the years during which I heard him (1884–96), Brahms had long ceased to practice regularly."[15] We have, alas, no account of Brahms's organ playing, unless Joachim's previously mentioned comment about joyfully tearing loose in one of the early fugues is somehow related to having heard him play a fugue on an organ. But we do have contemporary descriptions of his pianism, including his playing of Bach's organ works on the piano, and also some descriptions of his teaching methods. These give us a glimpse of his musicianship and perhaps a hint of how one should approach his organ works.

In the second half of the nineteenth century, there appear to have been two rather distinct schools of piano playing. The most popular, of course, was the flashy virtuosic style of Liszt and his acolytes; Brahms, from all accounts, occupied the other end of the spectrum, in which the music was all and the player its servant. Michael Musgrave, in a chapter on "Brahms the Pianist," cites several contemporary descriptions of Brahms's playing. Critic Eduard Hanslick, reviewing his first Vienna recital in 1862, observed that Brahms "only wishes to serve the composition, and he avoids almost to the point of shyness any semblance or suggestion of self-importance or show . . . [but] his playing is always heart-winning and convincing." Further on, he observes with slight disapproval that Brahms "plays more like a composer than a virtuoso" but nonetheless praises the "irresistible charm of his playing." Yet Brahms's playing style could be far from subservient or merely charming. In 1865, Viktor Widmann described it as "powerful," and in 1871, Florence May called it "stimulating to an extraordinary degree." But it was restrained power, and Musgrave notes that Brahms "shared Clara's belief in creating a beautiful tone by coaxing the sound from the instrument."[16] And the instrument Brahms preferred for his "fine shades of touch and tone" was the modern grand piano—preferably a Bechstein or a Steinway.[17]

These comments are, of course, somewhat subjective and say not as much as we would like about the finer details of Brahms's performance style. Some of these details, however, are captured by one of his more articulate students, the Englishwoman Florence May, who studied with him in the early 1870s. She mentions "a certain elasticity of tempo" in his playing of Bach and "use of the deep legato touch" to express sustained feeling in his Mozart. Good fingering was important, as was smooth phrasing, particularly in earlier music.[18] Neither should be overlooked by organists performing Brahms's music.

Brahms was surely a child of his times with regard to tempo, legato, and phrasing. In 1903, Brahms's contemporary, Joseph Bloch of the Budapest Conservatory, stated simply that "the main point of phrasing was to make the work more understandable to the listeners."[19] From all accounts, Brahms did just that. In 1881, Friedrich Chrysander praised Brahms's playing of contrapuntal music and his ability to bring out all the voices clearly.[20] "Elasticity of tempo," mentioned by May, can be another way of saying "rubato," which Bloch cites as a tool for outlining motivic and melodic structure, rather than something applied haphazardly as "a sentimental device." Excessive rubato can destroy the continuity of the rhythm, but, as the noted piano teacher Tobias Matthay wrote in 1913, the object is "to *bend* the time, but not break it."[21]

This would seem to be precisely what Fanny Davies heard in Brahms's playing, which she describes as "free, very elastic and expansive; but the balance was always there—one felt the fundamental rhythms underlying the surface rhythms." Recalling Brahms's performance in his C Minor Piano Trio (op. 101), she makes the interesting observation that at certain places "Brahms would lengthen infinitesimally a whole bar, or even a whole phrase, rather than spoil its quietude by making it up into a strictly metronomic bar." In this regard, Davies considers "this expansive elasticity" to be "in contradistinction to a real rubato"[22]—a rather subtle distinction indeed. A certain amount of this kind of "elasticity," judiciously and sensitively applied, could indeed help to bring out some of the finer melodic and motivic points of the Fugue in A-flat Minor and the Chorale Preludes. But overdone rubato, such as one sometimes hears in performances of *Es ist ein Ros' entsprungen,* can easily transform subtlety into shallow sentimentality—something Brahms viewed with disdain.

With regard to Brahms's "deep legato" piano touch, it should be noted that legato playing in the second half of the nineteenth century was hardly confined to the piano. It was also a cardinal element of organ technique in Germany, said to have been first seriously promulgated by the composer and theoretician Justin Heinrich Knecht (1752–1817) and certainly well established by Brahms's time. In 1845, a French journalist wrote disparagingly about the "legato fugal style" of contemporary German organ composers Rinck and Hesse.[23] During the second half of the nineteenth century, teachers such as Ernst Friedrich Richter, Karl August Haupt, and Julius Schneider were noted for their legato playing, Haupt being an early exponent of the use of the heel to facilitate legato pedal playing. Schneider, in his *Orgelschule,* states, "The principal means of expression are a strict attention to the accents, emphasis, syncopation, and a close observance of the *legato, staccato, crescendo* and *diminuendo.*"[24] In his 1868 *Katechismus,* Richter states that good organ touch demands that the fingers remain in contact with the keys for the full duration of each note and "the organ thus requires the strictest and most careful legato playing."[25] French organists apparently played in a somewhat more detached manner at the time. During the 1880s, Everett E. Truette, a German-trained American organist, visited Paris and attended several organ recitals there, commenting frequently in his notebook on what to him was an appalling lack of legato in the playing of some rather distinguished Parisian organists.[26]

Legato was, however, more of a tool for shaping phrases and *cantabile* lines in the nineteenth century, and not a be-all and end-all as it evolved in the early twentieth century with the increased usage of finger substitution and overlapping. Composers could freely indicate where they did not desire normal legato with accents, staccato marks, or, as Schumann does in his second B-A-C-H fugue of op. 60, by simply writing in "*non legato.*" This should be interpreted not as staccato, however, but rather as slightly detached. In the fifth B-A-C-H fugue, Schumann indeed indicates his desire for true staccato by placing dots above the notes of the dancing triple-time fugue subject whenever it occurs. Not surprisingly, the tempo marking for both of these fugues is *Lebhaft* (lively).

But organ staccato was not the same as piano staccato. Richter addresses this issue by describing staccato as firmly pressing (not striking) the keys, but "lingering for a shorter time" and drawing the fingers forward on the key "with precision" to release the note.[27] On a mechanical-action organ, this would initiate a sharp attack and, if what Richter means by "drawing the fingers forward" is slowing the rise of the key (and thus the pallet), a gentler release. The effect would be less like the percussive pianoforte staccato and more like what we today would regard as "detached." In other words, the quickly struck and released pianistic staccato would seem to have had no place in German organ playing of the nineteenth century. Indeed, Brahms even cautioned his student Eugenie Schumann against staccato on the piano, at least when playing Bach: "In any work by Bach, Brahms would occasionally permit an emphatic lifting of the notes (portamento) but never a staccato. 'You must not play Bach staccato,' he said to me."[28] This might suggest that Brahms did not approve of playing any contrapuntal music staccato, including his own—and if not on the piano, surely not on the organ.

Staccato and accent marks are in any case rare in Brahms's organ works, but where they exist, they clearly have special meaning. In the A Minor Prelude (WoO 9), a little seven-note figure appears in measures 5 and 6 in the left hand, repeated once in the right hand in measure 8. There is a slur over notes 4 and 5 and staccato marks over notes 6 and 7 (added editorially after the first iteration but clearly part of this figure whenever it recurs). To strike these two notes too sharply would be jarring following the implicit legato of the slur, but to simply detach them slightly would seem a more elegant way of calling attention to them. In measure 19 of the prelude, the forthcoming fugue subject is introduced in the pedal with both slurs and staccato marks. This again would seem to indicate only detachment, the slightest shortening of the notes, with perhaps a speck more detachment between the two slurs. It is possible that the detachment should continue through measure 20, for in the concluding two measures of the fugue subject (21 and 22), V-shaped accent marks appear in the pedal. These also occur in measures 23, 28, and 29, and all are below notes of half- or whole-note value. The use of accent rather than staccato marks here is not entirely clear, but it could either suggest a more forceful attack or perhaps imply slightly more detachment for these longer notes.

Interestingly, no staccato or accent marks appear in the A Minor Fugue or the G Minor Prelude, although the bravura passages and the chords of measures 31–35 of the latter would seem to ask for a certain amount of natural detachment. Slurred staccato marks appear again in the subject of the G Minor Fugue, however, and again would appear to merely indicate a slight detachment, which should presumably be observed in subsequent appearances of the subject. Only in these two early works, written in the brilliant *stylus fantasticus* idiom, does Brahms feel the need to use either staccato or accent. The other two more contemplative early works, and all eleven chorale preludes of Opus 122, are quite devoid of them.

It is in these more contemplative works that the player's sensitivity is required. Careful study of melodic lines, slurs, and phrasing (whether indicated or implicit) should dictate tempo, registration, and the amount of "elasticity" and legato to be employed. Especial attention should be paid to slurs. The type known as the phrasing slur occurs frequently in the chorale preludes, particularly numbers 1, 4, 7, 8, 10, and 11, although it is implicit in all of them. Less frequently used but as important are the articulation slurs, found in numbers 2, 3, 4, and 7—number 4 displaying a carefully worked-out combination of articulation and phrasing slurs. Slurs occur less frequently in the earlier works, appearing only sporadically in the A Minor and G Minor fugues and *O Traurigkeit* pair but quite consistently in the A-flat Minor Fugue. Van Oortmerssen calls attention to a technique called *abschleiffen,* mentioned in various nineteenth-century sources, which is the very slight shortening of the last note under a slur, which he regards as contributing to "a dynamic experience of the static organ sound."[29] The slurred four-note figure in measure 3 of the Prelude in A Minor is an example of a place where this would be effective, and it should be observed when this same figure occurs in the left-hand part in measures 10 and 11, where the same slurring is implied by the stemming.

According to Fanny Davies, "a strictly metronomic Brahms [was] unthinkable."[30] Static plodding and "notey-ness" have no more place in Brahms's organ music than in his songs, choral and piano music, chamber works, or symphonies. As in his other works, forward motion and the phrasing of melodic lines are of paramount importance. It would do no harm for organists to listen to some good performances of Brahms's symphonic or chamber works preliminary to studying the organ works, which contain many of the same elements, albeit in miniature.

APPENDIX A

Editions

(1) 1902: Simrock. *Elf Choralvorspiele für die Orgel, Opus 122,* edited by Eusebius Mandyczewski.

This was issued in two volumes and simultaneously published in London by Alfred Lengnick & Co. and in Paris by Max Eschig. Scholars seem agreed that this, the very first edition of the Eleven Chorale Preludes, was based solely on the "fair copy" of the first seven made for Brahms by Kupfer (with some corrections by Brahms), plus the final four with some editing only by Mandyczewski. Although Brahms inserted the chorale text only in no. 2, the editor has done the same for the other ten, a practice followed in most subsequent editions, excepting those by Biggs, Buszin/Bunjes, and Bozarth (all of which also omit the text in no. 2).

(2) 1927: Breitkopf & Härtel. *Sämtliche Orgelwerke,* also edited by Mandyczewski, and issued as volume 16 of Brahms's complete works.

This is the first edition to contain the entire organ works of Brahms, including the A-flat Minor Fugue and *O Traurigkeit* pair, published individually during Brahms's lifetime, as well as the previously unpublished (and at that time only recently discovered) Preludes and Fugues in A Minor and G Minor. The Eleven Chorale Preludes are substantially as they appear in the 1902 edition, save for a few minor corrections, and the A Minor Prelude and Fugue is on two staves, as it is in the only known holograph. This edition was later reprinted without any changes by Kalmus and others, including Dover.

(3) 1928: Novello & Co. *Eleven Chorale Preludes,* edited by John E. West. Later reprinted by H. W. Gray and G. Schirmer.

English translations have been inserted above the German chorale texts. Besides discarding the alto clef, West occasionally restaved notes, altered slurring and stemming, and added tempo, registration, and dynamic markings, although generally in editorial parentheses. The German numerical manual designations have been changed to "Gt.," "Sw.," and "Ch." (which somewhat blurs the hierarchical implications of Manuals I, II, and III), and in the Gray version, Hammond registrations have been added. Crescendo and decrescendo markings have been inserted where not indicated by Brahms, manual changes in no. 7 have been altered to require three manuals, and in no. 11 West suggests playing the tenor line of the last echo on the pedal. However, he has resisted making any other alterations relative to "lifting out" melodies. This edition is still in print, reasonably priced, and used by many church organists and students.

(4) 1948: Edward B. Marks. *Organ Works,* edited by Gerard Alphenaar, two volumes. Alphenaar, in his foreword, notes that his edition "marks the first American publication of Brahms' organ works in their entirety." However, this is essentially just a pirated version of the Breitkopf & Härtel edition, with no noticeable alteration beyond the elimination of the alto clef and the addition of English words to the chorales.

(5) 1949: Mercury Music. *Eleven Chorale Preludes,* edited by E. Power Biggs. Apparently based on the Breitkopf & Härtel edition. Manual indications, tempo, dynamics, and occasional registrations are added, but always in editorial brackets. In no. 1, three manuals are called for, rather than two. This is, further, the first edition in which the long-standing practice of "lifting out" chorale melodies and adding pedal parts is codified, in alternative versions arranged by Biggs—two of no. 6 and one each of nos. 5 and 7. In no. 8, the melodic "echoes" occurring in the inner parts of measures 5 and 6, and 15 and 16, are transferred to the pedal and (somewhat curiously) registered for the Clarinet stop. This is the only edition in which the fully harmonized version of the chorale is inserted before each chorale prelude.

(6) 1964: Edition Peters. *Complete Organ Works,* edited by Walter E. Buszin and Paul G. Bunjes and presumably also based on the Breitkopf & Härtel edition.
This is published in three volumes, one for the early works (substantially as found in the earlier edition, although with the A Minor Prelude and Fugue on three staves), one for the Eleven Chorale Preludes, and one for a supplement containing alternative versions of chorale preludes 2, 5, 6, and 7—again for the purpose of "lifting out" the melody (in one instance, by "thumbing") and adding pedal parts. The editors have also inserted their own manual changes in no. 4, which largely disagree with the obvious locations of manual changes indicated by the placement of Brahms's dynamic markings (which are retained). Perhaps the greatest weakness of this edition, however, is the insertion of inappropriate registrations based on a top-heavy, "neo-Baroque" stoplist, given in the preface.

(7) 1983: Breitkopf & Härtel. *Sämtliche Orgelwerke,* edited by Werner Jacob.
This is a single volume and part of a new series of Brahms's complete works. It is an update of the publisher's 1927 edition, with some corrections and new critical notes. It is unique among all editions in that the numbering of the first seven chorale preludes follows that of Brahms's original manuscript rather than of the first published edition. The preface and notes are in German and English.

(8) 1987: G. Henle Verlag. *Werke für Orgel,* edited by George S. Bozarth.
This is an urtext edition of the complete works, based on a careful reading of all available sources. It takes into consideration both versions of the first seven chorale preludes (Brahms's holograph and Kupfer's prepublication copy) and is the only edition to include as appendices the earlier versions of the A-flat Minor Fugue and *O Traurigkeit* chorale prelude. As in all editions since that of 1927, the use of the alto clef has been eliminated, but the editor has tried to be as faithful as possible to Brahms's slurring and (in most cases) stemming. Details of the manuscript sources and editorial process are given in the critical notes at the end, which are in English, German, and French. One minor criticism is that the version of the chorale melody stated before each of the chorale preludes is not always the

version used by Brahms—but then, neither are all of the versions included by Buszin/Bunjes and Biggs.

These editions are all still accessible, mostly still in print (or available in reprint form), and can be found in many larger libraries. Not listed are the original editions of the A-flat Minor Fugue and *O Traurigkeit* pair, long out of print but faithfully followed in subsequent editions of the complete works. In addition, certain excerpts from Brahms's organ works—largely chorale preludes, taken from the standard sources—have occasionally been included in various collections of organ music compiled for church use. Some chorale preludes (most popularly, no. 8) have also appeared from time to time in sheet music form. These versions, often heavily laced with rearranged parts and editorial tempo and registration suggestions, are now mostly out of print and are not considered here.

APPENDIX B

The Organs in Brahms's World

Guesswork, urban legends, and wishful thinking to the contrary, there is very little evidence to connect Brahms with any specific organs as a player. While still in his twenties, he admitted to having practiced on a small, anonymous organ in a Hamburg music store, and he is recorded as having played the organ in St. Michael's Church for a wedding. He may possibly have accompanied his Frauenchor on the organ in St. Peter's Church, at least for rehearsals, and may also have accompanied a Bach cantata for his friend Julius Grimm on an unknown organ in an unknown location in Göttingen. Vague references in early correspondence suggest that he may have "tried" or "practiced" some of his compositions on other, unknown organs. However, from his thirties on, and particularly after settling in Vienna, scholars—hard as some have tried—have not found a shred of evidence that Brahms ever placed a finger on an organ keyboard for the rest of his life. To the best of present knowledge, Brahms's actual hands-on organ-playing experience was quite short-lived and confined to his youthful years.

On the other hand, there is little question that Brahms *heard* organs on various occasions throughout his lifetime, probably more than are recorded. After all, a few of his acquaintances were organists, and in addition to his organ works, he had written three smaller choral works with independent organ accompaniment. He had also included organ parts not only in some of his own larger works (*Requiem, Triumphlied*) but also in his scoring of the orchestral accompaniments of certain Bach, Handel, and Mozart choral works as well. If nothing else, he would have heard an organ in the performances of these works when he conducted them, and perhaps even had to deal with matters of balance and registration in rehearsals.

Composers—and especially orchestral composers—must have a good memory for sounds and tone colors, or they would not be able to orchestrate effectively. We must thus take a small leap of faith and accept that none of Brahms's organ works were conceived in the abstract, but with the remembered sounds of familiar organs echoing in his mind's ear. Some of these organs are described here, with stoplists. They are cited in more or less chronological order, as they appeared in Brahms's life. Although none now exist, at least in the form in which Brahms knew them, their stoplists exemplify the types of tonal resources with which he would have been familiar.

St. Michael's Church [Michaeliskirche], Hamburg

There can be little question that the first organ young Brahms could have heard was the magnificent instrument completed for this church between and 1767 and 1771 by J. G. Hildebrandt, successor to the noted Central German builder Gottfried Silbermann. It was an imposing organ in one of Hamburg's most imposing church buildings, which just happened to be the parish church of the neighborhood in which Brahms was born and raised. Brahms was baptized and confirmed in this church and was friends with Pastor Johannes Geffcken, noted as a hymnologist, and Pastor von Ahlsen, for whose daughter's wedding he provided the organ accompaniment for a small choir. He could hardly have escaped hearing the splendid Hildebrandt organ, although nowhere did he ever record his impression of it.

The fame of this organ was such that it attracted visitors such as C. P. E. Bach, Felix Mendelssohn, and that most notable of British musical tourists, Charles Burney, who in 1775 described the chorus as "the most noble that can be imagined; but it is more striking by its force, and the richness of the harmony." He also observed that "a swell has been attempted," perhaps shortly after completion, as there is no mention of it in the original stoplist; Burney disparagingly noted that its three stops had so little effect that he could hardly discern the crescendo and diminuendo.[1] Another Englishman, E. J. Hopkins, who recorded the stoplist of the organ three quarters of a century later, described the swell as having four stops. Hopkins, however, seems to have been more impressed by the "handsome front" and the thirty-two-foot tin pedal pipes in it than anything else.[2]

HAUPTWERK [Man. I]
Principal 16'
Quintatön 16'
Octave 8'
Violadagamba 8'
Gemshorn 8'
Gedackt 8'
Quinte 6'
Octave 4'
Gemshorn 4'
Nasat 3'
Octave 2'
Sesquialtera, II rks [Rauschpfeife]
Mixtur, VIII rks
Scharf, V rks
Trompete 16'
[Oboe 8']

OBERWERK [Man. II]
Bourdon 16'
Principal 8'
Quintatön 8'
Spitzflöte 8'
Unda Maris 8'
Octave 4'
Spitzflöte 4'
Quinte 3'
Octave 2'
Rauschpfeife, II rks
Cimbel, V rks
Echo des Cornets, V rks
Trompete 8'
Vox Humana 8'
[Cremona 8']
[Glockenspiel 8']
Schwebung [Tremulant]

BRUSTWERK
Rohrflöte 16'
Principal 8'
Flötetraversiere 8' [Principal 8']
Kleingedackt 8'
Rohrflöte 8'
Octave 4'
Rohrflöte 4'

PEDAL
Principal 32'
Subbass 32'
Principal 16'
Subbass 16' (open)
[Subbass 16' (stopped)]
[Violone 16']
Rohrquinte 12'

Oktave 2'
Terze 2' [sic]
Quinte 1 1/3'
Sifflet 1' [Flachflöte 2']
Cimbel, V rks
Chalumeau 8'
[Trompete 4']

[ECHO/SCHWELLWERK]
[Octave 8']
[Octave 4']
[Cornet, II–V rks]
[Trompete 8']

Octave 8'
[Gedact 8']
Octave 4'
Mixture, X rks
Posaune 32'
Posaune 16'
Fagott 16'
Trompete 8'
Clairon 4'

This stoplist is taken from the earliest source, Jakob Adlung, *Musica Mechanica Organoedi* (Berlin, 1768). By 1775, the small "swell" (probably called Echo) had already been added, and a small number of further additions and alterations (in brackets) had been made by J. G. Wolfsteller in 1839–1841, which appear in the stoplist published in Hopkins and Rimbault, *The Organ, Its History, and Construction* (London, 1855). Further repairs and alterations were made in 1876. In 1906, the Hildebrandt organ was destroyed in a fire that did widespread damage to the church, and it was replaced in 1912 by an E. F. Walcker instrument of even greater size. In 1909, Marcussen had built a smaller organ in a side gallery, but it is not certain whether there had been a second organ in the church prior to the fire.

St. Peter's Church [Petrikirche], Hamburg

Brahms's Frauenchor, for which he wrote some music with organ accompaniment, gave concerts in this church in 1859 and 1860 and occasionally rehearsed there. Brahms himself remarked on how well they sounded with the organ and how they liked to sing with it. The church's organist, Georg Armbrust, accompanied the chorus in their concerts, but Brahms may sometimes have accompanied at rehearsals. Brahms liked the acoustics of the church and perhaps the sound of the organ as well.

St. Peter's Church was one of those that had been destroyed in the great Hamburg fire of 1842. After it was rebuilt, a two-manual organ by the local builder Johann Gottlieb Wolfsteller was installed in 1848. The same builder enlarged it in 1852 with the addition of a third manual division; during 1857–1859, this division was enclosed in a swell box, and additional stops placed in all divisions. We must wonder whether the presence of an enclosed division of respectable size was one of the reasons for the attractiveness of this organ as an accompanimental instrument.

HAUPTWERK [Man. I]

Bordun 16
Prinzipal 8'
Gemshorn 8'
Octave 4'
Gemshorn 4'
Octave 2'
Mixtur, IV rks

OBERWERK [Man. II]

Quintadena 16' (tenor C, added 1857)
Gedact 8'
Offene Flöte 8'
Viola da Gamba 8' (added 1857)
Prinzipal 4'
Offene Flöte 4'
Waldflöte 2'

Dulzian 16' (added 1857)
Trompete 8'

PEDAL
Subbaβ 32 (added 1857)
Prinzipal 16'
Subbaβ 16'
Octave 8'
Quint 6' (added 1857)
Octave 4'
Posaune 32'
Posaune 16'

Rauschpfeife, II rks
Dulcian 8'
Tremulant

UNTERWERK [Man. III] (enclosed)
Gedact 16'
Octav 8'
Gedact 8'
Rohrflöte 8'
Octave 4'
Spitzflöte 4'
Octave 2'
Mixtur, IV rks
Trompete 8'
Dulcian 8' (added 1857)

This stoplist, which depicts the organ as it was when Brahms knew it, is taken from Günter Seggermann, *Geschichte der Orgeln in der Hamburger Hauptkirche St. Petri* (Lauffen, 1992). Brahms's friend Georg Armbrust died in 1869, and the organist's position was taken by his son Carl Friedrich, who shortly afterward presided over a further enlargement of the organ by Wolfsteller. In 1885, however, this organ was replaced by a new and much larger Walcker instrument, subsequently rebuilt by Sauer and later replaced by von Beckerath. The Wolfsteller organ, however, was sold to the then new St. Thomas's Church in Hamburg-Rothenburg and may still have been there in 1943, when that building was destroyed by bombing during World War II.

St. Maximilian's Church, Düsseldorf

This organ was built in 1755 by Ludwig König. Although the Schumanns and Brahms heard this organ in concerts (at least one of which was directed by Robert Schumann), there is no direct evidence that any of them ever actually played it—although the close proximity of the church to the Schumanns' residence does raise that possibility.

HAUPTWERK [Man. I]
Bourdun 16' (divided)
Praestant 8'
Rohrgedakt 8'
Violdigamba 8'
Octav 4'
Quintgedakt 6'
Superoctav 2'
Sesquialtra, II rks
Mixtur, IV rks
Cornett, III rks (discant)
Trompett 8' (divided)

ECHO/OBERWERK [Man. III]
Grosgedakt 8'

POSITIV/UNTERWERK [Man. II]
Bourdun 8'
Flautraversier 8' (discant)
Principal 4'
Flauto douce 4'
Salicional 4'
Quint 3'
Superoctav 2'
Quintflaut 1 1/2'
Cymbel, III rks
Clarong Baβ 4' ("halbe clavier")
Hubois 8' (discant)
Vox Humana 8'
Tremolant

Kleingedakt 4'
Octav 2'
Vox angelica Baβ 1' [sic]
Carlion [Carillon] IIrks (discant)
Cymbal IIrks
Klein trompet 8' (discant)
Tremolant

PEDAL
Subbass 16'
Prästant 8'
Violdigamba Baβ 8'
Rohrflautten Baβ 8'
Mixtur [composition not given]
Posaune Baβ 16'
Trompetten Baβ 8'
Clarong Baβ 4'

This stoplist is taken from the original contract, cited in Oskar Gottlieb Blarr and Theodor Kersken, *Orgelstadt Düsseldorf* (Düsseldorf, 1982). It is not stated what, if any, alterations might have been made in the century before Brahms came to Düsseldorf, although at some unknown time, probably in the late nineteenth century, the compass of the pedal was increased from twenty notes to twenty-seven notes. This organ was damaged in World War I and extensively rebuilt and electrified in 1929. It was entirely replaced in 1977 by Firma Oberlinger, with only four König stops being retained.

St. Peter's Cathedral [St. Petri Dom], Bremen

On Good Friday in 1868, six movements of Brahms's *Deutsches Requiem* (minus the fifth movement, composed shortly thereafter) were performed at the Bremen Cathedral, where Brahms's friend Karl Reinthaler was organist. Brahms conducted, and his Hamburg friend Julius Stockhausen was the baritone soloist. For this occasion, Brahms added an organ part, subsequently printed with the full score, and he later commented to his old teacher Marxsen on the necessity of the organ in this work. The completed Requiem, along with the *Triumphlied* (likewise containing an organ part), was performed there in 1871, also on Good Friday, with Brahms again conducting.[3]

In 1849, an organ was completed for Bremen Cathedral by Johann Friedrich Schulze, replacing a Schnitger organ that had been rebuilt several times. Schulze, while grounded in the older Thuringian tradition of robust choruses, imitative Gambas, and gentle Gedackts, also espoused some of the newer theories of pipe scaling promulgated by theorists such as J. G. Töpfer. The British organist Edward John Hopkins, who visited it in 1852, found the effect of the Bremen organ "exceedingly solemn, grand, or soothing, according to whether I used the 16 and 8 ft. diapasons, the full organ, or the Flutes and Gedackts."[4] This may be the most modern organ Brahms had heard up to this point.

HAUPTWERK [Man. I]

Bordun 32'
Principal 16'
Bordun 16'
Principal 8'
Gambe 8'
Gedact 8'
Hohlflöte 8'
Quinte 6'
Octave 4'
Flöte 4'

BRUSTWERK [Man. II]

Bordun 32' (from tenor G)
Bordun 16'
Principal 8'
Salicional 8'
Gedact 8'
Flöte 8'
Octave 4'
Spitzflöte 4'
Quinte 3' & Octave 2'
Mixtur, V rks

Quinte 3' & Octave 2'
Cornett, IV rks
Mixtur, V rks
Cymbel, III rks
Trompete 16' [free reed]
Trompete 8' [free reed]

PEDAL
Principal 32'
Quintenbaβ 24'
Principalbaβ 16'
Majorbaβ 16'
Violon 16'
Subbaβ 16'
Quinte 12'
Octavbaβ 8'
Gedactbaβ 8'
Flötenbaβ 8'
Violoncello 8'
Octave 4'
Mixtur, V rks
Posaune 32' [free reed]
Posaune 16' [free reed]
Reim 16' [reed; wooden tongues]
Trompete 8' [free reed; changed to striking reed in 1855]

Scharf, III rks
Physharmonica 8' [free reed]

OBERWERK [Man. III, enclosed]
Lieblich Gedact 16'
Geigenprincipal 8'
Lieblich Gedact 8'
Harmonica 8'
Terpodion 8'
Flauto traverso 8'
Flageoletto 8'
Geigenprincipal 4'
Flauto traverso 4'
Zartflöte 4'
Quint 3' & Octave 2'
Scharf, III rks
Aeoline 8' [free reed]

This stoplist is as recorded in the *Neue Zeitschrift für Musik* (1849) and cited in Wolfram Hackel, "Die Schulze-Orgel im St. Petri Dom zu Bremen," in *Die Orgeln im St. Petri Dom zu Bremen* (Berlin, 2002). By the middle of the nineteenth century, German organs were beginning to have full-fledged expressive divisions and some of the newer stops such as free reeds (but the "Terpodion" was simply a soft flue stop of unorthodox construction, introduced earlier by Schulze). In 1855, this organ was rebuilt with Barker-machine action and some minor tonal alterations. It was replaced by Wilhelm Sauer in 1894, retaining only the casework and the pedal 32' principal.

Pauline Viardot Salon, Baden-Baden

In 1863, one of Clara Schumann's friends, the Parisian diva Pauline Viardot, moved to Baden-Baden with her family, and encouraged by Pauline, Clara purchased a modest summer home there also. The Viardots had brought with them their 1851 Cavaillé-Coll salon organ, which was subsequently featured in musicales held at their home. Upon attending one of these, Clara wrote to Brahms that she wished she also had an organ in her home, so that Brahms could play it when he came to visit. Brahms spent part of the summers of 1864, 1866, and 1869 in Baden-Baden. He also knew the Viardots and is said to have attended some of their musicales. He thus may have heard the organ that Clara so admired, although he is not known to have mentioned it—which is a pity, because it was surely the only French organ he is likely to have ever heard.

GRAND-ORGUE EXPRESSIF
Bourdon 16' (treble)
Flûte harmonique 8'
Flûte octaviante 4'
Octavin 2'
Trompette 8' (divided)
Basson/Hautbois 8' (divided)

PÉDALE
Bourdon 16'
Flûte 8'

RÉCIT
Principal 8'
Viole de gambe 8'
Bourdon 8'
Voix celeste 8'
Gambe 4'
Doublette 2'

This stoplist is as recorded by Carolyn Shuster-Fournier in her detailed monograph, *Les orgues de salon d'Aristide Cavaillé-Coll* (Paris, 1997). The Viardots fled to London in 1870 because of the Franco-Prussian war and returned to Paris in 1872, bringing the organ back from Baden-Baden. Louis Viardot died in 1883, and the following year Pauline moved to a smaller apartment and sold the organ to the Church of Notre-Dame in Melun, where it remains in use, although somewhat altered.

Gesellschaft der Musikfreunde, Vienna

Although it is always possible that Brahms could have heard organs elsewhere in Vienna during his long residence there, the only one that he is known for certain to have heard was the 1872 Friedrich Ladegast instrument in the Grosser Saal of the Gesellschaft der Musikfreunde, of which he was director from 1872 to 1875. Although contracted for by Bruckner and a committee three years prior to Brahms's appointment, the organ was first used in Brahms's inaugural concert, and Brahms was present at its official dedication recital shortly afterward. Subsequently, Brahms would have heard this state-of-the-art organ a number of times in concerts that he conducted or attended, although usually only in its accompanimental role. It is possible that he also was in attendance on December 2, 1882, when Josef Labor gave a recital on it that included his *O Traurigkeit* settings. The concert hall was then as now noted for its warm acoustics, which doubtless complemented the sound of the organ.

HAUPTWERK [Man. I]
1st Division
Principal 16'
Principal 8'
Octave 4'
Gemshorn 4'
Flauto minor 4'
Doublette 3' & 2'
Cornett, III–IV rks
Mixtur, III–IV rks
Trompete 8'
2nd Division
Bordun 16'
Gamba 8'
Rohrflöte 8'

OBERWERK [Man. II]
1st Division
Fugara 4'
Doppelflöte 4'
Octavflöte 4'
Nasat 2 2/3'
Waldflöte 2'
Progressio harmonica, II–IV rks
Clarinett 8' [free reed]
2nd Division
Quintatön 16'
Geigenprinzipal 8'
Salicional 8'
Flauto harmonique 8'
Doppelflöte 8'

Flauto amabile 8'
Piffaro 8'
Nasat 5 1/3'
Doublette 4' & 2'

PEDAL
1st Division
Principalbaβ 32'
Principalbaβ 16'
Baβquinte 10 2/3'
Octavbaβ 8'
Baβquinte 5 1/3'
Octavbaβ 4'
Posaune 16'
Trompete 8'
Clarinet 8'
2nd Division
Violon 16'
Subbaβ 16'
Cello 8'
Baβflöte 8'

Gedeckt 8'

ECHOWERK [Man. III](enclosed)
Lieblich Gedeckt 16'
Viola d'amour 8'
Lieblich Gedeckt 8'
Unda Maris 8'
Flauto dolce 8'
Piffaro 4'
Zartflöte 4'
Violine 2'
Harmonia aetheria, II–IV rks
Oboe 8' [free reed]

This disposition is recorded in Alois Forer, *Orgeln in Österreich* (Vienna, 1973). It is virtually identical to descriptions found in other sources. This organ had Barker-machine action and several combination pedals, as well as a crescendo mechanism and—interestingly—a *prolongement* device on the Echo manual. It was rebuilt and enlarged in 1907 by Gebrüder Rieger, and a fourth manual division on higher pressure was added in 1948. In 1968, it was completely rebuilt and enlarged to one hundred stops by Walcker. However, the classical gilded façade (with the original tin front pipes) still appears much as it did during Brahms's lifetime.

Evangelical Lutheran Church, Vienna

It must be said at the outset that there is no direct evidence that Brahms ever heard this organ, built in 1808 by the Viennese craftsman Friedrich Deutschmann and possibly rebuilt by the same firm in 1821. However, Brahms had many friends among the Lutheran community in Vienna, including Gustav Porubsky, the pastor of the church, whom Brahms had known in Hamburg, and whose daughter Bertha had sung in his Frauenchor there.[5] Although not known as a churchgoer, especially in his later years, Brahms may have attended the church and heard the organ on some occasion, even if only at a wedding or funeral of one of these friends. His own funeral service was held there, suggesting that he maintained some connection with the Lutheran Church. The church's online history boasts that this organ was played at various times by Vogler, von Weber, Meyerbeer, and even Bruckner. If Brahms had ever played it, that fact would doubtless have also been recorded; thus it is probably safe to assume that he never did.

HAUPTWERK [Man. I]
Principal 8'
Viola da Gamba 8'

OBERWERK [Man. II]
Coppel 8'
Principal 4'

Flauto 8'
Octave 4'
Fugara 4'
Quinte 2 2/3'
Superoctave 2'
Mixtur, IV rks
Hautbois 8' (discant)
Fagotto 8' (bass)

Dulciana 4'
Octave 2'
Superoctave 1'
Vox Humana 8'
Tremulant

PEDAL
Bordun 16' (added 1821 or 1907?)
Subbaβ 16'
Principalbaβ 8'
Violon 8'
Octavebaβ 8'
Octav 4' (added 1821 or 1907?)
Posaune 16'
Trompete 8'

The 1808 stoplist is cited in Günter Lade, *Orgeln in Wien* (Vienna: G. Lade, 1990); a slightly different version, presumably reflecting later alterations, is recorded by E. J. Hopkins and published in Hopkins and Rimbault, *The Organ, Its History, and Construction* (London, 1855). The history of the organ since then is somewhat obscure, although alterations in 1821 and 1907 are recorded. However, the specification of the organ in 1907 (when the church was substantially remodeled), cited by Lade, is virtually the same as the original and is the version given here. Both the 1855 and 1907 versions of the stoplist give the pedal compass as CC to A (twenty-two notes). The organ now occupying the Deutschmann case was built in 1965 by Walcker.

St. Nicholas Church [Nikolauskirche], Bad Ischl

In 1888 a new organ was built for this church by Matthäus Mauracher of Salzburg, having thirty-three stops on three manuals and pedal. While Brahms may possibly have heard this organ on some occasion, no further description of it has been found. It would, however, have been similar in its tonal resources to other German or Austrian Romantic organs of the late nineteenth century. Mauracher replaced it in 1909 by a larger organ that utilized the older casework.

APPENDIX C

Organ Transcriptions of Works by Brahms

Although some of Brahms's organ works have been transcribed for piano and various instrumental ensembles, his piano, chamber, and orchestral works were not as popular as transcriptions for the organ as were those of certain other composers (notably Mozart, Schubert, Beethoven, and Wagner). Wallace Goodrich transcribed all four movements of the Second Symphony (op. 73) for Aeolian organ player rolls, but this transcription is not believed to have been published. Edwin H. Lemare approached this feat with his transcriptions of opp. 80 (somewhat abridged) and 81, as, more recently, did Klaus Uwe Ludwig, with a more complete transcription of op. 80, and Lionel Rogg, who transcribed Opus 56 and the last movement of Opus 98. Most other organ transcriptions from Brahms are of shorter and lighter works.

As early as 1895, Horatio Parker published two short organ transcriptions, and two years later, Brahms's publisher, Simrock, began to publish (and may even have commissioned) a series of transcriptions for organ from Brahms's orchestral, chamber, piano, and vocal compositions by the British recitalist Edwin H. Lemare. A decade later, three more transcriptions by Alfred J. Silver, another by Lemare, one by Reginald Goss-Custard, and one by Healey Willan had been added to Simrock's catalog. Interestingly, all of the transcriptions in the Simrock catalog were done by Britons. At some time during the first decade of the twentieth century, Rieter-Biedermann published organ transcriptions of three choral works, but despite the general popularity of transcriptions as recital pieces in the early twentieth century, the incidence of subsequent Brahms transcriptions has been slight.

By Horatio Parker [in *A Collection of Organ Arrangements* (G. Schirmer, 1895)]
    Op. 45. *In modo di marcia* (2nd movement of *Deutsches Requiem*)
    Op. 49, No. 4. *Cradle Song* (*Wiegenlied*)
By Edwin H. Lemare [Simrock]
    Op. 11. *Scherzo* (from *Serenade*), 1898
    Op. 80. *Akademische Festouvertüre*, 1898
    Op. 81. *Tragische Ouvertüre*, 1913
    Op. 96, No. 2. *Wir wandelten, wir zwei zusammen*, 1898 (?)
    Op. 101. *Andante Grazioso* from *Piano Trio in C Minor*, 1897
    Op. 108. *Adagio* from *Sonata in D Minor* for violin, 1897
    Op. 116. *Intermezzo No. 4*, 1897
    Op. 116. *Intermezzo No. 6*, 1897
    Op. 117. *Intermezzo No. 1*, 1897

WoO. *Hungarian Dance No. 1*, 1897
WoO. *Hungarian Dance No. 5*, 1897
By Ebenezer Prout [Augener & Co., ca. 1900]
   Op. 12. *Ave Maria*
By Rudolf Bibl [Breitkopf & Härtel, ca. 1900; "Harmonium or Organ"]
   Op. 31, No. 1. *Wechsellied zum Tanze*
   Op. 31, No. 3. *Der Gang zum Liebchen*
By Healey Willan (listed as "H. Willau" in early catalogs) [Simrock, 1906]
   Op. 67. *Andante* from *String Quartet in B-flat Major*
By John E. West [Novello, 1906–1907]
   Op. 1. *Andante* from *Sonata in C major* for piano
   Op. 5. *Andante* from *Sonata in F minor* for piano
   Op. 45. *Deutsches Requiem*, Movements 1, 2, and 4
By Alfred J. Silver [Simrock, 1908]
   Op. 90. *Andante* from *Symphony in F Major*
   Op. 73. *Allegretto grazioso* from *Symphony in D Major*
   Op. 117. *Intermezzo No. 3*
By Reginald Goss-Custard [Simrock, 1908]
   Op. 49, No. 4. *Wiegenlied*
By Theodor Kirchner [Rieter-Biedermann, pre-1910]
   Op. 12. *Ave Maria*
By Rob. Schaab [Rieter-Biedermann, pre-1910]
   Op. 45. Two movements [4 & 5] from *Deutsches Requiem*
By Phillips [Rieter-Biedermann, pre-1910]
   Op. 45. Movement 1 from *Deutsches Requiem*
By James H. Rogers [in *Thirty Offertories for the Organ* (Oliver Ditson, 1914)]
   Op. 94, No. 4. *Sapphische Ode*
By Gordon Balch Nevin [Theodore Presser, 1917]
   Op. 94, No. 4. *Sapphic Ode*
By Fr. E. Thiele [Simrock, 1921, for violin and organ]
   Op. 108. *Adagio* from *Sonata in D Minor* for violin
By J. Stuart Archer [Paxton, 1929]
   Op. 71, No. 5. *Minnelied*
By Albert E. Weir [in *Symphonic Pieces for Organ* (Harcourt, Brace & Co., 1935)]
   Op. 11. *Serenade*
   Op. 73. *Allegretto Grazioso* from *Symphony in D Major*
By Albert C. Tysoe [Oxford University Press, 1940]
   Op. 98. *Andante moderato* from *Symphony in E. Minor*
By Clarence Kohlmann [in *Album of Duets for Piano and Organ* (Theodore Presser, 1943)]
   Op. 68. *Andante* from *First Symphony*
By N. Lindsay Norden [Associated Music Publishers, ca. 1950]
   Op. 68. *Andante sostenuto* from *Symphony in C Minor*
Transcriber unknown (possibly a pirated version of the Kirchner or Prout transcription) [Carl Fischer, 1958]
   Op. 12. *Ave Maria*
By Stainton deB. Taylor [Hinrichsen Edition, 1961]
   Op. 56. *Chorale and Three Variations* from *Variations on a Theme by Haydn*
By Homer Whitford [Lorenz Publishing Co., 1971]
   Op. 56. "*St. Anthony's Chorale*" from *Variations on a Theme of Haydn*

By Lionel Rogg
    Op. 56. *Variations on a Theme of Haydn* [United Music Publishers, 1994]
    Op. 98. *Finale (Chaconne)* from *Symphony in E Minor* [Éditions Delatour, 2004]
By Klaus Uwe Ludwig [Breitkopf & Härtel, 2003]
    Op. 80. *Academic Festival Overture*

The foregoing list, chronologically arranged by publication date, makes no pretense of being complete, particularly with regard to abbreviated excerpts or virtual note-for-note transcriptions of short piano pieces or songs occasionally appearing in "service music" collections. Compared with the plethora of pieces transcribed from Wagner (who, ironically, never wrote any actual organ music himself), it is rather slight—and indeed a bit surprising, considering the "organlike" sonorities that Brahms often incorporated into his symphonic works.

Notes

Chapter One

1. Walter Niemann, *Brahms* (New York: Alfred A. Knopf, 1929), p. 251.
2. H. William Hawke, "Lynnwood Farnam; His Life," *American Organist* 47/7 (July 1964): 22.
3. E. Power Biggs, preface to *Eleven Chorale Preludes, a Comprehensive Edition* (New York: Mercury Music, 1949).
4. Edwin Evans, *Handbook to the Pianoforte Works of Johannes Brahms* (London: Reeves, 1912), p. 298.
5. Gotthold Frotscher, *Geschichte des Orgelspiels und der Orgelkomposition* (Berlin: Merseberger, 1959), pp. 1214–1215.
6. Review of Biggs edition in *American Organist* 33/1 (January 1950): 10.
7. Marilou Kratzenstein, *Survey of Organ Literature and Editions* (Ames: Iowa State University Press, 1980), p. 49.
8. Niemann, *Brahms*. For a translation of Schumann's laudatory article, see p. 43.
9. John M. Burk, *Clara Schumann. A Romantic Biography* (New York: Random House, 1940), p. 234.
10. Gerd Nauhaus, ed., *The Marriage Diaries of Robert and Clara Schumann,* trans. Peter Ostwald (Boston: Northeastern University Press, 1993), p. 8.
11. Cited in introduction to Robert Schumann, *The Complete Works for Organ and Pedal Piano,* ed. Wayne Leupold (New York: McAfee Music, 1978), p. 8.
12. Nauhaus, *Marriage Diaries,* p. 133.
13. Ibid., p. 193.
14. Cited in Joan Chissell, *Schumann Piano Music* (Seattle: University of Washington Press, 1972), p. 59.
15. Cited in Andreas Seiling, "Der Dresdner Hoforganist Johann Gottlob Schneider," in *Zur deutschen Orgelmusik des 19. Jahrhunderts,* ed. Hermann J. Busch and Michael Heinemann (Sinzig, Germany: Studio, 1998), p. 187.
16. Cited in Johannes Rossner, "Robert Schumanns Bezüge zur Orgel—Neue Erkentnisse," *Freiburger Studien zur Orgel Nr. 5.* (Altenburg, Germany: Verlag Kaus-Jürgen Kamprad, 1997), pp. 41–42.

17. Barbara Harbach, "Editor's Note" to Clara Schumann, *Prelude and Fugue for Organ* (Pullman, WA: Vivace, 1993).

18. Victor Basch, *Schumann: A Life of Suffering* (New York: Tudor, 1936), p. 178.

19. Burkhard Meischein, "'Nach Dichterweise ausgeführt': Robert Schumanns Werke für Orgel oder Pedalklavier," in *Zur deutschen Orgelmusik des 19. Jahrhunderts*, ed. Hermann J. Busch and Michael Heinemann (Sinzig, Germany: Studio, 1998), p. 195.

20. Max Kalbeck, *Johannes Brahms* (Berlin: Deutsches Brahms-Gesellschaft, 1915), vol. 2, p. 323.

21. Berthold Litzmann, ed., *Clara Schumann Johannes Brahms Briefe an den Jahren 1853–1896* (Leipzig: Breitkopf & Härtel, 1927), vol. 1, p. 32.

22. Letter from Wm. A. Little, February 9, 2005.

23. Heinrich Reimann, *Johannes Brahms*, 3rd ed. (Berlin, 1903), p. 21, quoted in Vernon Gotwals, "Brahms and the Organ," *Music/The A.G.O.-R.C.C.O. Magazine* 4/4 (April 1970).

24. Litzmann, *Schumann-Brahms Briefe*, vol. 1, pp. 183–184.

25. Ibid., vol. 1, p. 187.

26. Ibid., vol. 1, pp. 187–188.

27. Christian Ahrens, ed., *Zur Geschichte der Konzertsaalorgel in Deutschland* (Frankfurt am Main: Erwin Bochinsky, 1999), p. 17.

28. Andreas Moser, ed., *Johannes Brahms in Briefwechsel mit Joseph Joachim*, vol. 1 (Berlin, 1908), p. 139.

29. Michael Musgrave, *The Music of Brahms* (Oxford: Clarendon, 1996), p. 296.

30. Wm. A. Little, "Brahms and the Organ—Redivivus," in *The Organist as Scholar: Essays in Memory of Russell Saunders* (Stuyvesant, NY: Pendragon, 1994), p. 287.

31. Berthold Litzmann, *Clara Schumann: Ein Künstlerleben* (Leipzig: Breitkopf & Härtel, 1907), vol. 2, p. 282.

32. Cited in David Brodbeck, "The Brahms-Joachim Counterpoint Exchange, or, Robert, Clara, and 'the Best Harmony between Jos. and Joh,'" in David Brodbeck, ed., *Brahms Studies*, vol. 1 (Lincoln: University of Nebraska Press, 1994), p. 73.

33. Burk, *Clara Schumann*, p. 286.

34. Oskar Gottlieb Blarr and Theodor Kersken, *Orgelstadt Düsseldorf* (Düsseldorf: Tritsch Verlag, 1982), pp. 27–29.

35. Roland Eberlin, "Dispositionanalyse," *Ars Organi* 46/4 (December 1998): 194–202.

36. Litzmann, *Schumann-Brahms Briefe*, vol. 1, p. 197.

37. Otto Biba, "Orgel und Orgelspiel in Leben und Schaffen von Johannes Brahms," *Ars Organi* 31/4 (December 1983): 215–221.

38. Quoted in Niemann, *Brahms*, p. 69.

39. Sophie Drinker, *Brahms and His Women's Choruses* (Merion, PA: Sophie Drinker, 1952), p. 74.

40. Richard Barth, ed., *Johannes Brahms im Briefwechsel mit Julius Otto Grimm*, p. 62, cited in Little, "Brahms and the Organ" and Gotwals, "Brahms and the Organ."

41. Ibid., p. 73, cited in Little, "Brahms and the Organ."

42. W. L. Sumner, "Organs of St. Michael's Church, Hamburg," *Organ* 26/102 (October 1946): 82.

43. Jacob Adlung, *Musica Mechanica Organoedi* (Berlin: Friedrich Wilhelm Birnstiel, 1768), pp. 241–242.

44. Drinker, *Women's Choruses*, p. 20.

45. Little, "Brahms and the Organ," p. 284.

46. Günter Seggermann, *Geschichte der Orgeln in der Hamburger Hauptkirche St. Petri vom 16. Jahrhundert bis Heute* (Lauffen, Germany: Orgelbau-Fachverlag Rensch, 1992).

47. Drinker, *Women's Choruses*, p. 22.
48. Ibid., p. 23.
49. Ibid., p. 28.
50. Ibid., p. 41.
51. Ibid., p. 30.
52. Ibid., p. 37.
53. Karl Geiringer, *Brahms, His Life and Work* (New York: Doubleday, 1961), p. 73.
54. Michael Musgrave, *A Brahms Reader* (New Haven, CT: Yale University Press, 2000), pp. 162–163.
55. Ernst Kern, "Johannes Brahms und die Orgel," *Zur Orgelmusik im 19, Jahrhundert* (Innsbruck: Musikverlag Helbling, 1983), p. 129.
56. Litzmann, *Schumann-Brahms Briefe*, vol. 1, p. 256.
57. Ibid., p. 408.
58. Cited in Jan Swafford, *Johannes Brahms: A Biography* (New York: Alfred A. Knopf, 1997), p. 239.
59. Ibid., pp. 230, 274.
60. Carolyn Shuster-Fournier, *Les Orgues de Salon d'Aristide Cavaillé-Coll* (Paris: L'Orgue Cahiers et Memoires, 1997), pp. 25–40.
61. Burk, *Clara Schumann*, chapter 24.
62. Litzmann, *Schumann-Brahms Briefe*, vol. 1, p. 474.
63. April Fitzlyon, *The Price of Genius: A Life of Pauline Viardot* (London: John Calder, 1964), p. 381.
64. Shuster-Fournier, *Les Orgues*, p. 39.
65. Litzmann, *Schumann-Brahms Briefe*, vol. 1, p. 325.
66. Gotwals, "Brahms and the Organ," p. 41.
67. Kern, "Brahms und Orgel," p. 129.
68. Max Rudolf, "A Recently Discovered Composer-Annotated Score of the Brahms Requiem," *Bach* 7/4 (October 1976): 2–13.
69. Siegfried Ochs, "Encounter with Bruckner and Brahms," *American Choral Review* 14/4 (October 1972): 12–15.
70. Joachim Walter, *"This Heaving Ocean of Tones": Nineteenth-Century Organ Registration Practice at St. Marien, Lübeck* (Göteborg: Göteborg University, 2000), p. 25.
71. Gotwals, "Brahms and the Organ," p. 41.
72. Alois Forer, *Orgeln in Österreich* (Vienna: Verlag Anton Schroll, 1983), p. 58.
73. Hermann J. Busch, "Die Orgeln Mendelssohns, Liszts und Brahms," in *Proceedings of the Göteborg International Organ Academy, 1994* (Göteborg: Göteborg University, 1995), p. 245.
74. E-mail message from Alexander Koschel, May 7, 2003.
75. Emile Rupp, *Die Entwicklungsgeschichte der Orgelbaukunst* (Einseideln, Switzerland: Benziger, 1929), p. 146.
76. Little, "Brahms and the Organ," p. 288.
77. Rudolf Quoika, *Die Orgelwelt um Anton Bruckner* (Ludwigsburg, Germany: Verlag E. F. Walcker, 1966), p. 30.
78. Walter Ladegast, ed., *Friedrich Ladegast, Der Orgelbauer von Weissenfels* (Stockach am Bodensee, Germany: Weidling Verlag, 1998), p. 96.
79. Busch, "Orgeln Mendelssohn," p. 246.
80. Cited in Little, "Brahms and the Organ," p. 298.
81. Niemann, *Brahms*, p. 103.
82. Cited in Jacques Barzun, ed., *Pleasures of Music* (New York: Viking, 1951), p. 596.
83. Musgrave, *Music of Brahms*, p. 303.

84. Hellmut Federhofer, "Georg Friedrich Händels Oratorium 'Saul' in der Bearbeitung von Johannes Brahms," in *Brahms-Kongress Wien 1983. Kongressbericht* (Tutzing, Germany: Hans Schneider, 1988), p. 133.
85. Busch, "Orgeln Mendelssohns."
86. David Sanger, "My Fascination with the Sources—4," *Organists' Review* 86/4 (November 2000): 364–365.
87. Musgrave, *Brahms Reader*, p. 125, citing C. V. Stanford.
88. Quoika, "Orgelwelt," p. 57.
89. Gotwals, "Brahms and the Organ," p. 42.
90. A. Maczewski, in George Grove, ed., *A Dictionary of Music and Musicians*, vol. 1 (London: Macmillan, 1889), p. 270.
91. Raymond Kendall, "Brahms's Knowledge of Bach's Music," *PAMS*, 1941, cited by Gotwals.
92. Russell Stinson, *J. S. Bach's Great Eighteen Organ Chorales* (New York: Oxford University Press, 2001), p. 123.
93. Ethel Smyth, *Impressions That Remained* (New York: Alfred A. Knopf, 1946), p. 238.
94. Klaus Sonnleitner, "Die Restaurierung der Kaiserjubiläumsorgel in Bad Ischl," *Osterreichisches Orgelforum* 1–3 (1993): 489.
95. Ibid., p. 490.
96. Little, "Brahms and the Organ," p. 276.
97. Robert Haven Schauffler, *The Unknown Brahms* (New York: Crown, 1940), p. 204.
98. Quoika, "Orgelwelt," p. 79.
99. Harry W. Gay, "Study of Brahms' Works Expanded by Vivid Detail," *Diapason* 50/4 (March 1959): 38.
100. Quoted in Gotwals, "Brahms and the Organ," p. 45.
101. Otto Biba, preface to Heinrich von Herzogenberg, *Sechs Choräle für Orgel, Op. 67* (Vienna: Ludwig Doblinger, 1976).
102. Little, "Brahms and the Organ," p. 291.
103. Kurt Hofmann, *Die Bibliothek von Johannes Brahms* (Hamburg: Musikhandel Wagner, 1974).
104. Martin Weyer, *Die Orgelwerke Max Regers* (Wilhelmshaven, Germany: Florian Noetzel Verlag, 1989), p. 14, cited by Little.
105. Walter Frisch, "The 'Brahms Fog': On Tracing Brahmsian Influences," *American Brahms Society Newsletter* 7/1 (Spring 1989): 1–3.

Chapter Two

1. Hugh Wood, "A Photograph of Brahms," in *The Cambridge Companion to Brahms* (Cambridge: Cambridge University Press, 1999), p. 285.
2. Gustav Jenner, "Johannes Brahms as Man, Teacher, and Artist," in *Brahms and His World* (Princeton, NJ: Princeton University Press, 1990), p. 189.
3. Nora Bickley, ed. and trans., *Letters from and to Joseph Joachim* (London: Macmillan, 1914), p. 121.
4. Joachim Dorfmüller, preface to *Edvard Grieg: Choralbearbeitungen und Fugen für Orgel* (Frankfurt: C. F. Peters, 2002).
5. David Brodbeck, "The Brahms-Joachim Counterpoint Exchange; or, Robert, Clara, and 'the Best Harmony between Jos. and Joh.,'" in *Brahms Studies*, vol. 1 (Lincoln: University of Nebraska Press, 1994), p. 33.
6. Siegfried Mauser, "Brahms und die vorklassische Instrumentalmusic," in *Brahms-Kongress Wien 1983. Kongressbericht* (Tutzing, Germany: Hans Schneider, 1988), p. 368.

7. Michael Musgrave, *The Music of Brahms* (Oxford: Clarendon, 1996), p. 53.
8. Malcolm MacDonald, *The Master Musicians: Brahms* (New York: Oxford University Press, 2001), p. 175.
9. Musgrave, *Music of Brahms*, pp. 295, 297, 298, 299.
10. Max Kalbeck, *Johannes Brahms*, vol. 1 (Vienna: Wiener Verlag, 1904), p. 264.
11. Cited in MacDonald, *Master Musicians: Brahms*, p. 150.
12. Virginia Hancock, "Brahms's Early Music Studies and His Sacred Choral Music," *American Organist* 17/5 (May 1983): 41.
13. Musgrave, *Music of Brahms*, pp. 82–84.
14. Jan Swafford, *Johannes Brahms: A Biography* (New York: Alfred A. Knopf, 1997), p. 151.
15. Ibid., p. 619.
16. Charles S. Terry, "Bach Gesellschaft," in *Grove's Dictionary of Music and Musicians*, 3rd ed. (New York: Macmillan, 1935), pp. 186–187.
17. Robert Ricks, "A Possible Source for a Brahms Ground," *American Brahms Society Newsletter* 23/1 (Spring 2005): 1.
18. Musgrave, *Music of Brahms*, p. 225.
19. Brodbeck, "Brahms-Joachim," p. 74 fn.
20. Daniel Beller-McKenna, "Brahms, the Bible, and Robert Schumann," *American Brahms Society Newsletter* 13/2 (Autumn 1995): 1–4.
21. MacDonald, *Master Musicians: Brahms*, p. 380.
22. Russell Stinson, *Bach: The Orgelbüchlein* (New York: Schirmer, 1996), p. 155.
23. Daniel Beller-McKenna, "Brahms's Motet 'Es ist das Heil uns kommen her' and the 'Innermost Essence of Music,'" in *Brahms Studies* (Lincoln: University of Nebraska Press, 1998), p. 35.
24. Robert Pascall, "Brahms's *Missa Canonica* and Its Recomposition in His Motet 'Warum' Op. 74 No. 1," in *Brahms 2: Biographical, Documentary and Analytical Studies* (Cambridge: Cambridge University Press, 1987), p. 121.
25. Hancock, "Brahms's Early Music Studies," pp. 40–43.
26. Percy M. Young, *The Choral Tradition* (New York: W. W. Norton, 1971), p. 244.
27. Alec Robertson, *Requiem: Music of Mourning and Consolation* (New York: Frederick A. Praeger, 1967), p. 179.
28. Musgrave, *Music of Brahms*, p. 82.
29. Daniel Beller-McKenna, "The Scope and Significance of the Choral Music," in *The Cambridge Companion to Brahms* (Cambridge: Cambridge University Press, 1999), p. 181.
30. Musgrave, *Music of Brahms*, pp. 68, 313.
31. Robert Haven Schauffler, *The Unknown Brahms* (New York: Crown, 1940), p. 339.

Chapter Three

1. Cited in Jan Swafford, *Johannes Brahms* (New York: Alfred A. Knopf, 1997), p. 420.
2. Malcolm MacDonald, "'Veiled Symphonies?' The Concertos," in *The Cambridge Companion to Brahms* (Cambridge: Cambridge University Press, 1999), pp. 158–160.
3. Malcolm MacDonald, *The Master Musicians: Brahms* (New York: Oxford University Press, 2001), p. 315.
4. Robert Haven Schauffler, *The Unknown Brahms* (New York: Crown, 1940), p. 19.
5. Swafford, *Johannes Brahms*, p. 379.
6. Robert Pascall, "The Editor's Brahms," in *The Cambridge Companion to Brahms* (Cambridge: Cambridge University Press, 1999), pp. 250–251.

7. George S. Bozarth, "Brahms's Posthumous Compositions and Arrangements: Editorial Problems and Questions of Authenticity," in *Brahms 2: Biographical, Documentary and Analytical Studies* (Cambridge: Cambridge University Press, 1997), p. 59.

8. Michael Musgrave, *The Music of Brahms* (Oxford: Clarendon, 1996), p. 81.

9. Ibid., p. 201.

10. William Horne, "Brahms's Düsseldorf Suite Study and His Intermezzo, Op. 116, No. 2," *Musical Quarterly* 73/2 (1989): 249–283.

11. Swafford, *Johannes Brahms*, p. 449.

12. Karl Geiringer, *Brahms: His Life and Work* (New York: Doubleday, 1961), p. 131.

13. MacDonald, *Master Musicians: Brahms*, pp. 338–340.

14. Berthold Litzmann, ed., *Clara Schumann Johannes Brahms Briefe aus den Jahren 1853–1896* (Leipzig: Breitkopf & Härtel, 1927), vol. 1, p. 369.

15. Otto Biba, preface to *Messe für sechstimmige gemischten Chor und Continuo* (Vienna: Doblinger, 1984).

16. Pascall, "Editor's Brahms," p. 251.

17. Daniel Beller-McKenna, "The Scope and Significance of the Choral Music," in *The Cambridge Companion to Brahms* (Cambridge: Cambridge University Press, 1999), p. 174.

18. Cited in Timothy P. Kinsella, "From Königgrätz to My Lai: Brahms *in tempore belli*," *American Brahms Society Newsletter* 23/2 (November 2005): 3.

19. Virginia Hancock, "Brahms's Early Music Studies and His Sacred Choral Music," *American Organist* 17/5 (May 1983): 42.

20. Geiringer, *Brahms, His Life and Work*, p. 163.

21. MacDonald, *Master Musicians: Brahms*, p. 1.

22. Musgrave, *Music of Brahms*, caption of plate 3.

23. Ibid., p. 170.

24. Ibid., p. 255.

25. Camilla Cai, "Brahms's Exercises for Piano: Rethinking Their Place and Purpose," *American Brahms Society Newsletter* 20/1 (Spring 2002): 1–4.

26. Cited in David Pacun, "Brahms and the Sense of Ending," *American Brahms Society Newsletter* 22/1 (Spring 2004): 1–4.

27. Daniel Beller-McKenna, "Reminiscence in Brahms's Late Intermezzi," *American Brahms Society Newsletter* 22/2 (Autumn 2004): 6–9.

28. Pacun, "Sense of Ending," p. 3.

Chapter Four

1. Berthold Litzmann, *Clara Schumann: Ein Kunstlerleben* (Leipzig: Breitkopf & Härtel, 1907–1910), vol. 2, p. 404.

2. Berthold Litzmann, ed., *Clara Schumann Johannes Brahms Briefe aus den Jahren 1853–1896* (Leipzig: Breitkopf & Härtel, 1927), vol. 1, p. 73.

3. Letter to Joseph Joachim, cited in David Brodbeck, "The Brahms-Joachim Counterpoint Exchange," in *Brahms Studies*, vol. 1 (Lincoln: University of Nebraska Press, 1994), p. 34.

4. Nora Bickley, ed. and trans., *Letters from and to Joseph Joachim* (London: Macmillan, 1914), p. 120.

5. Quoted in Styra Avins, ed., *Johannes Brahms Life and Letters* (New York: Oxford University Press, 1997), p. 137.

6. Letter to Joseph Joachim, cited in Wm. A. Little, "Brahms and the Organ—Redivivus," in *The Organist as Scholar* (Stuyvesant, NY: Pendragon, 1994), p. 281.

7. Brodbeck, "Brahms-Joachim," p. 60.

8. Cited in Hans Gal, ed., *The Musician's World: Letters of Great Composers* (New York: Thames & Hudson, 1978), p. 304.

9. Litzmann, *Clara Schumann*, vol. 2, p. 412.

10. Ibid.

11. Andreas Moser, ed., *Johannes Brahms in Briefwechsel mit Joseph Joachim* (Berlin: Deutsches Brahms-Gesellschaft, 1912), vol. 1, p. 143.

12. Avins, *Brahms Life and Letters*, p. 133.

13. Max Kalbeck, cited in Vernon Gotwals, "Brahms and the Organ," *American Organist* 4/4 (April 1970): 45.

14. George Bozarth, "Brahms's Organ Works: A New Critical Edition," *American Organist* 22/6 (June 1988): 51.

15. Susan Testa, "A Holograph of Johannes Brahms's Fugue in A-flat Minor for Organ," *Current Musicology* 19 (1975): 101.

16. Ibid., p. 95.

17. Litzmann, *Schumann-Brahms Briefe*, vol. 1, p. 460.

18. Carolyn Shuster-Fournier, *Les Orgues de Salon d'Aristide Cavaillé-Coll* (Paris: L'Orgue Cahiers et Memoires, 1997), p. 29.

19. John Daverio, *Crossing Paths: Schubert, Schumann, and Brahms* (New York: Oxford University Press, 2002), p. 110.

20. Hermann J. Busch, "Die Orgelwerke von Johannes Brahms," *Ars Organi* 11/22 (July 1963): 583.

21. Brodbeck, "Brahms-Joachim," p. 74.

22. Gwilym Beechey, "The Organ Music of Brahms," *American Organist* 17/5 (May 1983): 44.

23. Jacques van Oortmerssen, "Johannes Brahms and 19th-Century Performance Practice in a Historical Perspective," in *Proceedings of the Göteborg International Organ Academy 1994* (Göteborg: Göteborg University, 1995), p. 362.

24. Arthur Birkby, "Lean Brahms Organ Output Other Than Opus 122 Discussed," *Diapason* 49/12 (November 1958): 9.

25. Malcolm MacDonald, *The Master Musicians: Brahms* (New York: Oxford University Press, 2001), p. 93.

26. Günter Hartmann, "Zur Orgelfuge in as-Moll von Johannes Brahms," *Brahms-Studien, Band* 7 (1987): 9.

27. W. Wright Roberts, "Brahms: The Organ Works," *Music and Letters* 14/2 (April 1933): 105.

28. Quoted in Bozarth, "Brahms's Organ Works," p. 51.

29. Brodbeck, "Brahms-Joachim," p. 51.

30. Ibid., p. 67.

31. Jan Swafford, *Johannes Brahms: A Biography* (New York: Alfred A. Knopf, 1997), p. 157.

32. Brodbeck, "Brahms-Joachim," p. 51.

33. MacDonald, *Master Musicians: Brahms*, p. 92.

34. Beechey, "Organ Music," p. 43.

35. Bozarth, "Brahms's Organ Works," p. 51.

36. Robert Pascall, "Brahms's Solo Organ Works," *Royal College of Organists Journal* 3 (1995): 100.

37. MacDonald, *Master Musicians: Brahms*, p. 92.

38. Beechey, "Organ Music," p. 43.

39. Birkby, "Lean Brahms," p. 9.

40. Sophie Drinker, *Brahms and His Women's Choruses* (Merion, PA: Sophie Drinker, 1952), p. 74.

41. Ibid.

42. Litzmann, *Brahms-Schumann Briefe*, vol. 1, p. 223.
43. Bozarth, "Brahms's Organ Works," p. 53.
44. Max Kalbeck, ed., *Johannes Brahms: The Herzogenberg Correspondence*, trans. Hannah Bryant (New York: Da Capo, 1987), p. 52.
45. Litzmann, *Brahms-Schumann Briefe*, vol. 2, p. 9.
46. Bozarth, "Brahms's Organ Works," p. 53.
47. *Brahms Briefwechsel*, vol. 16, p. 51. Cited in Bozarth, "Brahms's Organ Works," p. 53.
48. *Brahms Briefwechsel*, vol. 14, cited in Pascall, "Brahms's Solo," p. 101.
49. Wilhelm Altman, ed., *Johannes Brahms im Briefwechsel mit Karl Reinthaler, Max Bruch, Hermann Dieters, Friedr. Heimfoeth, Karl Reinecke, Ernst Rudorff, Bernhard und Luise Scholz* (Berlin: Deutsche Brahms-Gesellschaft, 1908), p. 72.
50. Pascall, "Brahms's Solo," p. 102.
51. Relf Clark, "A Note on the Chorale Preludes of Ethel Smyth," *BIOS Journal* 29 (2005): 188–189.
52. Ethel Smyth, *Impressions That Remained* (New York: Alfred A. Knopf, 1946), p. 158.
53. Review in *American Organist* 32/1 (January 1949): 6.
54. Review in *Diapason* 40/3 (February 1949): 16.
55. Cited in MacDonald, *Master Musicians: Brahms*, p. 583.
56. Letter from Max Miller, October 31, 2006.

Chapter Five

1. Von Bülow is said to have been the originator of the "Three B's" quotation linking Brahms to Bach and Beethoven.
2. John M. Burk, *Clara Schumann: A Romantic Biography* (New York: Random House, 1940), p. 429.
3. Michael Musgrave, *The Music of Brahms* (Oxford: Clarendon, 1985), p. 264.
4. Karl Geiringer, *Brahms, His Life and Work* (New York: Doubleday, 1961), p. 175.
5. Bernard D. Sherman, "How Different Was Brahms's Playing Style from Our Own," in *Performing Brahms* (Cambridge: Cambridge University Press, 2003), p. 9.
6. Otto Biba, "Orgel und Orgelspiel im Leben und Schaffen von Johannes Brahms," *Ars Organi* 31/4 (December 1983): 219.
7. Jan Swafford, *Johannes Brahms: A Biography* (New York: Alfred A. Knopf, 1997), p. 600.
8. Ibid., p. 612.
9. Florence May, *The Life of Johannes Brahms* (London: William Reeves, n.d.), p. 659.
10. Jacques van Oortmerssen, "Johannes Brahms and 19th-Century Performance Practice in a Historical Perspective," in *Proceedings of the Göteborg International Organ Academy 1994* (Göteborg: Göteborg University, 1995), p. 365.
11. Vernon Gotwals, "Brahms and the Organ," *Music/The A.G.O.-R.C.C.O. Magazine* 4/4 (April 1970): 46.
12. Cited in Ludwig Karpath, "Der musikalisches Nachlass von Johannes Brahms," *Signale für die Musikalische Welt* 60/21 (March 26, 1902): 354.
13. Robert Haven Schauffler, *The Unknown Brahms* (New York: Crown, 1940), p. 292.
14. Hans-Hubert Schönzeler, *Bruckner* (New York: Grossman Publishers, n.d.), p. 108.
15. Walter Niemann, *Brahms* (New York: Tudor, 1937), p. 155.
16. Cited in Hans Joachim Moser, *Orgelromantik* (Ludwigsburg, Germany: Verlag E. F. Walcker, 1966), p. 45.
17. Max Kalbeck, ed., *Brahms Briefwechsel XII: Johannes Brahms und Fritz Simrock* (Berlin: Deutsches Brahms-Gesellschaft, 1919), p. 197.

18. Ivor Keys, *Brahms Chamber Music* (Seattle: University of Washington Press, 1974), p. 17.
19. Swafford, *Johannes Brahms*, p. 259.
20. Hans Georg Bertram, *Geheimnisvoller Brahms* (Kassel, Germany: Edition Merseberger, 2000), p. 17.
21. George S. Bozarth, "Brahms's Organ Works: A New Critical Edition" *American Organist* 22/6 (June 1988): 54.
22. Cited in van Oortmerssen, "Brahms and 19th-Century Performance," p. 364.
23. Wm. A. Little, "Brahms and the Organ—Redivivus," *The Organist as Scholar: Essays in Memory of Russell Saunders* (Stuyvesant, NY: Pendragon, 1994), p. 293.
24. Max Kalbeck, *Johannes Brahms*, vol. 4 (Berlin: Deutsches Brahms-Gesellschaft, 1915), p. 469.
25. Harry W. Gay, "Study of Brahms' Works Expanded in Vivid Detail," *Diapason* 50/4 (March 1959): 58.
26. Little, "Brahms and the Organ," p. 294.
27. Michael Musgrave, *The Music of Brahms* (Oxford: Clarendon, 1996), p. 245.
28. Biba, "Orgel und Orgelspiel," p. 38.
29. Robert Pascall, "Brahms's Solo Organ Works," *RCO Journal* 3 (1995): 105.
30. A modern edition of this is still in print, available from Breitkopf & Härtel.
31. Andreas Schröder, "Johannes Brahms und die Orgel," *Freiberger Studien zur Orgel*, Nr. 5 (Altenburg, Germany: Klaus-Jurgen Kamprad, 1997), p. 109.
32. Lorene Banta, "Brahms in the Church Organist's Repertoire," *Journal of Church Music* 2/3 (March 1960): 9.
33. Gay, "Study of Brahms," p. 58.
34. Hans Joachim Moser, *Die Evangelische Kirchenmusik in Deutschland* (Berlin: Carl Merseberger, 1954), p. 448.
35. Geiringer, *Brahms*, p. 204.
36. Wilfrid Mellers, *Man and His Music: The Sonata Principle* (New York: Schocken, 1969), p. 120.
37. R. W. S. Mendl, *The Divine Quest in Music* (New York: Philosophical Library, 1957), p. 146.
38. Ivor Keys, *Johannes Brahms* (Portland, OR: Amadeus, 1989), p. 244.
39. Musgrave, *Music of Brahms*, p. 245.
40. Eileen Coggin, "'Mein Jesu, der du mich': Analysis of the Compositional Techniques Used in Building the Climax," *American Organist* 53/3 (April 1970): 14.
41. Cited in Pascall, "Brahms's Solo," p. 106.
42. Gotwals, "Brahms and the Organ," p. 48.
43. Wilfrid Mellers, "Brahms's Opus Ultimum," *Choir and Organ* 5/2 (March 1997): 20–24.
44. "Bridegroom" is a biblical allegory for Jesus, derived from the parable of the wise and foolish virgins; it is encountered in other chorale texts, notably the Advent chorale *Wachet auf*.
45. W. Wright Roberts, "Brahms: The Organ Works," *Music and Letters* 14/2 (April 1933): 108.
46. Bozarth, "Brahms's Organ Works," p. 54.
47. Niemann, *Brahms*, p. 254.
48. Roberts, "Brahms: The Organ Works," p. 109.
49. Bozarth, "Brahms's Organ Works," p. 55.
50. Max B. Miller, "The Brahms Chorale Preludes: Master Lesson," *American Organist* 13/4 (April 1979): 44.
51. Ernst Kern, "Johannes Brahms und die Orgel," *ZurOrgelmusik im 19. Jahrhundert* (Innsbruck: Musikverlag Helbling, 1983), p. 130.
52. Kalbeck, *Brahms*, vol. 4, p. 471.

53. Miller, "Brahms Chorale Preludes," p. 44.
54. Gotwals, "Brahms and the Organ," p. 49.
55. Erika Steinbach, ed., *Neues Chorbuch für Mädchen-, Frauen- und Knabenstimmen* (Kassel, Germany: Bärenreiter Verlag, 1957), p. 42.
56. Roberts, "Brahms: The Organ Works," p. 108.
57. Bozarth, "Brahms's Organ Works," p. 55.
58. Archibald Farmer, "The Organ Music of Brahms," *Musical Times* 72 (1931): 503.
59. Ann Bond, "Brahms Chorale Preludes, op. 122," *Musical Times* 112/1543 (September 1971): 899.
60. Roberts, "Brahms: The Organ Works," p. 109.
61. Jack C. Goode, *Pipe Organ Registration* (Nashville: Abingdon, 1964), p. 130.
62. Miller, "Brahms Chorale Preludes," p. 45.
63. Bozarth, "Brahms's Organ Works," p. 56.
64. Miller, "Brahms Chorale Preludes," p. 45.
65. Ann Bond, booklet notes to Nicholas Danby's CD "Johannes Brahms, The Complete Organ Music," CRD Records, 1982.
66. Kees van Houten, "Het laatse opus van Johannes Brahms (1833–1897)" (2), *Het Orgel* 93/5 (May 1997): 6.
67. Gotwals, "Brahms and the Organ," p. 49.
68. Wijnand van de Pol, "L'insostenibile malinconia del distacco. Gli 11 Preludi-corali Op. 122 per organo de Johannes Brahms," *Arte Organaria/Organistica* 4/4 (1997): 57.
69. Van Houten, "Het laatse opus," p. 7.
70. Bertram, *Geheimnisvoller Brahms*, p. 17.
71. Robert Arnold Jordahl, "A Study of the Use of the Chorale in the Works of Mendelssohn, Brahms and Reger," Ph.D. dissertation, University of Rochester, 1965, p. 381.
72. J. A. Fuller-Maitland, "Brahms," in H. C. Colles, ed., *Grove's Dictionary of Music and Musicians*, 3rd ed., vol. 1 (New York: Macmillan, 1935), p. 452.
73. Hermann J. Busch, "Die Orgelwerke von Johannes Brahms," *Ars Organi* 22 (July 1963): 584.
74. Musgrave, *Music of Brahms*, p. 246.
75. John Holler, ed., *A Lovely Rose Is Blooming* (New York: H. W. Gray, 1935).
76. Bozarth, "Brahms's Organ Music," p. 57.
77. Max Kalbeck, *Johannes Brahms*, vol. 4 (Berlin: Deutsches Brahms-Gesellschaft, 1915), p. 476.
78. Miller, "Brahms Chorale Preludes," p. 48.
79. John Butt, "Choral Culture and the Regeneration of the Organ," in Jim Samson, ed., *The Cambridge History of Nineteenth-Century Music* (Cambridge: Cambridge University Press, 2001), p. 539.
80. Bozarth, *Music of Brahms*, p. 57.
81. Gotwals, "Brahms and the Organ," p. 50.
82. Wilfrid Mellers, "Brahms's Opus Ultimum," *Choir and Organ* 5/2 (March 1997): 22.
83. A. C. Delacour de Brisay, *The Organ and Its Music* (London: Kegan Paul, Trench, Trubner, 1934), p. 60.
84. Ludwig Karpath, "Der musikalisches Nachlass von Johannes Brahms," *Signale für die Musikalische Welt* 60/21 (March 26, 1902): 353.
85. Daniel Gregory Mason, "The Posthumous Organ-Preludes of Brahms," *Church Music Review* 1/9 (July 1902): 97.
86. William Osborne, *Clarence Eddy (1851–1937), Dean of American Organists* (Richmond, VA: Organ Historical Society, 2000), p. 82.

87. Relf Clark, *Elgar and the Three Cathedral Organists* (Oxford: Positif, 2002), p. 13.
88. Andreas Stock, "Brahms' Opus Posthumum," *Signale für die Musikalische Welt* 60/23 (April 9, 1902): 402.
89. Eugen Segnitz, "Kritischer Anhang," *Musikalisches Wochenblatt* 33/40 (September 25, 1902): 574.
90. R. Walker Robson, *The Repertoire of the Modern Organist* (London: Musical Opinion, 1925), p. 13.
91. Latham True, "By Brahms, yet Barely Known," *American Organ Monthly* I/8 (December 1920): xxx–xxxi.
92. Carl Dahlhaus, *Nineteenth-Century Music,* trans. J. Bradford Robinson (Berkeley: University of California Press, 1989), p. 258.
93. Gotwals, "Brahms and the Organ," p. 54.
94. Virgil Thomson, review in *New York Herald Tribune,* August 5, 1945, cited in program notes for a concert given by the Juilliard Orchestra on November 8, 1957.
95. Antonius Bittmann, *Max Reger and Historicist Modernisms* (Baden-Baden: Verlag Valentin Koerner, 2004), p. 17.
96. Ibid., p. 37.
97. Christopher Anderson, "Once Again Johannes Brahms—Max Reger: Brahms among the Organists," *American Brahms Society Newsletter* 23/2 (Fall 2005): 7.
98. Ibid., p. 8.
99. Jeremy Dibble, *C. Hubert H. Parry: His Life and Music* (Oxford: Clarendon, 1992), p. 345.
100. Ibid., p. 446.
101. *A Little Organ Book in Memory of Hubert Parry* (London: Year Book, 1924).

Chapter Six

1. For a detailed discussion of the registration practices of Bach, Walther, and others, see Thomas Harmon, *The Registration of J. S. Bach's Organ Works* (Buren, Netherlands: Frits Knuf, 1978.
2. Hermann J. Busch, "Zur Registrierkunst der deutschen romantischen Orgel," in *Zur deutschen Orgelmusik des 19. Jahrhunderts* (Sinzig, Germany: Studio, 1998), p. 59.
3. Ibid., pp. 62–63.
4. Ernst Friedrich Richter, *Katechismus der Orgel* [1868], ed. Hans Menzel (Leipzig: J. J. Weber, 1896), chapter 13.
5. Hugo Riemann, *Katechismus der Orgel* (Leipzig: Hesse, 1888), pp. 58–62.
6. Carl Locher, *An Explanation of Organ Stops,* trans. Agnes Schauenburg (London: Kegan Paul, Trench, 1888), pp. 7–8.
7. *Johannes Brahms: Briefwechsel* (Berlin: Deutsches Brahms-Gesellschaft, 1907–22), vol. 5, p. 142.
8. Otto Biba, "Orgel und Orgelspiel in Leben und Schaffen von Johannes Brahms," *Ars Organi* 31/4 (December 1983): 216.
9. Carl Piutti, *Zweihundert Choralvorspiele für die Orgel* (Berlin: H. C. Schroeder, 1900), p. 172.
10. Perhaps most notably Harald Vogel and Anton Heiller, as expressed in classes attended by the author.
11. Letter from Brahms to Henschel, cited in Stephen M. May, "Tempo in Brahms' Op. 122," *Diapason* 82/3 (March 1991): 12.
12. Styra Avins, "Performing Brahms's Music: Clues from His Letters," in *Performing Brahms* (Cambridge: Cambridge University Press, 2003), p. 25.

13. May, "Tempo in Brahms," p. 12.
14. Max B. Miller, "The Brahms Chorale Preludes: Master Lesson," *American Organist* 13/4 (May 1979): 43.
15. Fanny Davies, "Some Personal Recollections of Brahms as Pianist and Interpreter," in *Cobbett's Cyclopedic Survey of Chamber Music*, vol. 1 (New York: Oxford University Press, 1963), p. 183.
16. Cited in Michael Musgrave, *A Brahms Reader* (New Haven, CT: Yale University Press, 2000), pp. 122–125.
17. George S. Bozarth and Stephen H. Brady, "The Pianos of Johannes Brahms," in *Brahms and His World* (Princeton, NJ: Princeton University Press, 1990), p. 60.
18. Musgrave, *Brahms Reader*, pp. 128–129.
19. Jon W. Finson, "Performing Practice in the Late Nineteenth Century, with Special Reference to the Music of Brahms," *Musical Quarterly* 70/4 (Fall 1984): 473.
20. Jacques van Oortmerssen, "Johannes Brahms and 19th-Century Performance Practice in Historical Perspective," in *Proceeedings of the Göteborg International Organ Academy 1994* (Göteborg: Göteborg University, 1995), p. 357.
21. Tobias Matthay, *Musical Interpretation* (Boston: Boston Music, 1913), p. 63.
22. Davies, "Personal Recollections," p. 184.
23. Graham Barber, "German Organ Music after 1800," in *The Cambridge Companion to the Organ* (Cambridge: Cambridge University Press, 1998), p. 250.
24. *Schneider's Practical Organ School* (Boston: Oliver Ditson, n.d.), p. 20. [N.B.: This particular edition is a "pirated" English-language version, published around 1875.]
25. Richter, *Katechismus*, p. 227.
26. Everett E. Truette, ms. "Notebook A" (unpaged) in Boston Public Library Special Collections.
27. Richter, *Katechismus*, p. 227.
28. Eugenie Schumann, *The Schumanns and Johannes Brahms* (New York: Dial, 1927), p. 145.
29. Van Oortmerssen, "Brahms and 19th-Century Performance," p. 370.
30. Davies, "Personal Recollections," p. 182.

Appendix B

1. Percy A. Scholes, ed., *Dr. Burney's Musical Tours in Europe*, vol. 2 (London: Oxford University Press, 1959), p. 221.
2. Edward J. Hopkins and Edward F. Rimbault, *The Organ, Its History, and Construction* (London: Robert Cocks, 1855), p. 368.
3. Michael Musgrave, *The Music of Brahms* (Oxford: Clarendon, 1996), p. 300.
4. C. W. Pearce, *The Life and Works of Edward John Hopkins* (London, 1910), p. 66.
5. Otto Biba, *Johannes Brahms in Wien* (Vienna: Gesellschaft der Musikfreunde, 1983), p. 14.

Bibliography

General

Adler, Guido. "Johannes Brahms: His Achievement, His Personality, and His Position." *Musical Quarterly*, 19/2 (April 1933): 113–150.

Adlung, Jacob. *Musica Mechanica Organoedi*. Berlin: Birnstiel, 1768.

Ahrens, Christian, ed. *Zur Geschichte der Konzertsaalorgel in Deutschland*. Frankfurt am Main: Erwin Bochinsky, 1999.

Altman, Wilhelm, ed. *Johannes Brahms im Briefwechsel mit Karl Reinthaler, Max Bruch, Hermann Dieters, Friedr. Heimfoeth, Karl Reinecke, Ernst Rudorff, Bernhard und Luise Scholz*. Berlin: Deutsche Brahms-Gesellschaft, 1908.

Anderson, Christopher. *Max Reger and Karl Straube: Perspectives on an Organ Performing Tradition*. Aldershot, UK: Ashgate, 2003.

Arnold, Corliss Richard. *Organ Literature: A Comprehensive Survey* (3rd edition). Metuchen, NJ: Scarecrow, 1995.

Avins, Styra, ed. *Johannes Brahms Life and Letters*. New York: Oxford University Press, 1997.

———. "Performing Brahms's Music: Clues from His Letters." In *Performing Brahms*, edited by Michael Musgrave and Bernard D. Sherman. Cambridge: Cambridge University Press, 2003: 11–47.

Barber, Graham. "German Organ Music after 1800." In *The Cambridge Companion to the Organ*, edited by Nicholas Thistlethwaite and Geoffrey Webber. Cambridge: Cambridge University Press, 1998: 250–262.

Basch, Victor. *Schumann: A Life of Suffering* (trans. Catherine Allison Phillips). New York: Tudor, 1936.

Beller-McKenna, Daniel. "Brahms, the Bible, and Robert Schumann." *American Brahms Society Newsletter*, 13/2 (Autumn 1995): 1–4.

———. "Brahms's Motet 'Es ist das Heil uns kommen her' and the 'Innermost Essence of Music.'" In *Brahms Studies*, edited by David Brodbeck. Lincoln: University of Nebraska Press, 1998: 31–49.

Biba, Otto. *Johannes Brahms in Wien*. Vienna: Gesellschaft der Musikfreunde, 1983.

———. "New Light on the Brahms *Nachlass*." In *Brahms 2: Biographical, Documentary, and Analytical Studies*, edited by Michael Musgrave. Cambridge: Cambridge University Press, 1987: 39–47.

———. Preface to *Messe für sechstimmige gemischten Chor und Continuo*. Vienna: Doblinger, 1984.
Bickley, Nora, ed. and trans. *Letters from and to Joseph Joachim*. London: Macmillan, 1914.
Bittmann, Antonius. *Max Reger and Historicist Modernisms*. Baden-Baden: Verlag Valentin Koerner, 2004.
Blarr, Oskar G., and Theodor Kersken. *Orgelstadt Düsseldorf*. Düsseldorf: Tritsch Verlag, 1982.
Botstein, Leon. *The Compleat Brahms*. New York: W. W. Norton, 1999.
Bozarth, George S. "Brahms's Posthumous Compositions and Arrangements: Editorial Problems and Questions of Authenticity." In *Brahms 2: Biographical, Documentary, and Analytical Studies*, edited by Michael Musgrave. Cambridge: Cambridge University Press, 1987: 59–85.
Brahms, Johannes, compiler. *Des jungen Kreislers Schatzkästlein*, edited by Carl Krebs. Berlin: Verlag der Deutschen Brahmsgesellschaft, 1909.
Brahms, Johannes. *Werke für Orgel*, edited by George S. Bozarth. Munich: G. Henle Verlag, 1988.
Burk, John H. *Clara Schumann: A Romantic Biography*. New York: Random House, 1940.
Busch, Hermann J., and Michael Heinemann, eds. *Zur deutschen Orgelmusik des 19: Jahrhunderts*. Sinzig, Germany: Studio, 1998.
Butt, John. "Choral Culture and the Regeneration of the Organ." In *The Cambridge History of Nineteenth-Century Music*, edited by Jim Samson. Cambridge: Cambridge University Press, 2001: 522–543.
Chissell, Joan. *Schumann Piano Music*. Seattle: University of Washington Press, 1972.
Clark, Relf. "A Note on the Chorale Preludes of Ethel Smyth." *BIOS Journal*, 29 (2005): 185–191.
Clarke, F. R. C. *Healey Willan: Life and Music*. Toronto: University of Toronto Press, 1983.
Cobbett, Walter Willson, ed. *Cobbett's Cyclopedic Survey of Chamber Music*. Vol. 1. New York: Oxford University Press, 1963.
Crichton, Ronald, ed. *The Memoirs of Ethel Smyth*. New York: Viking, 1987.
Dahlhaus, Carl. *Nineteenth-Century Music*, translated by J. Bradford Robinson. Berkeley: University of California Press, 1989.
Daverio, John. *Crossing Paths: Schubert, Schumann, and Brahms*. New York: Oxford University Press, 2002.
Davies, Fanny. "Some Personal Recollections of Brahms as Pianist and Interpreter." In *Cobbett's Cyclopedic Survey of Chamber Music*, vol. 1, edited by Walter Willson Cobbett. New York: Oxford University Press, 1963: 182–184.
Dedel, Peter. *Johannes Brahms: A Guide to His Autograph in Facsimile*. MLA Index & Bibliography Series, Number 18.
Delacour de Brisay, A. C. *The Organ and Its Music*. London: Kegan, Paul, Trench, Trubner, 1934.
Drinker, Sophie. *Brahms and His Women's Choruses*. Merion, PA: Sophie Drinker, 1952.
Eberlin, Roland. "Dispositionanalyse." *Ars Organi*, 46/4 (December 1998): 194–202.
Faber, Rudolf, and Philip Hartmann. *Handbuch Orgelmusik: Komponisten—Werke—Interpretation*. Kassel, Germany: Bärenreiter, 2002.
Fagius, Hans. "The Organ Works of Mendelssohn and Schumann and Their Links to the Classical Tradition." In *Proceeedings of the Göteborg International Organ Academy 1994*, edited by Hans Davidson and Sverker Jullander. Göteborg: Göteborg University, 1995: 325–352.
Federhofer, Hellmut. "Georg Friedrich Handels Oratorium 'Saul' in der Bearbeitung von Johannes Brahms." In *Brahms-Kongress Wien 1983. Kongressbericht*, edited by Susanne Antonicek and Otto Biba. Tutzing, Germany: Hans Schneider, 1988: 125–138.

Fellinger, Imogen. "Brahms's 'Way': A Composer's Self-View." In *Brahms 2: Biographical, Documentary, and Analytical Studies*, edited by Michael Musgrave. Cambridge: Cambridge University Press, 1987: 49–58.

Finson, Jon W. "Performing Practice in the Late Nineteenth Century, with Special Reference to the Music of Brahms." *Musical Quarterly*, 70/4 (Fall 1984): 457–475.

Fitzlyon, April. *The Price of Genius: A Life of Pauline Viardot*. London: John Calder, 1964.

Forer, Alois. *Orgeln in Österreich*. Vienna: Verlag Anton Schroll, 1983.

Frisch, Walter. "The 'Brahms Fog': On Tracing Brahmsian Influences." *American Brahms Society Newsletter*, 7/1 (Spring 1989): 1–3.

———, ed. *Brahms and His World*. Princeton, NJ: Princeton University Press, 1990.

Frotscher, Gotthold. *Geschichte des Orgelspiels und der Orgelkomposition*. Berlin: Merseberger, 1959.

Fuller-Maitland, J. A. *Brahms*. London: Methuen, 1911.

———. "Brahms." In *Grove's Dictionary of Music and Musicians*, 3rd edition, vol. 1, edited by H. C. Colles. New York: Macmillan, 1935: 444–453.

Fusner, Henry. "Brahms and the von Beckerath Family." *American Organist*, 17/5 (May 1983): 47–48.

Gal, Hans. *Johannes Brahms: His Work and Personality*. New York: Knopf, 1963.

———. *The Musician's World: Letters of the Great Composers*. London: Thames & Hudson, 1978.

Geiringer, Karl. *Brahms, His Life and Work*. New York: Doubleday, 1961.

———. "Brahms as Reader and Collector." *Musical Quarterly*, 19/2 (April 1933): 158–168.

———. "Johannes Brahms in Briefwechsel mit Eusebius Mandyczewski." *Zeitschrift für Musikwissenschaft*, 8/15 (May 1933): 337–370.

———. *Symbolism in the Music of Bach*. Washington, DC: Library of Congress, 1956.

Geiringer, Karl, and Irene Geiringer. "The Brahms Library in the 'Gesellschaft der Musikfreunde,' Wien." MLA *Notes*, 30/1 (September 1973): 1–14.

Green, Douglass M. *Form in Tonal Music*. New York: Holt, Rinehart, and Winston.

Hackel, Wolfram. "Die Schulze-Orgel im St. Petri Dom zu Bremen." In *Die Orgeln im St. Petri Dom zu Bremen*, edited by Uwe Pape. Berlin: Pape Verlag, 2002: 39–50.

Hancock, Virginia. "Brahms's Early Music Studies and His Sacred Choral Music." *American Organist*, 17/5 (May 1983): 40–43.

———. "The Growth of Brahms's Interest in Early Choral Music and Its Effect on His Own Choral Compositions." In *Brahms*, edited by Robert Pascall. Cambridge: Cambridge University Press, 1963.

Haselböck, Hans. "Ein Klangdokument der Elsässischen Reform. Zur Wiederherstellung der Orgel im Grossen Saal des Wiener Konzerthauses." *Ars Organi*, 31/1 (März 1983): 43–50.

Helms, Siegmund. "Johannes Brahms und Johann Sebastian Bach." *Bach-Jahrbuch* 57 (1971), 13–81.

Hill, Robert. "Overcoming Romanticism: On the Modernization of Twentieth-Century Performance Practice." In *Music and Performance during the Weimar Republic*, edited by Bryan Gilliam. Cambridge: Cambridge University Press, 1994: 37–58.

Hofmann, Kurt. *Die Bibliothek von Johannes Brahms*. Hamburg: Musikhandel Wagner, 1974.

Hopkins, Edward J., and Edward F. Rimbault, *The Organ, Its History, and Construction*. London: Robert Cocks, 1855.

Horne, William. "Brahms's Düsseldorf Suite Study and His Intermezzo, Op. 116 No. 2." *Musical Quarterly*, 73/2 (1989): 249–283.

Jacobsen, Christiane, ed. *Johannes Brahms: Leben und Werk*. Wiesbaden: Breitkopf & Härtel, 1983.

Kalbeck, Max, ed. *Brahms Briefwechsel XII: Johannes Brahms und Fritz Simrock*. Berlin: Deutsches Brahms-Gesellschaft 1919.

———. *Johannes Brahms*. Vol. 1. Vienna: Wiener Verlag, 1904.

———. *Johannes Brahms*. Vol. 4. Berlin: Deutsches Brahms-Gesellschaft, 1915.

———, ed. *Johannes Brahms. The Herzogenberg Correspondence*, translated by Hannah Bryant. New York: Da Capo, 1987.

Keys, Ivor. *Brahms Chamber Music*. Seattle: University of Washington Press, 1974.

———. *Johannes Brahms*. Portland, OR: Amadeus, 1989.

Klek, Konrad. "Heinrich von Herzogenberg—nach hundert Jahren im Kommen?" *Musik und Kirche*, no. 5 (2000): 309–316.

Klinda, Ferdinand. *Orgelregistrierung. Klanggestaltung der Orgelmusik*. Leipzig: VEB Breitkopf & Härtel, 1987.

Knapp, Raymond. "Brahms's Revisions Revisited." *Musical Times*, 129/1749 (November 1988): 584–588.

Komorn, Maria. "Brahms, Choral Conductor." *Musical Quarterly*, 19/2 (April 1933): 151–157.

Kratzenstein, Marilou. *Survey of Organ Literature and Editions*. Ames: Iowa State University Press, 1980.

Kunzel, Hans. *Brahms in Göttingen*. Göttingen: Edition Herodot, 1985.

Lade, Günter. *Orgeln in Wien*. Vienna: Günter Lade, 1990.

Ladegast, Walter, ed. *Friedrich Ladegast, Der Orgelbauer von Weissenfels*. Stockach am Bodensee, Germany: Weidling Verlag, 1998.

Litzmann, Berthold, ed. *Clara Schumann: Ein Kunstlerleben*. Leipzig: Breitkopf & Härtel, 1907.

———. *Clara Schumann Johannes Brahms Briefe aus den Jahren 1853–1896*. Leipzig: Breitkopf & Härtel, 1927.

Locher, Carl. *An Explanation of Organ Stops,* translated by Agnes Schauenburg. London: Kegan Paul, Trench, 1888.

Lohman, Ludger. "Hugo Riemann and the Development of Musical Performance Practice." In *Proceedings of the Göteborg International Organ Academy 1994*, edited by Hans Davidson and Sverker Jullander. Göteborg: Göteborg University,1995: 251–284.

MacDonald, Malcolm. *The Master Musicians: Brahms*. New York: Oxford University Press, 2001.

Matthay, Tobias. *Musical Interpretation*. Boston: Boston Music, 1913.

Mauser, Siegfried. "Brahms und der vorklassische Instrumentalmusik." In *Brahms-Kongress Wien 1983. Kongressbericht,* edited by Susanne Antonicek and Otto Biba. Tutzing, Germany: Hans Schneider, 1988: 367–378.

May, Florence. *The Life of Johannes Brahms*. London: William Reeves, n.d.

McCorkle, Donald. *Johannes Brahms: Variations on a Theme of Haydn*. New York: Norton, 1976.

Melamed, Daniel R., and Virginia Hancock. "Brahms's Kyrie and *Missa Canonica*. Two Discussions of the Mass Movements and Their Publication. *American Brahms Society Newsletter*, 3/1 (Spring 1985).

Mellers, Wilfrid. *Man and His Music. Vol. III: The Sonata Principle*. New York: Schocken, 1969.

Mendl, R. W. S. *The Divine Quest in Music*. New York: Philosophical Library, 1957.

Meredith, Victoria. "The Pivotal Role of Brahms and Schubert in the Development of the Women's Choir." *Choral Journal*, 37/9 (February 1997).

Moser, Andreas, ed. *Johannes Brahms in Briefwechsel mit Joseph Joachim*. Berlin: Deutsches Brahms-Gesellschaft, 1912.

Moser, Hans Joachim. *Die Evangelische Kirchenmusik in Deutschland*. Berlin: Merseberger, 1954.

———. *Orgelromantik*. Ludwigsburg, Germany: Verlag E. F. Walcker, 1961.

Musgrave, Michael. *A Brahms Reader.* New Haven, CT: Yale University Press, 2000.

———, ed. *The Cambridge Companion to Brahms.* Cambridge: Cambridge University Press, 1999.

Nauhaus, Gerd, ed. *The Marriage Diaries of Robert and Clara Schumann,* translated by Peter Ostwald. Boston: Northeastern University Press, 1993.

Niemann, Walter. *Brahms,* translated by Catherine A. Phillips. New York: Alfred Knopf, 1929.

Ochs, Siegfried. "Encounter with Bruckner and Brahms," translated by Tamara Trykar. *American Choral Review,* 14/4 (October 1972): 12–15.

"Die Orgel der Hofkirche Luzern." *Vox Humana,* 3/10 (September 2001): 6–7.

Osborne, William. *Clarence Eddy (1851–1937): Dean of American Organists.* Richmond, VA: Organ Historical Society, 2000.

Pacun, David. "Brahms and the Sense of Ending." *American Brahms Society Newsletter,* 22/1 (Spring 2004): 1–4.

Pape, Uwe, and Winfried Topp. *Orgeln und Orgelbauer in Bremen.* Berlin: Pape Verlag, 1998.

Pascall, Robert. Brahms's *Missa Canonica* and Its Recomposition in His Motet 'Warum' Op. 74 No. 1." In *Brahms 2: Biographical, Documentary, and Analytical Studies,* edited by Michael Musgrave. Cambridge: Cambridge University Press, 1987: 111-136.

Peterson, John David. "Schumann's Fugues on B-A-C-H: A Secret Tribute." *Diapason* (May 1983): 11–12.

Platt, Heather. *Johannes Brahms: A Guide to Research.* New York: Routledge, 2003.

Quigley, Thomas. *Johannes Brahms: An Annotated Bibliography of the Literature through 1982.* Metuchen, NJ: Scarecrow, 1990.

———. *Johannes Brahms: An Annotated Bibliography of the Literature from 1982 to 1996.* Lanham, MD: Scarecrow, 1998.

Quoika, Rudolf. *Die Orgelwelt um Anton Bruckner.* Ludwigsburg, Germany: Verlag E. F. Walcker, 1966.

Reiber, Joachim. *Musikverein Wien.* Vienna: Gesellschaft der Musikfreunde, 1999.

Richter, Ernst Friedrich. *Katechismus der Orgel.* Leipzig: J. J. Weber, 1868.

Ricks, Robert. "A Possible Source for a Brahms Ground." *American Brahms Society Newsletter,* 23/1 (Spring 2005): 1–5.

Riemann, Hugo. *Katechismus der Orgel.* Leipzig: Hesse, 1888.

Robertson, Alec. *Requiem: Music of Mourning and Consolation.* New York: Frederick A. Praeger, 1967.

Robson, R. Walker. *The Repertoire of the Modern Organist.* London: Musical Opinion, 1925.

Röhring, Klaus, ed. *Max Reger 1873–1973. Ein Symposion.* Wiesbaden: Breitkopf & Härtel, 1974.

Rossner, Johannes. "Robert Schumanns Bezüge zur Orgel—Neue Erkenntnisse." *Freiberger Studien zur Orgel Nr. 5.* Altenburg: Klaus-Jürgen Kamprad, 1997: 37–48.

Rudolf, Max. "A Recently Discovered Composer-Annotated Score of the Brahms Requiem." *Bach,* 7/4 (October 1976): 2–13.

Rupp, Emile. *Die Entwicklungsgeschichte der Orgelbaukunst.* Einseideln, Switzerland: Benziger, 1929.

Russell, Tilden A. "Brahms and *Wer nur den lieben Gott lässt walten:* A New Contribution." *American Brahms Society Newsletter,* 6/2 (Autumn 1988).

Sanger, David. "My Fascination with the Sources—4." *Organists' Review,* 86/4 (November 2000): 364–365.

Sceats, Godfrey. *The Liturgical Use of the Organ.* London: Musical Opinion, 1922.

Schauffler, Robert Haven. *Florestan: The Life and Work of Robert Schumann.* New York: Henry Holt, 1945.

———. *The Unknown Brahms.* New York: Crown, 1940.

Schmidt, Christian Martin. *Reclams Musikführer: Johannes Brahms*. Stuttgart: Philipp Reclam, 1994.
Schönzeler, Hans-Hubert. *Bruckner*. New York: Vienna House, 1970.
Schou, Larry. "Brahms and His Cultural Milieu." *Diapason*, 88/4 (April 1997): 15–18.
Schouten, Hennie. *Voordracht en Registratie der Orgelliteratur*. Amsterdam: H. J. Paris, 1947.
Schumann, Eugenie. *The Schumanns and Johannes Brahms*. New York: Dial, 1927.
Schumann, Robert. *The Complete Works for Organ and Pedal Piano*, edited by Wayne Leupold. New York: McAfee Music, 1978.
Seggermann, Günter. *Geschichte der Orgeln in der Hamburger Hauptkirche St. Petri vom 16: Jahrhundert bis Heute*. Lauffen, Germany: Orgelbau-Fachverlag Rensch, 1992.
Sherman, Bernard D. "How Different Was Brahms's Playing Style from Our Own?" In *Performing Brahms*, edited by Michael Musgrave and Bernard D. Sherman. Cambridge: Cambridge University Press, 2003: 1–10.
Shuster-Fournier, Carolyn. *Les Orgues de Salon d'Aristide Cavaillé-Coll*. Paris: L'Orgue Cahiers et Memoires, 1997.
Sittard, Alfred. *Das Hauptorgelwerk und die Hilfsorgel der Grossen St. Michaelis-Kirche in Hamburg*. Hamburg: Bonsen & Maasch, 1912.
Smyth, Ethel. *Impressions That Remained*. New York: Alfred A. Knopf, 1946.
Sonnleitner, Klaus. "Die Restaurierung der Kaiserjubiläumsorgel in Bad Ischl." *Osterreichisches Orgelforum*, 1–3 (1993): 489–495.
Stinson, Russell. *Bach: The Orgelbüchlein*. New York: Schirmer, 1996.
———. *J. S. Bach's Great Eighteen Organ Chorales*. New York: Oxford University Press, 2001.
Stojowski, Sigismond. "Recollections of Brahms." *Musical Quarterly*, 19/2 (April 1933): 143–149.
Stuifbergen, Lourens, and Hennie Schouten. *Voordracht en Registratie der Orgelliteratur*. Naarden, Netherlands: A. J. G. Strengholt, 1938.
Stulken, Marilyn Kay. *Hymnal Companion to the Lutheran Book of Worship*. Philadelphia: Fortress, 1981.
Sumner, W. L. "More Austrian Organs." *The Organ*, 41/163 (January 1962): 113–120.
———. "Organs of St. Michael's Church, Hamburg." *The Organ*, 26/102 (October 1946): 81–87.
Swafford, Jan. *Johannes Brahms: A Biography*. New York: Alfred A. Knopf, 1997.
Terry, Charles S. "Bach Gesellschaft." In *Grove's Dictionary of Music and Musicians* (3rd edition), edited by H. C. Colles. New York: Macmillan, 1935: 182–188.
Van Wageningen, Cor. "Max Reger's Chorale Preludes." *Het Orgel*, 95/5 (1999): 5–13.
Walsh, Stephen. "Schumann and the Organ." *Musical Times*, 1529/8 (July 1970): 741–743.
Walter, Joachim. "*This Heaving Ocean of Tones*": *Nineteenth-Century Organ Registration Practice at St. Marien, Lübeck*. Göteborg: Göteborg University, 2000.
Weigl, Bruno. *Handbuch der Orgelliteratur*. Leipzig: Leuckart, 1931.
Wetschky, Jürgen. *Die Kanontechnik in der Instrumentalmusik von Johannes Brahms*. Regensburg: Gustav Bosse Verlag, 1967.
Weyer, Martin. *Die Orgelwerke Max Regers*. Wilhelmshaven, Germany: Florian Noetzel Verlag, 1989.
Wills, Arthur. *Organ*. New York: Schirmer, 1984.

The Organ Works

Anderson, Christopher. "Once Again Johannes Brahms—Max Reger: Brahms among the Organists." *American Brahms Society Newsletter*, 23/2 (Fall 2005): 6–9.
Banta, Lorene. "Brahms in the Church Organist's Repertoire." *Journal of Church Music*, 2/3 (March 1960): 9–12.

Beechey, Gwilym. "The Organ Music of Brahms." *American Organist*, 17/5 (May 1983): 43–46.

Bertram, Hans Georg. *Geheimnisvoller Brahms. Versuch über die 7 Klavierfantasien op. 116; Versuch über die 11 Choralvorspiele für Orgel op. 122*. Kassel, Germany: Merseburger, 2000.

Biba, Otto. "Brahms, Bruckner und die Orgel." In *Bruckner Symposion. Johannes Brahms und Anton Bruckner*, edited by Othmar Wessely. Linz, Austria: Anton Bruckner-Institut, 1985: 191–196.

———. "Orgel und Orgelspiel in Leben und Schaffen von Johannes Brahms." *Ars Organi*, 31/4 (December 1983): 215–221.

Birkby, Arthur. "Lean Brahms Organ Output Other Than Opus 122 Discussed." *Diapason*, 49/12 (November 1958): 9.

Bond, Ann. "Brahms Chorale Preludes, Op. 122." *Musical Times*, 112/1543 (September 1971): 898–900.

———. Booklet notes to Nicholas Danby's CD "Johannes Brahms, The Complete Organ Music." CRD Records, 1982.

Bozarth, George S. "Brahms's Organ Works: A New Critical Edition." *American Organist*, 22/6 (June 1988): 50–59.

———. "Editorial Problems in the Music of Johannes Brahms (with a Special Focus on the Organ Works)." (unpublished lecture handout, circa 1998).

———. Preface to *Johannes Brahms: Werke für Orgel*. München: G. Henle Verlag, 1988.

Brodbeck, David. "The Brahms-Joachim Counterpoint Exchange; or, Robert, Clara, and 'the Best Harmony between Jos. and Joh.'" In *Brahms Studies*, vol. 1, edited by David Brodbeck. Lincoln: University of Nebraska Press, 1994: 30–80.

Busch, Hermann J. "Die Orgeln Mendelssohns, Liszts und Brahms." In *Proceedings of the Göteborg International Organ Academy, 1994*, edited by Hans Davidsson and Sverker Jullander. Göteborg: Göteborg University, 1995: 235–250.

———. "Die Orgelwerke von Johannes Brahms." *Ars Organi*, 11/22 (July 1963): 582–584.

Calflisch, Ursina. "Johannes Brahms' Orgelwerke." *Musik und Gottesdienst*, 51/3 (1997): 98–104.

Coggin, Eileen. "'Mein Jesu, der du mich': An Analysis of the Compositional Techniques Used in Building the Climax." *American Organist*, 53/3 (April 1970): 14–20.

Douglas, Charles Winfred. *The Chorales from the Organ Works of Brahms, Edited and Harmonized for Chorus of Mixed Voices, with an Introduction on the Organ Music of Brahms*. New York: H. W. Gray, 1945.

Evans, Edwin. *Handbook to the Pianoforte Works of Johannes Brahms*. London: Reeves, 1912.

Farmer, Archibald. "The Organ Music of Brahms." *Musical Times* 72/1059–1062 (May–August 1931): 406–408, 501–503, 596–598, 693–696.

Gay, Harry W. "Study of Brahms' Works Expanded by Vivid Detail." *Diapason*, 50/4 (March 959): 38.

Gehring, Holger. *Deutsche Orgelmusik der Romantik*. Vienna: Österreichisches Orgelforum (double number 1994/2–1995/1): 13–75.

Gotwals, Vernon. "Brahms and the Organ." *Music/the A.G.O.-R.C.C.O. Magazine*, 4/4 (April 1970): 38–55.

Harbach, Barbara. Preface to Clara Schumann, *Prelude and Fugue for Organ, Op. 16 No. 3*. Pullman, WA: Vivace, 1993.

Hartmann, Günter. "Zur Orgelfuge in as-Moll von Johannes Brahms." *Brahms-Studien*, Band 7 (1987): 9–19.

Heinemann, Michael. "'*Ganz eigentlich für meine Clara.*' Zur Orgelmusik von Johannes Brahms." In *Zur deutschen Orgelmusik des 19. Jahrhunderts*, edited by Hermann J. Busch and Michael Heinemann. Sinzig, Germany: Studio, 1998: 75–78.

Horning, Joseph. "Brahms' Chorale Preludes." *Diapason*, 88/5 (May 1997): 13–17.

Hughes, Sarah Mahler. "The Oboe and the Titan: Two Chorale Settings by Dame Ethel Smyth and Johannes Brahms." *Diapason*, 88/6 (June 1997): 13–15.
Jordahl, Robert Arnold. "A Study of the Use of the Chorale in the Works of Mendelssohn, Brahms and Reger." Ph.D. dissertation, University of Rochester, 1965.
Karels, J. C. "De Orgelwerken van Johannes Brahms (1833–1897)." *Kirche und Musik*, No. 2 (March/April 1998).
Karpath, Ludwig. "Der musikalische Nachlass von Johannes Brahms." *Signale für die Musikalische Welt*, No. 21 (March 26, 1902): 353–355.
Kern, Ernst. "Johannes Brahms und die Orgel." In *Zur Orgelmusik im 19. Jahrhundert*, edited by Walter Salmen. Innsbruck: Musikverlag Helbling, 1983: 127–131.
Little, Wm. A. "Brahms and the Organ—Redivivus." In *The Organist as Scholar: Essays in Memory of Russell Saunders*. Stuyvesant, NY: Pendragon, 1994: 273–297.
Mason, Daniel Gregory. "The Posthumous Organ-Preludes of Brahms." *Church Music Review*, 1/9 (July 1902): 96–97.
May, Stephen M. "Tempo in Brahms' Op. 122." *Diapason*, 82/3 (March 1991): 12–13.
Mealli, Enrico. "La forma del sentimento: Le opere giovanili per organo di Johannes Brahms." *Arte Organaria/Organistica*, 4/4 (1997): 56–59.
Mellers, Wilfrid. "Brahms's Opus Ultimum." *Choir and Organ*, 5/2 (March/April 1997): 20–24.
Miller, Max. "The Brahms Chorale Preludes: Master Lesson." *American Organist*, 13/4 (April 1979): 43–47.
Musgrave, Michael. *The Music of Brahms*. Oxford: Clarendon, 1996.
Owen, Barbara. "Brahms's 'Eleven': Classical Organ Works in a Romantic Age." *Journal of Church Music* (November 1983): 5–9.
Pascall, Robert. "Brahms's Orgelwerke." In *Johannes Brahms: Leben und Werk*, edited by Christiane Jacobsen. Wiesbaden: Breitkopf & Härtel, 1983: 123–124.
———. "Brahms's Solo Organ Works." *Royal College of Organists Journal*, No. 3 (1995): 97–120.
Paterson, Donald R. M. "The Organ Works of Johannes Brahms." *Crescendo*, 22/8 (May 1958): 4–7; 22/9 (June 1958): 4–5.
Roberts, W. Wright. "Brahms: The Organ Works." *Music and Letters*, 14/2 (April 1933): 104–111.
Saint, David. "Technical Tips: Mendelssohn and Brahms." *Organists' Review*, 90/2, No. 354 (May 2004): 166–168.
Schröder, Andreas. "Johannes Brahms und die Orgel." In *Freiberger Studien zur Orgel*, Nr. 5. Altenburg, Germany: Klaus-Jurgen Kamprad, 1997: 105–111.
Schroeder, Hermann. "Die Orgelkompositionen von Johannes Brahms." *Musica Sacra*, 103 (1983): 196–201.
Schuneman, Robert. "Brahms and the Organ: Some Reflections on Modern Editions and Performance." *Music/the A.G.O.-R.C.C.O. Magazine*, 6/9 (September 1972): 30–34.
Segnitz, Eugen. "Kritischer Anhang." *Musikalisches Wochenblatt*, 40/25 (September 1902): 574.
Stock, Andreas. "Brahms' Opus posthumum." *Signale für die Musikalische Welt*, No. 23 (April 9, 1902): 401–403.
Testa, Susan. "A Holograph of Johannes Brahms's Fugue in A-flat Minor for Organ." *Current Musicology*, 19 (1975): 89–102.
Thomas, Anne Marsden. "Organ Lesson IX: Brahms, Es ist ein Ros' entsprungen." *American Organist*, 35/11 (November 2001): 54–55.
True, Latham. "By Brahms, yet Barely Known." *American Organ Monthly*, I/8 (December 1920): xxx–xxxi.
van de Pol, Wijnand. "L'insostenibile malinconia del distacco. Gli 11 Preludi-corali Op. 122 per organo de Johannes Brahms." *Arte Organaria/Organistica* 4/4 (1997): 50–55.

van Houten, Kees. "Het laatste opus van Johannes Brahms (1833–1897)." *Het Orgel,* 93/4 (April 1997), 6–14; 93/5 (May 1997): 6–11.

van Oortmerssen, Jacques. "Johannes Brahms and 19th-Century Performance Practice in a Historical Perspective." In *Proceedings of the Göteborg International Organ Academy 1994,* edited by Hans Davidson and Sverker Jullander. Göteborg: Göteborg University, 1995: 354–367.

Discography

Although many recordings of Brahms's organ works can be found on older 78 rpm and LP records, these are now difficult to find, save in library collections. Thus all recordings listed here are in the currently more accessible CD medium, although no claim of completeness can be made. The recordings are listed without comment, but those that the author has sampled display a surprisingly wide range of interpretation, particularly with regard to tempo and registration. Although a few titles include works by other composers, Brahms is well represented in these (e.g., all Eleven Chorale Preludes on the Parshin CD). Not listed are recordings in which only three or fewer Brahms works appear.

Jean-Charles Ablitzer. *Brahms: Intégrale pour Orgue.* Organ of St. Christophe, Belfort (Harmonic Records)
Luc Antonini. *Johannes Brahms: Oeuvre pour Orgue.* Organ of the Basilica of Daurade (Soli Deo Verita/RCA Victor)
Georges Athanasaides. *Brahms: Das Orgelwerke.* Organ of Stiftsbasilika Waldsassen (Tudor 790)
Robert Bates. *Brahms: Complete Organ Works.* Bond organ, Holy Rosary Church, Portland, OR. (Pro Organo 7060)
Kevin Bowyer. *Brahms: Complete Organ Works.* Organ of Odense Cathedral (Nimbus NI5262)
Ursina Calflisch. *Brahms Orgelwerke.* 1872 Kuhn organ, Neumünster, Zürich (Coronata IFO49)
Bernard Coudurier. *Johannes Brahms: Das Orgelwerk.* 1878 Walcker organ, Votivkirche, Vienna. (Scam/BNL 112885)
George Edward Damp. *Last Works for Organ by Brahms and Franck.* Organ of Sage Chapel, Cornell University (Calcante CAL 004)
Nicholas Danby. *Brahms: Complete Organ Music.* Organ of Immaculate Conception Church, London (CRD Records 3404)
Jonathan Dimmock. *The Romance of the Organ.* (Arkay AR6113)
Alexander Fiseisky. *Bach and German Romantic Music.* Klais organ, Stadtkirche, Rotenburg/Wümme (Lammas 108D)
Lorenzo Ghielmi. *Bach and the Romanticist: Johann Sebastian Bach and Johannes Brahms.* 1888 Walcker organ in Stadtkirche, Winterthur (Music Edition: Winter & Winter 910 114-2)

Rudolf Innig. *Brahms Complete Organ Works*. Klais organ. (Dabringhaus & Grimm)

Bernard Lagacé. *Brahms: Chorale Preludes Op. 122 & Fugue in A-flat Minor*. Wolff organ (Titanic Ti38)

Jean-Pierre Leguay. *Brahms: Intégrale des Oeuvres pour Orgue*. Cavaillé-Coll Organ of St. Ouen, Rouen (Euromuses 2008)

François Menissier. *Johannes Brahms: Forte ma dolce; l'Oeuvre pour Orgue*. Organs of Sint Maarten, Zaltbommel and St. Maria, Schram (Editions Hortus 031)

Bruno Morin. *Brahms und Reubke*. 1888 Walcker organ, Stadtkirche, Winterthur (Triton TRI331103)

Kare Nordstoga. *Brahms: Complete Organ Works*. Ryde & Berg organ, Oslo Cathedral (Simax PSC 1137)

Robert Parkins. *Brahms Organ Works*. Flentrop organ, Duke University Chapel (Naxos NX-824)

Alexsei Parshin. *Die Grosse historische Röver-orgel in die Evangelischen Baptistenkirche in Moskau*. 1898 Röver organ (Psallite CD60481)

Herman Schäffer. *Brahms: Das Orgelwerke* (Motette CDM 10711)

Ulfert Smidt. *Johannes Brahms: Das gesamte geistliche Werk für Chor und Orgel*. 1885 Ladegast organ, St. Johanniskirche, Wernigerode. 2 disks (Thorofon DCTH 2301)

Ulfert Smidt. *Norddeutsche Orgelmusik*. Organ of Stadtkirche, Bückeburg (Thorofon 2411)

Carole Terry. *Carole Terry in Schwerin*. 1871 Ladegast organ, Schwerin Cathedral (Gothic CD1021-ARC)

Jacques van Oortmerssen. *Brahms Organ Works*. 1906 Setterquist organ, Kristine Church, Falun, Sweden (BIS CD497)

Kari Vuola. *Brahms: Complete Organ Works*. Paschen organ, Kerava Church, Finland (Alba ABCD 121)

John Weaver. *For All the Saints*. Reuter organ, University Presbyterian Church, Seattle (Pro Organo POCD 7124)

Jurgen Wolf. *Werke von Brahms und Reubke*. Organ of Nikolaikirche, Leipzig (Musikwelt)

Index

Ahlsen, Pastor von, 15, 143
Albrechtsberger, J. G., 54
Allgemeine musikalische Zeitung, 56
Alphenaar, Gerard, 75, 140
American Organist, 75
Archer, Frederick, 69
Armbrust, Carl Friedrich, 145
Armbrust, Georg H. F., 17, 28, 102, 144–145
Arnim, Gisela von, 56
Atkins, Ivor, 114, 120

Bach, C. P. E., 54, 143
Bach, Johann Sebastian, 4, 6–8, 17–18, 23–24, 28, 32, 33, 37, 47, 62, 66, 68, 70–71, 76, 82, 84, 89–90, 101, 114, 121–122
  Actus Tragicus (Trauerode), 47, 109
  cantatas, 14, 18, 35–37, 42, 93
  chorale preludes, 6, 27–28, 36–37, 54, 98–99, 102, 110, 115, 131–132
  Clavierübung, 36
  Kunst der Fuge, 35, 54
  Orgelbüchlein, 37, 53, 70, 85, 87, 93–94, 97–98, 100, 109, 114, 130–132
  preludes and fugues, 24, 27, 33, 35–36, 53, 66
  St. Matthew Passion, 36, 91, 93–94, 106
  violin works, 35–37
  Wohltemperierte Klavier, 19, 66, 69
Bach-Gesellschaft, 36, 42
Bad Ischl, 27–28, 78–79, 86, 89, 117, 122, 150
Baden-Baden, 19, 28, 59, 122

Bagge, Selmar, 56–57
Banta, Lorene, 88
Beckerath, Alwin von, 79
Beechey, Gwilym, 63, 66, 68
Beethoven, Ludwig van, 18, 57, 81, 114, 151
Beller-McKenna, Daniel, 49
Berlin Philharmonische Chor, 21
Bertram, Hans, 103
Biba, Otto, 13, 31, 78, 87, 103, 130
Bibl, Rudolf, 23, 29, 124, 129–130, 152
Bible, the, 37, 77, 82, 88–89
Biggs, E. Power, 3, 95, 99, 102, 140
Billam, Peter, 116
Billroth, Theodor, 24, 77
Birkby, Arthur, 64
Bittmann, Antonius, 117
Bloch, Joseph, 135
Bogler, 70
Bond, Ann, 96, 98, 101
Bonn, 13, 78
Bos, Coenraad V., 77
Bozarth, George, 58, 68, 83, 91, 93, 97, 99, 105, 108
Brahms, Elise, 13, 17, 77
Brahms, Johannes
  Academic Festival Overture, 39, 44, 82
  Adoremus, 16
  Alto Rhapsody, 20
  Auf dem Kirchhofe, 38
  Ave Maria, 14, 16–17
  Ballades, 9, 53

Brahms, Johannes (*continued*)
  Begräbnisgesang, 38
  Cello Sonata in E Minor, 44
  Cello Sonata in F Major, 44
  Chorale Prelude and Fugue on *O Traurigkeit*, 14, 26–27, 29, 41, 46, 50, 55, 69–75, 81, 85, 87, 89–90, 100, 104, 107, 109, 131, 141, 148
  Clarinet Quintet in B Minor, 48
  Clarinet Trio in A Minor, 48
  Deutsche Volkslieder, 37, 44–45, 49, 82
  Deutsches Requiem, 20–22, 29, 35–37, 39, 41, 44, 46, 62, 64, 81–82, 95, 109, 132, 146
  Drei Geistliche Chöre, 35, 44
  Eleven Chorale Preludes, 3, 28, 37, 43, 46, 49–50, 76, 78–79, 81–89, 91, 109, 113, 122–124, 130–133, 135, 137, 139–141
    1. *Mein Jesu, der du mich*, 89–92
    2. *Herzliebster Jesu*, 92–94
    3. *O Welt, ich muss dich lassen*, 94–96
    4. *Herzlich thut much erfreuen*, 96–98
    5. *Schmücke dich, o liebe Seele*, 98–100
    6. *O wie selig seid ihr doch, ihr Frommen*, 100–101
    7. *O Gott, du frommer Gott*, 101–103
    8. *Es ist ein Ros' entsprungen*, 103–106
    9. *Herzlich thut mich verlangen*, 106–108
    10. *Herzlich thut much verlangen*, 108–111
    11. *O Welt, ich muss dich lassen*, 111–113
  Fahr Wohl, 80
  Fantasias, 82
  Fest und Gedenksprüche, 35
  First String Sextet, 14
  Fugue in A-flat Minor, 10–11, 20, 42, 55–65, 69, 72, 74–75, 81, 87, 89, 129–131, 135, 141
  Geistliche Lied, 20, 35, 39, 44, 55–56, 65
  Geistliches Wiegenlied, 104
  Gesang des Parzen, 82
  Hungarian Dances, 76
  Intermezzi, 49
  Marienlieder, 17, 46, 82, 104
  Missa Canonica, 45, 47, 87
  motets, 37–38, 44–47, 71, 87, 89–90
  Nänie, 35
  O Bone Jesu, 16
  Piano Concerto in D Minor, 41, 43–44
  piano exercises, 49
  Piano Quartet in A Major, 42, 95
  Piano Quintet in F Minor, 63, 97
  Piano Sonata in C Major, 49
  Piano Sonata in F Minor, 53
  Piano Trio in B Major, 44, 48, 53
  Piano Trio in C Minor, 96
  piano works, 49, 53
  Prelude and Fugue in A Minor, 11, 13, 20, 55–56, 64–67, 104, 123, 131, 136–137
  Prelude and Fugue in G Minor, 20, 55, 67–69, 86, 130–131, 137
  Psalm XIII, 14, 17, 44, 56
  Rhapsodie No. 1, 103
  Rinaldo, 41
  Sarabande and Gavotte, 11
  Schicksalslied, 24
  Schumann Variations, 53
  Serenades, 14
  Six Vocal Quartets, 48
  Sonatas for Clarinet and Piano, 48, 50, 82
  String Quartet in G Major, 48, 80
  String Quintet in F Major, 35, 44, 48
  Symphony No. 1, 39, 41, 46, 64, 102
  Symphony No. 2, 46
  Symphony No. 3, 102
  Symphony No. 4, 36, 42, 63, 80
  Thirteen Canons, 35, 48
  Three Vocal Quartets, 45
  Tragic Overture, 44, 62, 82
  Trio in B Major, 35
  Triumphlied, 22, 24, 29, 38
  Variations and Fugue on a Theme by Handel, 35, 66
  Variations on a Theme by Haydn, 43, 46
  Vier ernste Gesänge, 37, 39, 49–50, 66, 77–79, 84
  Volks-Kinderlieder, 49
Breitkopf & Härtel, 5, 57, 75–76, 104, 139–140
Bremen, St. Petri Cathedral, 21, 28–29, 121–122, 146–147
Breslau University, 44
Brisay, A. C. Delacour de, 113
Bruch, Max, 38
Bruckner, Anton, 23, 26–29, 40, 80, 149
Buck, Dudley, 34
Budapest Conservatory, 135
Buhrman, T. Scott, 4, 75

Bülow, Hans von, 31, 47, 77
Bunjes, Paul, 99, 102, 122, 140
Burney, Charles, 143
Busch, Hermann J., 23, 25, 62, 105
Busoni, Ferruccio, 116
Buszin, Walter, 99, 122, 140
Butt, John, 109
Buxtehude, Dieterich, 31, 37, 39, 68, 76, 121

Cavaillé-Coll, Aristide, 19–20, 59, 147
Chemnitz, Jakobikirche, 20
Cherubini, Luigi, 6
chorale fugue, 71
chorales, 14, 16, 33, 37–40, 78, 87, 115, 117, 132–133
Christmas, 104
Chrysander, Friedrich, 135
Church Music Review, 119
"Clara" theme, 65–66
Coggin, Eileen, 89
concert-hall organs, 10, 22, 122
counterpoint, 6–8, 11–14, 20, 33–36, 54–55, 64, 67, 71, 75, 86–87, 89–90, 95, 98, 130
Couperin, François, 37
Crüger, Johann, 87, 93, 98, 100

Dahlhaus, Carl, 116
Daverio, John, 61
Davies, Fanny, 134–135, 137
Denkmäler deutscher Tonkunst, 32
Dessoff, Otto, 133
Detmold, 13, 16
Deutschmann, Friedrich, 25, 86, 149
Diapason, 75
Dibble, Jeremy, 119
Dietrich, Albert, 5, 13
Dohnanyi, Ernst von, 114
Dresden, 6
Dresden, Hofkirche, 7, 18
Düsseldorf, 9–11, 96,
 churches, 11, 121
 St. Maximilian, 86, 122, 145–146
Dvorák, Antonin, 30

Eddy, Clarence, 114
Eschig, Max, 139
Evans, Edwin, 116

Farmer, Archibald, 97
Farnam, Lynnwood, 3
Fellinger family, 79–80
Fink, Christian, 40
Fischer, Karl August, 23, 31
Flatz, Ida, 48
Flemming, Paul, 20, 55
folk songs, 24, 37, 43, 54, 79, 96, 104–106, 133
Forer, Alois, 149
Franck, César, 76
Frankfurt am Main, 78
Freiberg, Cathedral, 6
Fritsch, E. W., 71
Frotscher, Gotthold, 4, 117
Fuller-Maitland, J. A., 105, 115

Gade, Niels, 8, 34
Gay, Harry W., 30, 86, 88
Geffcken, Johannes, 143
Gehring, Holger, 25
Geiringer, Karl, 18, 77, 88
Gerhardt, Paulus, 106
Gesellschaft der Musikfreunde, 18–19, 22, 24, 26, 46, 54, 57, 74, 93, 105, 122, 148–149
Goode, Jack C., 99
Goodrich, Wallace, 151
Goss-Custard, Reginald, 151–152
Göttingen, 14–15, 36, 142
Gotwals, Vernon, 21, 90, 96, 101, 110, 116
Grädener, Hermann, 30
Grädener, Karl, 16–17, 30, 54
Gray, H. W., 139
Grieg, Edvard, 34
Grimm, Julius Otto, 10, 14–15, 38, 43, 45, 142
Grünberger, Dr., 80

Haas, Friedrich, 18
Hackel, Wolfram, 147
Hamburg, 4, 8, 13, 36, 48
 Böhme's music store, 9, 55, 70, 72, 142
 Philharmonic Society, 17
 St. Michael's Church, 6, 15, 28, 37, 86, 102, 121–122, 142–144
 St. Peter's Church, 16–17, 28, 86, 102, 121–122, 142, 144–145
 St. Thomas's Church, 145
 Tonhalle, 10
Hamburger Frauenchor, 15–17, 25, 29, 35, 44, 48, 69, 94, 144, 149

Hancock, Virginia, 47
Handel, Georg Friedrich, 15, 18, 23–24, 27, 33
Hanslick, Eduard, 134
Harbach, Barbara, 8
harmonium, 114, 116
harpsichord, 53, 122
Hartmann, Günter, 64
Haupt, Karl August, 31, 135
Hauptmann, Moritz, 11, 34
Henle Verlag, 58, 83, 140
Henschel, George, 41, 43, 74, 132
Herzog, Johann Georg, 126
Herzogenberg, Elisabet von, 30, 37, 70–71, 75, 77
Herzogenberg, Heinrich von, 27, 30, 32, 40, 46, 74, 80, 84
  compositions, 31, 104, 129
Hesse, Adolph Friedrich, 31, 39, 124, 129
Heuberger, Richard, 77–80, 84, 89
Hildebrandt, J. G., 14, 86, 122, 143
Holler, John, 106
Hopkins, Edward John, 143, 146, 150
Houten, Kees van, 101, 103

Isaac, Heinrich, 94, 96
Ischl. *See* Bad Ischl

Jenner, Gustav, 33
Joachim, Amalie, 24
Joachim, Joseph, 5, 11–12, 24, 31, 34, 43, 54, 57, 64, 68, 80, 86, 119, 134
Jordahl, Robert, 105
Juilliard Orchestra, 116
Juon, Paul, 116

Kalbeck, Max, 21, 39, 42, 84–87, 94, 103, 108
Karg-Elert, Sigfrid, 3, 119–120, 130
Karlsbad, 80, 117
Karpath, Ludwig, 114–115
Kaufmann, Georg Friedrich, 121
Keller, Robert, 77
Kendall, Raymond, 27
Keys, Ivor, 82, 89
Kirchner, Theodor, 18–19, 30, 70, 152
Kirnberger, Johann Philipp, 34, 54
Kittel, Johann Christian, 102
Klinger, Max, 77
Knecht, Justin Heinrich, 135

König, Ludwig, 11, 86, 122, 145
Koschel, Alexander, 23
Kratzenstein, Marilou, 4
Krebs, Johann Ludwig, 4
Kuntsch, Johann, 7
Kupfer, William, 81, 83, 91, 93, 97, 102

Labor, Josef, 29, 74, 148
Lachner, Franz, 32
Lade, Günter, 150
Ladegast, Friedrich, 22–23, 71, 122, 148
Lange, Samuel de, 24, 30, 32, 37, 40
Leipzig
  Bachverein, 31
  Conservatory, 5, 7, 30, 34, 74, 126–127
  Gewandhaus, 34
  Nikolaikirche, 74
  Thomaskirche, 4, 16, 34, 40, 118, 126
Lemare, Edwin H., 151–152
Lemmens, J.-N., 31
Lengnick, Alfred, 139
Lester, William, 75
Levi, Hermann, 71
Leyen, Rudolf von der, 78
Liszt, Franz, 3, 8, 23–24, 40, 113, 118, 134
Little, Wm. A., 9, 31, 86–87
Locher, Carl, 128
London, 10, 11
Lübeck, Marienkirche, 22
Lucerne, Hofkirche, 18–19
Ludwig, Klaus Uwe, 151–152
Luther, Martin, 38, 89

MacDonald, Malcolm, 37, 64, 66, 68
Maczewski, A., 27
Malibran, Maria, 19
Mandyczewski, Eusebius, 4, 33, 79, 81, 84, 92, 105, 113, 116, 139
Marks, Edward B., 140
Marpurg, Friedrich Wilhelm, 31, 34, 54
Marxsen, Eduard, 4, 21, 34
Mason, Daniel Gregory, 114
Mattheson, Johann, 34, 54
Mauracher, Matthias, 27, 150
May, Florence, 78, 134–135
May, Stephen, 133
McCorkle, Donald, 43
Meier, Camilla, 17

Meier, Franziska, 16
Mellers, Wilfrid, 88, 90, 112
Melun, Notre-Dame Church, 148
Mendelssohn, Felix, 5–7, 10, 23, 30, 34, 38–40, 66, 98
  organ works, 8, 40, 102, 118, 124
Mendl, R. W. S., 89
Merkel, Gustav, 31, 39, 125
metronome, 76, 132–133, 137
Miller, Max, 75, 94–95, 99–100, 108, 133
Moser, Hans Joachim, 88
Mozart, Wolfgang Amadeus, 18, 24, 33, 134, 151
Muffat, Georg, 30–31, 37
Mühlfeld, Richard, 31, 48
Musgrave, Michael, 18, 39, 49, 77, 87, 89, 105, 134
Musikalisches Wochenblatt, 71

Neue Zeitschrift für Musik, 5–6, 37, 147
Niemann, Walter, 3, 93
Norden, N. Lindsay, 152
Novello, 139

Ochs, Siegfried, 21–22
Oortmerssen, Jacques van, 64, 137
organ, Romantic, 123
organ compass, 85–86
organ recitals, 6, 8, 10, 18–19, 23, 29, 74–75, 114–115, 136, 148
organ registration, 22, 25, 37, 59, 61, 66, 72, 76, 94, 98–99, 101, 112, 121–131
organ stops, 12, 19, 59–60, 65, 71, 99, 122–123, 126, 129–130
Orgel ad libitum, 22
Orgelbewegung, 76
ornaments, 66–67, 69
Osterholdt, G. D. W., 28

Pachelbel, Johann, 4, 39, 90, 98, 118
Pacun, David, 49
Paris, 19–20, 136
Parker, Horatio, 151
Parratt, Walter, 74
Parry, C. Hubert H., 119
Pascall, Robert, 43, 45, 68, 74, 85, 87
pedal piano, 5, 7–8, 11–12
performance practice, 133–138
Peters Edition, 122, 140

phrygian cadence, 58
piano, 4, 9, 11–13, 18–20, 26–28, 31, 33, 43, 57, 70, 74, 84, 114–115, 133–134, 137, 151
picardy third, 63, 73, 88, 107
Piutti, Carl, 40, 126, 129–130, 132
Pol, Wijnand van de, 103
Porubsky, Bertha, 149
Porubsky, Gustav, 25, 149
Praetorius, Hieronymus, 104
Prague, 30
Prout, Ebenezer, 152

Quoika, Rudolf, 23

Rebbeling, Louis, 125
Reger, Max, 3, 32, 40, 76, 119, 121, 129–130, 132
  compositions, 117–118, 129
Reimann, Heinrich, 40, 115, 117
Reinhard, August, 116
Reinthaler, Karl, 29, 71, 74, 146
Remenyi, Eduard, 5
Reubke, Julius, 3, 113
Rhaw, Georg, 96
Rheinberger, Josef, 3, 40, 118, 125–126, 130
Richter, Ernst Friedrich, 34, 127, 135–136
Rieger, 149
Riemann, Hugo, 117, 128
Rinck, J. C. H., 39, 102, 115, 125, 132
Ritter, August Gottfried, 40
Ritter, J. C., 102
Roberts, W. Wright, 64, 91, 93, 96, 99
Robson, R. Walker, 115
Rogg, Lionel, 151–152
Ruckert, Friedrich, 48
Rupp, Emile, 23

Sauer, Wilhelm, 126, 147
Schauffler, Robert Haven, 29, 39, 42
Scheidt, Samuel, 31–32, 47, 98, 121
Schneider, Johann Gottlob, 18, 30–31
Schneider, Julius, 135
Schnitger, Arp, 15, 122, 146
Schoenberg, Arnold, 75–76
Schröder, Andreas, 87
Schubert, Franz, 32, 40, 48, 81, 151
Schubring, Adolf, 12, 37
Schulze, Johann Friedrich, 10, 21, 121–122, 146

Schumann, Clara, 5, 11, 13–14, 18–20, 26, 28,
   30–31, 34, 42–43, 50, 53, 55–57, 59,
   64–65, 70, 72, 77–78, 82, 86, 94, 103,
   119, 134, 147
  concerts, 8, 10, 13
  correspondence, 10, 18, 67–68
  Fugues, 7
  organ playing, 8–9
Schumann, Eugenie, 136
Schumann, Marie, 77
Schumann, Robert, 5, 7–8, 11, 13–14, 18, 20,
   36–37, 53, 55, 57, 78, 98, 121, 145
  Album für die Jugend, 34, 40
  B-A-C-H Fugues, 11, 53, 62–63, 68, 129,
   136
  Drei Fantastiestücke, 48
  Manfred Overture, 62
  pedal piano studies, 7–8, 12, 35, 53
Schuneman, Robert, 25
Schütz, Heinrich, 47
Schweitzer, Albert, 93
Seggermann, Günter, 145
Segnitz, Eugen, 115
Serkin, Rudolf, 42
Signale, 114–115
Silbermann, Gottfried, 6, 14, 143
Silver, Alfred J., 151–152
Simrock, Fritz, 30, 49, 81, 83, 91, 113–114, 139,
   151
Singverein, 24, 36, 80, 104
Sittard, Alfred, 75
slurs, 91, 95, 97, 100, 105–106, 112–113, 137
Smidt, Ulfert, 83
Smyth, Ethel, 27, 33, 74–75
Spies, Hermine, 77
Spitta, Philipp, 18, 31, 46–47, 71, 77
Stanford, Charles Villiers, 120
Stock, Andreas, 115
Stockhausen, Julius, 18–19, 31, 43, 146
Straube, Karl, 118
Strauss, Johann Jr., 81
stylus fantasticus, 67–69, 130, 137
Swafford, Jan, 36, 43, 78, 82
symbolism, 57–58, 61–62, 65, 82, 93, 95, 100,
   102, 107, 109

Tappe, Peter, 10
Tausig, Karl, 27
Taylor, Stainton de B., 152
tempo, 58, 62, 71–73, 92, 95, 100, 111, 131–133
Teschemacher, 12
Testa, Susan, 59
Thalberg, Sigismund, 8
Thomson, Virgil, 116
Töpfer, J. G., 39, 146
True, Latham, 115
Truette, Everett E., 136
Truxa, Frau, 42
Tucher, Gottlieb von, 38

Viardot, Louis, 19
Viardot, Pauline, 19–20, 59, 122, 147–148
Vienna, 17, 21–22, 31, 45, 56, 79, 133
  Conservatory, 105
  Karlskirche, 25, 80
  Lutheran Church, 25, 80, 86, 122, 149–150
  Piaristenkirche, 25
  St. Stephen's Cathedral, 25
  Singakademie, 18, 44, 94
  Votivkirche, 25–26
Vierling, Johann Gottfried, 54
Völckers, Marie, 15

Wagner, Friedchen, 14, 59, 69–70
Wagner, Richard, 24, 151, 153
Walcker, E. F., 16, 25, 144, 149, 150
Walther, Johann Gottfried, 39
West, John E., 95, 139, 152
Widmann, Viktor, 134
Willan, Healey, 120, 151–152
Winterfeld, Carl von, 38
Winterthur, 19
Wittgenstein, Karl, 29
Wolf, Hugo, 24, 33
Wolfrum, Philipp, 32
Wolfsteller, Johann Gottlieb, 16, 86, 144

Young, Percy, 39

Zimmermann, Pastor, 80
Zürich, 20